WITHDRAWN

Sinan

Architecture alone of all the arts can give space its full volume. It can surround us with a void of true dimensions: and whatever delight may be derived from that is the gift of architecture alone.

Geoffrey Scott, *The Architecture of Humanism*

Godfrey Goodwin

SINAN
Ottoman Architecture and its Values Today

Saqi Books

British Library Cataloguing-in-Publication Data
Goodwin, Godfrey, *1921–*
  Sinan : Ottoman architecture and its values today
  I. Title
  723.3

ISBN 0-86356-172-1

First published 1993 by
Saqi Books, 26 Westbourne Grove
London W2 5RH

© Godfrey Goodwin 1993

Typeset by Contour Typesetters, Southall, London

Printed in Great Britain by Redwood Press Limited, Melksham, Wiltshire

To Gillian

Contents

Acknowledgements	9
Turkish Pronunciation	10
Glossary	11
Preface	13
Elements of a Life	16
Before Sinan	20
Patronage and Sites	29
The Royal Architect	31
Süleymaniye Complex (1551-8)	36
Other Buildings	45
Kara Ahmad Pasha Complex (1561-2)	46
Üç Şerefeli Mosque, Edirne (*c.* 1450)	47
Mosques of Mihrimah Sultan, Üsküdar (1547-8) and Edirnekapı (*c.* 1565-70)	49
Rüstem Pasha Mosque (1561-2)	50
Zal Mahmud Pasha Mosque (*c.* 1580)	51
Sokollu Mehmed Pasha Mosque, Kadırga (1571-2)	52
Sokollu Mehmed Pasha Mosque, Azapkapı (1577-8)	53
Sokollu Mehmed Pasha Mosque, Lüleburgaz (1569-70)	54
Civil Buildings	55
Bridge at Büyükçekmece (1566-8)	56
Students and Disciples	56
Selim II Mosque, Karapınar (1563-4)	57
Süleyman Mosque, Damascus (1554-5)	58
Lala Mustafa Pasha Mosque, Erzerum (1562-3)	59
Murad III Mosque, Manisa (1586-7)	61
Other Mosques	62
Sultan Ahmad Mosque (1609-16)	64
The Importance of Light	66
Light and the Selimiye Mosque (1572-5)	69
The Dome	72
The Minaret	79
Problems of Interior Space	82
Galleries	82
Conflict of Dome and Mihrab	84
Space and Form	84
The Recognition of Apsidal Form	88
The Courtyard	90
Measuring the Void	98
Decoration	99
Tiles	104
Mathematics and Architecture	107

Contents

No Building is an Island	108
The Dimensions of Genius	110
The Common Denominator of Ottoman Architecture	111
Counting the Dead	114
Notes	116
Ottoman Sultans and their Mothers, 1444-1595	120
An Abbreviated List of Sinan's Buildings	121
A. Monuments Built by Sinan	122
B. Monuments Built to Plans by Sinan	123
C. Monuments Planned (but never Seen) by Sinan	123
D. Minor Works	123
List of Illustrations	124
Index	128

Maps

I.	Sinan's Turkey	133
II.	Istanbul: Location of Principal Monuments Mentioned in the Text	134
III.	Edirne: Location of Principal Monuments Mentioned in the Text	135

Acknowledgements

First I must thank my wife for the magical encouragement which she gave me during the writing of this book.

Peter Campbell was kinder than one could expect a friend to be. Professor Don Antonio Fernández-Puertas and David Castillejo have supported me warmly while Alison and Peter Smithson took the trouble to write critical appraisals. Professor J.M. Rogers, also, kindly checked the text. I am equally grateful to Sir Philip Dowson and Sherban Cantacuzino for their appraisals. Many others have helped me in many different ways; in particular, I must thank Mary Berkmen, Professor John Carswell, Charles Cooper, Dr Howard Crane, Özer and Ayma Kabaş, Dr Attilio Petruccioli, Venetia Porter and Professor Günsal Renda.

Graeme Gardiner photographed the Gurlitt plates for me and then spent a week in Istanbul and Edirne when he had many better things to do. To Ara Güler I owe the magnificent jacket. André Gaspard has been the most understanding of publishers and Jana Gough an equally humane editor.

When I awoke to the genius of Sinan in 1957, I met Professor Aptullah Kuran to whose profound study of his work I owe much, not least when we disagree. Professor Hilary Sumner-Boyd is dead but it is impossible to forget him whenever and wherever one strolls in Istanbul.

Turkish Pronunciation

c pronounced *j* as in jam
ç pronounced *ch* as in church
ğ not pronounced; lengthens the preceding vowel
ı akin to the pronunciation of *u* in radium
ö pronounced as in the German word *König*
ş akin to the *sh* in shall
ü as the French *u* in *tu*

Glossary

Turkish terms have been translated into English where possible in the text (and italicized at the first mention) but the glossary may help readers when in the country. (Hence the inclusion of a few items which do not appear in the text.)

acemioğlan	cadet
alem	horned crest
arasta	parade of shops
bend	dam
bımarhane	hospital, asylum
cami	Friday mosque as opposed to a *mescid*
gazi	fighter for the Faith; hero
hamam	ritual bath-house
han	inn or entrepôt for merchants
ımaret	soup kitchen
ivan	hall
kalfa	assistant architect; superintendent
kervansaray	large inn or caravanserai
kible	see *mihrab*
külliye	complex of educational and charitable buildings attached to a mosque
medrese	detached building with a courtyard which serves a department of a university both for teaching and for residence (a college)
mescid	small mosque formerly without a *mimber*
meydan	open space; square
mihrab (kible)	niche, sometimes like a grand portal, which indicates the direction of prayer
mimar	architect, hence *mimarbaşi* or chief architect
mimber (minber, minbar)	hooded pulpit reached by lofty stairs from which the Friday sermon is pronounced
orta	regiment
revak	domed or vaulted colonnade enclosing a court
şadırvan	ritual ablution fountain
sadrazam	grand vezir or chancellor
saray	palace
tabhane	hospice for dervishes (and later other guests) in a complex
tekke	dervish complex
türbe	tomb
ulema	elite judiciary and religious educationalists
valide sultan	mother of the sultan (directed the palace and could influence ministers)
vezir	(Turkish spelling of vizier) minister of state
vezirazam	chief vezir whose power grew until the title *sadrazam* delegated much of the sultan's rule to him
zaviye	dervish hospice attached to a mosque

Preface

Architecture will never again take an established form, whether classical or romantic. At such a time, it is worth considering the works of one of the greatest architects of the sixteenth century, Sinan Abdülmennan, who is little known in the West. They demonstrate how one mind absorbed and developed established ideas, using their strengths to evolve revolutionary forms. Such was the grandeur of these achievements that Sinan wielded absolute authority even over those who were unable to understand them in intellectual terms. In this there are sure and certain lessons for the architectural barnyard. Here I seek to show how a forerunner came to crow.

At the beginning, Sinan's career was based on inherited Ottoman building methods: a tradition based on structure. At the end this had been transformed by an awareness of the psychology of space, incomprehensible to his predecessors and, it must be said, to some architectural historians and critics here and now.[1] Art and architecture reveal how people persist in viewing others in their own image.

This book is an analysis of Sinan's development, based on a comparative study of certain of his buildings. Supreme amongst these is the mosque of Selim II at Edirne, second capital of the Ottoman empire. It assumes throughout that a figure of the Renaissance was one capable of logical thought matched by creative sensitivity.[2]

It is not a life, for the materials of biography are not available. Even so Western-orientated an outrider of Islam as the Ottoman empire was careless with individual records, rarely writing or preserving letters for

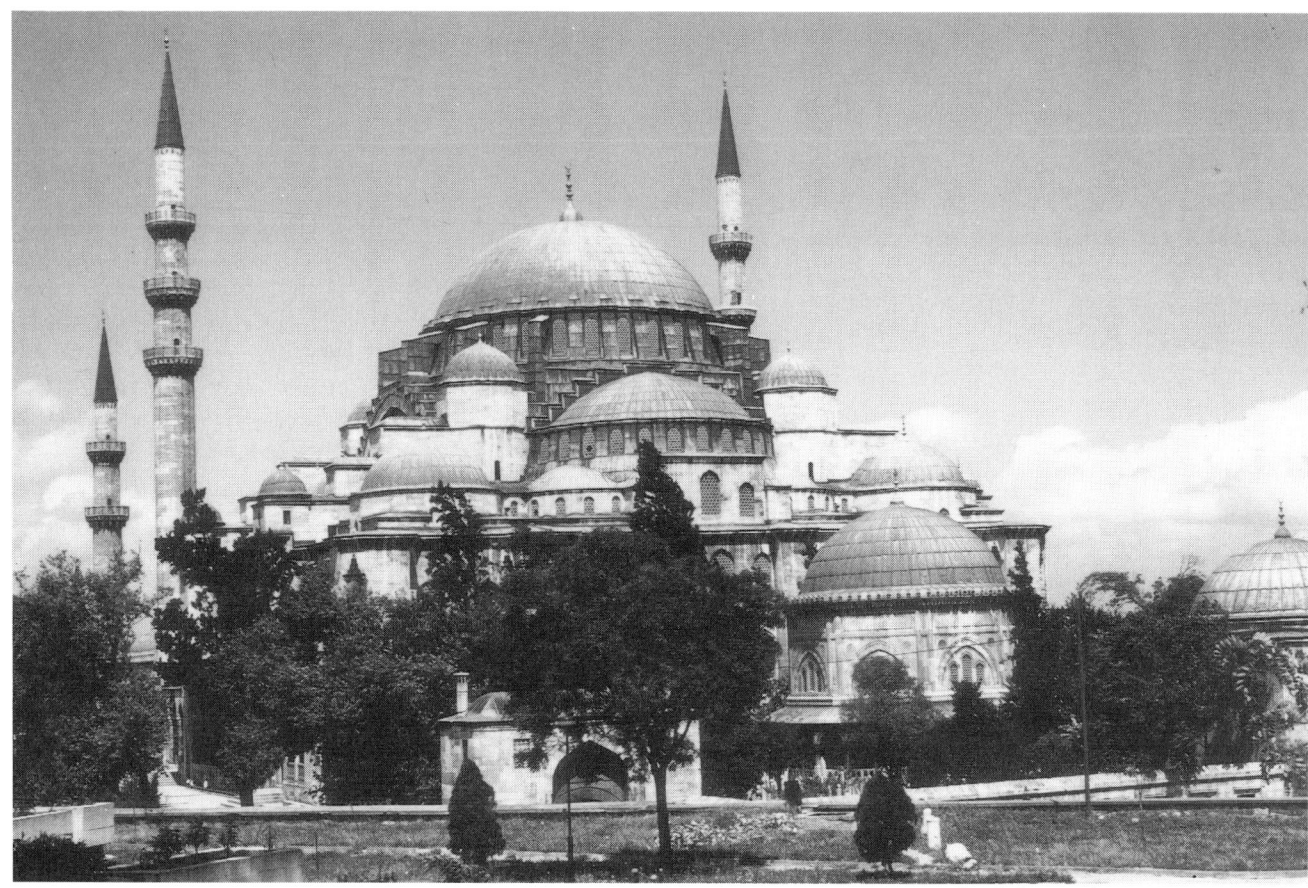

2. Süleymaniye mosque, Istanbul

their own sake and even more rarely conserving family papers as mementoes. Outside religion and philosophy there are no records of ideas. Official decisions are documented, but their interpretation takes years of work. The publication, thanks to the diligence of Professor Barkan,[3] of the full account books for the building of the Süleymaniye complex is a unique event; most of the other facts about Sinan must be gleaned from a few Orders-in-Council here and conflicting lists of buildings there.

Sinan's careers as soldier and architect were so successful that his life was undramatic but his astonishing ability to escape death on numerous battlefields, and his inexorable advance to senior offices of a society so absolute, and therefore so dangerous for able men, are evidence of a remarkable personality and high abilities. In his own day he was clearly regarded as a colossus. He was to die in his bed when other architects were killed in battle, like Ahmad Pasha, or executed, like Davud Agha,[4] as were able and ambitious Grand *Vezirs* and princes such as the unique Ibrahim Pasha and Sinan's one-time patron Kara Ahmad Pasha.[5]

Sinan's great projects used workforces of 25,000 men and more, which included recruits, galley slaves and artisans of different nationalities. The process of building, from the digging of the deep foundations of the minarets to the placing of the final dome, required the interplay of hoists, building materials and human hands. All this had to be scheduled, and the schedule achieved according to the seasons of the year. A taskmaster with an infectious spirit and vision was required for such work; today the results of this vision cannot be ignored.

Photographs of the Süleymaniye mosque in Istanbul constantly appear on posters and travel brochures. This monumental building on the skyline of the Golden Horn is the stage set for that Islamic world which Europeans regarded as romantic until the resurgence of fundamentalism made it frightening, a cunning foe, the enemy of the questioning individual mind—just such a mind by which the Süleymaniye itself was conceived. The precarious balance between dogma and curiosity, the mass instinct to engulf and the individual's desire to emerge and be recognized was the inward conflict of sixteenth-century Ottoman society. If history were a desert, to be traversed at the pace of the pilgrimage, the united community could define its own future. But Sinan rode no camel among the thousands in the caravan. He led the host from so far in advance that he was out of sight. He was lucky to die when the early liberalism of the Ottoman house expired with the last breath of the melancholy Murad III.

Despite the absence of documents a discussion of Sinan's work which is based on something more than speculation is possible. Underlying his architectural concepts are the mathematical theories and practices of classical Greece.[6] He shared these ideals of proportion and balance with builders in the West and, however different the results may be, his buildings and those of Bramante, Palladio[7] or other members of the great confraternity whose lives ran parallel to his must be seen as part of the same intellectual revolution.

But Sinan walked alone. Whatever he may have heard about the monuments of Venice, Rome or Florence—and there is no reason to suppose he was totally unaware of their existence—he had certainly not read Alberti.[8] He began his career with the advantage of a mature masonry tradition, and if he seems to follow Vitruvius this is the evidence of his training rather than his reading. He worked in the tradition of consistently sound and practical building common to the Ottoman architects. The paradox, inevitably, was that tradition was not enough and he had to recast and reform it with that confidence that is shared by fools and geniuses: and nobody could imagine Sinan to be a fool.

Elements of a Life

Sinan died on 17 July 1588 aged 100 or in the 100th year of his life, which since these were Muslim years suggests that he was born in 1492. As this fits with his retirement from the army at the correct age for an officer of field rank it would seem to be the probable date. He was born at Agyrnas, in Kayseri province, which is still barely worthy of the name of a small town. (It was renamed Mimarsinanköy, 'Village of the Architect Sinan', in his honour.) It possesses no monuments except for the two fountains which Sinan endowed and (probably) built there. Down by the river, however, boys still play with stone blocks in the caves as if they were toy bricks.[9]

The village was Orthodox Christian and its people were of peasant stock whose roots were lost in the Anatolian past. Thus it was that when Sinan was recruited in 1511 he was eligible to join the janissaries. He was well over the usual age of 8 to 12 or so, however, which may account for the fact that he was not sent to the Enderun Kolej, or Palace School, at Topkapısaray, but to the second establishment in the earlier Ibrahim Pasha *Saray* facing onto the Hippodrome at Istanbul.

The levy of 1511 was exceptional or it would never have taken place in Anatolia at all. Selim I extended the levy there for the first time because he foresaw that he would have to muster a much enlarged army which would suffer many casualties in the years of campaign ahead. For his intention (in which he succeeded) was to take over the whole of Anatolia and then destroy the Mamluk empire from Aleppo and Damascus to Cairo. He could not hope to raise enough youths in the Balkans, for the recruiting officers were restricted by rules which were applied equally strictly in Anatolia. They could not levy tradesmen or only sons and the boy could not be an Armenian, Jew, Kurd, gypsy or an Arab. Townsfolk too were exempt. Thus the recruits could only be Greek Orthodox boys, or Franks who were hardly to be found in Anatolia, rules that were not to be broken until much later in the century. It would not have been surprising were the age limit stretched, particularly if the man in question was eager to escape the restraints of peasant life for the opportunities and rewards of the capital.

Sinan's father was said to have been a carpenter; the evidence suggests that the family were not poor and were likely to have owned land. They could not have been highly skilled else Sinan would not have been eligible for the levy since, at 19, he would have begun his apprenticeship to a craft or trade. As an *acemioğlan* (cadet) he would not have gone on campaign in the conquering years between 1514 and 1517 but would have been left behind in the capital to guard and police the city. He would also have been drafted to work on the maintenance of monuments and walls and on any new building erected for the sultan or his government. Selim had little time for building, however, and his own mosque was piously built for him by his son, Süleyman, after his death. By 1520 Sinan was 28 years old so he could certainly have worked on the complex. He himself was to employ thousands of recruits on the Süleymaniye complex in the 1550s. The work toughened up the young men and kept them out of idle mischief to some degree although records of drunkenness and insubordination during the building of the Selimiye mosque at Edirne and the Muradiye at Manisa show that where the older janissaries were employed this was not always the case.

From his first campaign, it is likely that Sinan was employed on siegeworks and fortifications. The advance on Mohacs[10] was interrupted by the capture of several strongholds which needed scientific breaching by mines and then repair. While he was employed in this work, Sinan could hardly have failed to learn about the behaviour of masonry and the limits of its ability to withstand pressure and stress. He would need to know how stone behaved and what were its functional limits. By the time that he was appointed Royal Architect in 1538 he had built bridges and even supply barges, in addition to causeways and redoubts. He had served in the Household Brigade and so was known to his sovereign; moreover, he had commanded an *orta* (regiment) of the janissaries besides brigades of Anatolian troops. His last commander in the field was Lutfi Pasha whose patronage he enjoyed and who was briefly in office as Grand Vezir when the office of Royal Architect fell vacant.

Since Sinan's abilities were well known and his friends at court many, and the sultan also knew of him, his appointment was not a surprise. In the sixteenth century, experience of command in war was important to the chief architect. An experienced commander had learnt how to organize supplies so that they arrived in the right quantities in the right place at the right time and how to get men to do what they were told. Sinan's student and eventual successor, Ahmad Agha, was to be recalled to the colours and to die a pasha in the field against Anatolian rebels. When Sinan was appointed, no major building had been erected for fifteen years and there was no one trained to control men in their thousands. It was not simply the logistics of controlling large numbers. There were companies of specialized, skilled workers of all kinds and nationalities besides the unskilled recruits. Prefabricated units had also to arrive on time. These included window grilles and locks and bolts and various sizes of tiles for the floors. Rope and poles for scaffolding and haulage gear were constantly growing or contracting. The Süleymaniye complex had approximately 550 domes: each needed to be crowned with its *alem* (horned crest) of gilded bronze of the proportionate size as soon as the masonry was complete.

In the history of war, the quartermaster's department has all too often been responsible for defeat. The Ottoman armies in the sixteenth and seventeenth centuries were brilliantly supplied by long-established assembly points and depots. These gathered beasts of burden from mules to expensive (and thus hired) water buffalo and flocks of sheep for food and fleece-mats, besides military materials, along the two major routes: the equivalent of the present London Road through the Balkans for when the army marched west and the trans-Anatolian road for when it marched east. Without this experience of handling supplies and men, the great sixteenth-century Ottoman works of architecture could not have been achieved whatever the wealth of the sultan and however many slaves he could employ. And, apart from galley slaves during the three winter months, his labour force of military recruits was much more a matter of loyal members of his household than slaves in the sense that applied to the helots of classical Greece.

The importance of his long military career for Sinan the Architect was that he was confident of having the competence to build and to bridge difficult terrain and so control deep foundations. Above all he had the personality with which to command men. In this, his career has some relationship to that of the eighteenth-century German architect Balthasar Neumann.

What Sinan's campaigns in the Balkans and his forays to Corfu and Apulia did not do was to educate him in the forms or decoration of Western architecture. It is not possible to guess what structural details he may have studied when repairing fallen fortresses, but there is no trace whatsoever of any influence from the ecclesiastical

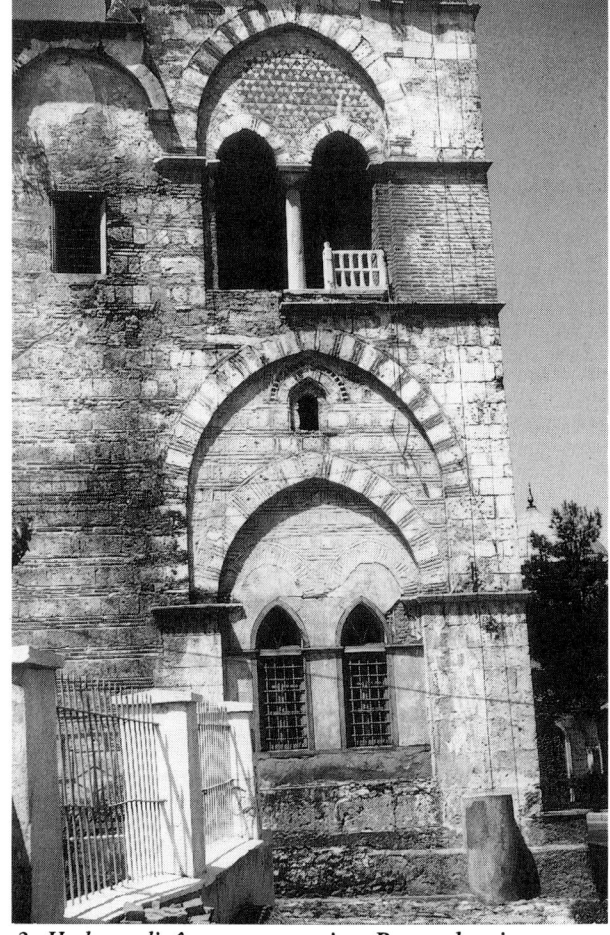

3. *Hudavendigâr mosque-zaviye, Bursa: loggia*

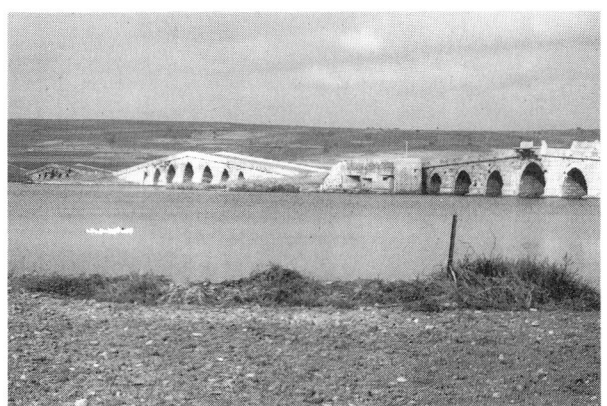

4. Bridge at Büyükçekmece

Right:
5. Thirteenth-century Seljuk bridge at Çeşnıgar

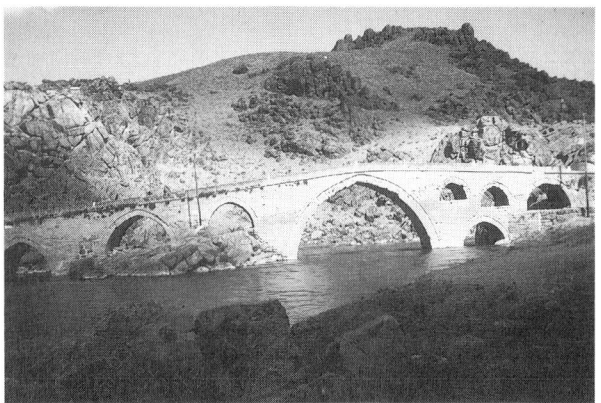

or domestic monuments of Europe. There had been in the past.

The mosque of Hudavendigâr, Murad I, built in the 1370s at Çekirce above Bursa, has a loggia over its pierced portico that clearly owes its inspiration to the architecture of the Ragusan coast and the cathedral at Ohrid. But with Sinan there is nothing to trace. There are two reasons for this. First, major Christian monuments did not abound on the route to Buda, along which there were those self-same churches and monasteries that were familiar to anyone living in Istanbul. The Byzantine monuments of the capital had already made their lasting impression on all aspects of Ottoman architecture, such as the use of alternating courses of stone and brick as an economy measure, rather than for elasticity, when building walls. More important aesthetically was Sinan's understanding of the liberating force of the exedra.

At what moment he studied bridges is not known but he repaired them during the Mohacs campaign and the floating bridge weighed down by the city's bells (used to anchor the pontoons) at Buda is attributed to him because genius accretes the works of lesser men. Many of the structures which he helped to repair were Roman in origin. Their even-handed and straightforward disposition of main arches and relieving arches, reducing weight and letting floodwaters flow, was to be reflected in his much-repaired bridge at Visegrád across the Dvina river although it does change direction in the Seljuk manner: if only once. Yet the only one of his monuments chosen to be inscribed on his tombstone is the bridge at Büyükçekmece. It is a masterpiece of engineering, unique because the marsh had never been spanned until Sinan did this with his four donkey-backs in the 1560s. It is astonishing rather than beautiful and it would be churlish to gainsay its indebtedness to the great Seljuk engineers who were precursors of the Ottomans in Anatolia. Their bridges used the spurs and outcrop of riverbanks, with the islets of the bed like stepping stones, in order to reduce the span of their arches and therefore their height as they zigzagged in sympathy with the contours of the land. Büyükçekmece runs straight from shore to shore.

Before Sinan

Until Sinan, Ottoman architecture had been a reading of parts. This is not to disparage the robust style that had nevertheless achieved some contrast of light within a building. There is also a reading of parts in Western architecture, as at the church of St Clement Danes in London. To talk of kiosks and pavilions would be another matter but even here the building is not disguised; it is never a folly or a protest against classical forms. The only Ottoman follies were cardboard forts put up at festivals. These were closer to stage scenery than to buildings and they were not intended to survive.

Sinan broke down the distinct forms that created a rigidity in larger buildings in a manner which would have been inconceivable in the relatively modest *zaviye*-mosques of the fifteenth century. He freed interior space and exterior form simultaneously. There was no deception.

Sinan lived in the sixteenth century when Ottoman architecture had achieved an immediately recognizable style. This had emerged in the fourteenth century, to reach aesthetic coherence and simple grandeur between 1450 and 1525. Sinan transformed it.

In the first half of the fourteenth century, Seljuk rule disappeared in Anatolia and the Mongol overlords withdrew. A little fiefdom led by Ertuğrul Bey achieved independence in the area of Iznik (Nicaea) and his son Osman (who gave his name to the dynasty) died at the capture of Bursa by his own son, Orhan Gazi. This important trading city enriched the new state and its army crossed the Sea of Marmara to take Adrianople, now Edirne, and Thrace. Later, the other Balkan territories were subjected. Under Selim I at the beginning of the sixteenth century, the Mamluk empire in Syria and Egypt was acquired and nominal Ottoman rule extended across the north coast of Africa as far as Morocco.

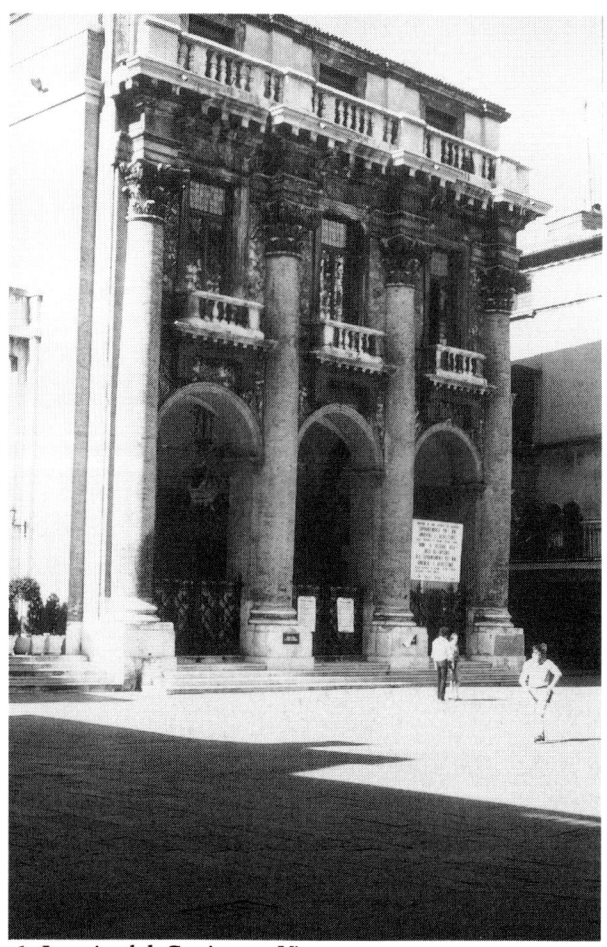
6. Loggia del Capitano, Vicenza

Before Sinan

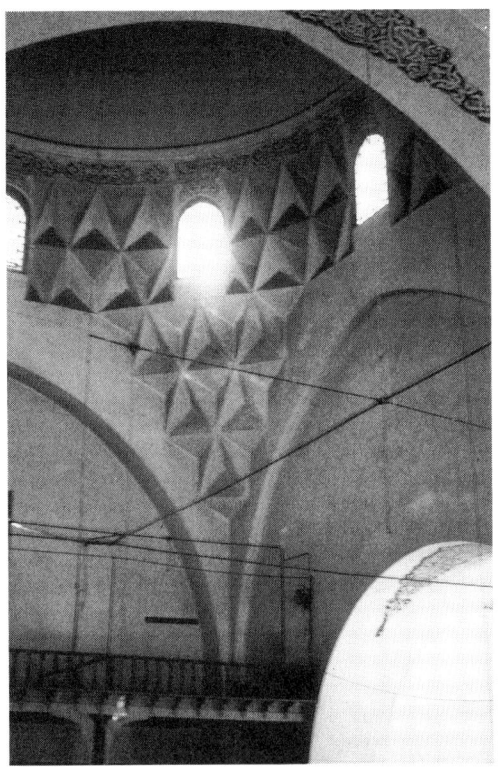

7. *Muradiye mosque, Bursa: support for subsidiary dome*

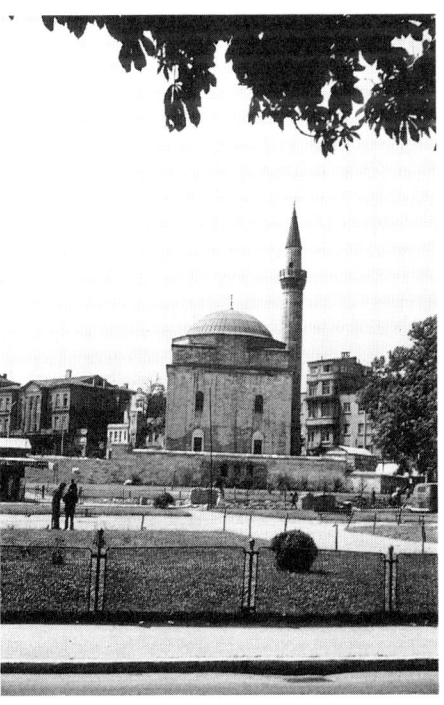

8. *Firuz Agha mosque, Istanbul: a single-domed unit*

The early Ottoman leaders were sustained by the dervishes, some of whom had roots in Turkish homelands in Central Asia. The sects varied in their beliefs and some were fighters for the Faith (*gazis*) while others influenced central government. The other important ally was the brotherhood of the Ahis, who were both democratic and also the more prosperous leaders of the Anatolian communities either under local emirs or, as at Ankara, as an independent government.

In 1402 Timur came out of Asia and broke up the Ottoman lands in Anatolia. He could do nothing to weaken Ottoman power in the Balkans, however, and the Anatolian territories, never completely lost, were to be reunited after Mehmed I, who became sultan in 1413. Expansion renewed its energy and the conquest of the enfeebled Constantinople (Konstantiniyye or New Rome) in 1453 had symbolic significance. Sultan Fatih Mehmed II ('the Conqueror') could imagine himself a Roman emperor who would one day enter Old Rome as a caesar and re-establish the Pantheon as the repository of all the religions of his dominions. But the westward ride of the Ottomans did not penetrate Italy for long. Mehmed II's cavalry swept past Venice and the gates of Vicenza were closed against them, but Rome was logistically beyond his reach.[11] Nor was Vienna to fall to Süleyman if only because his march was delayed by Balkan floods in May 1526. Thus the Danube became the frontier of the vast empire.

This Western world outlook meant that until the end of the fifteenth century there were exchanges of ideas, however hostile the intellectual outlooks may have been, between Europe and Ottoman grandees. That there was always an alternative Eastern policy is not important to this monograph.

The core of Ottoman architecture was the elemental symbolism of the perfect hemisphere set on a cube. This required the transitional zone of support for the dome: the curiously Ottoman triangulations which later became ordinary squinches and were finally replaced by Byzantine-type pendentives. The mosque, the most important of buildings, was such a unit. Added to it to form the so-called zaviye or convent mosque was a closed court with a fountain under an oculus. This was flanked by two open-sided *ivans* (halls) connecting to chambers for rest. They were hospices or even residences for dervishes and Ahi supporters of the sultans. This conglomerate of six domed units was contrived—with that of the mosque raised higher than the rest. In front of the zaviye was a portico or colonnade of some five or

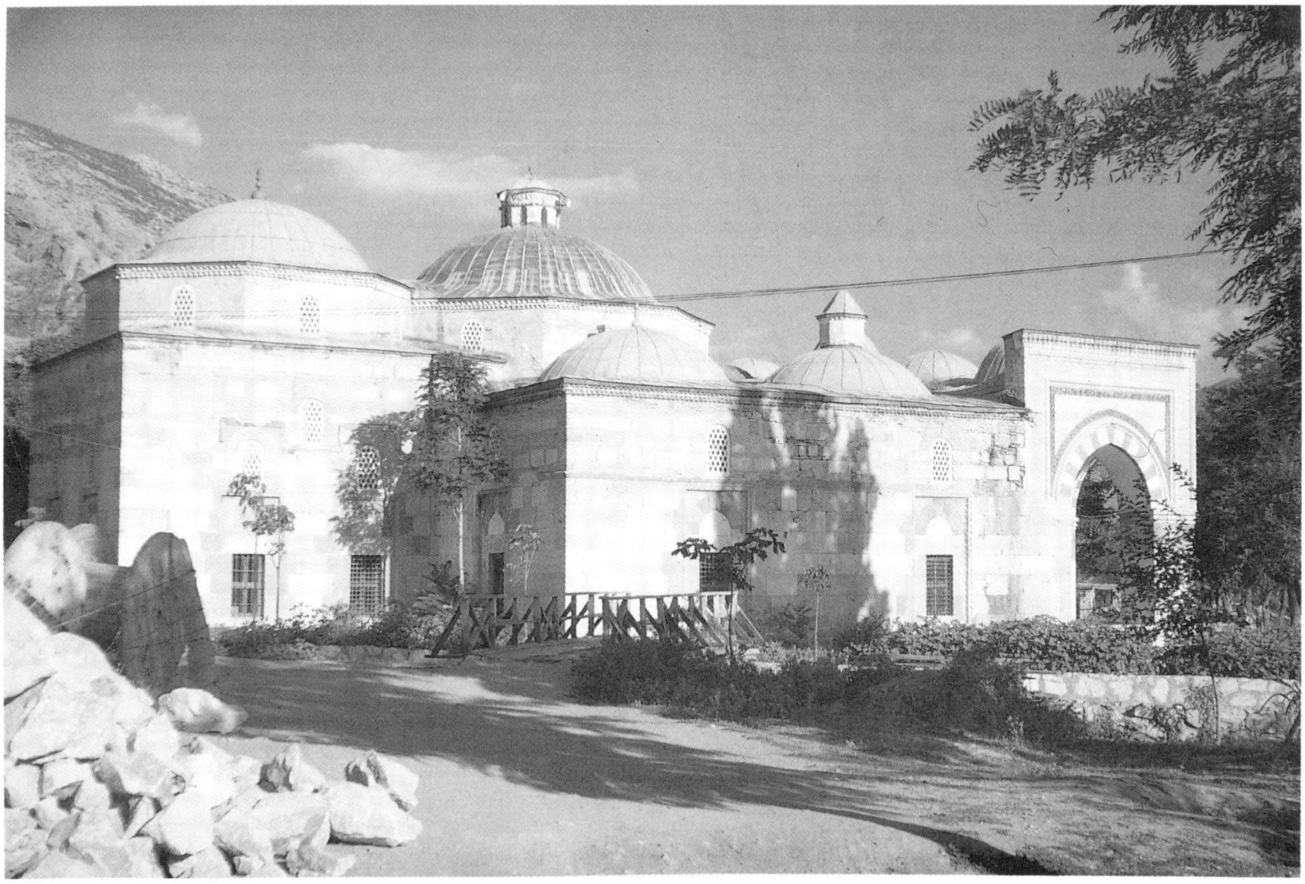

Sinan

9. Bayazid Pasha mosque-zaviye, Amasya. The dome (left) is the prayer-hall, the dome (centre) is the inner court and the two below are dervish rooms. The portico (right) served as the living area by day.

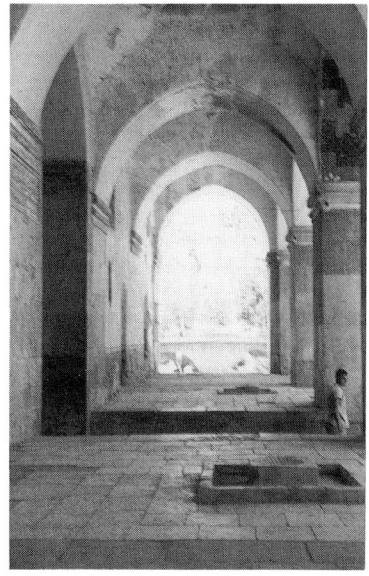

10. Bayazid Pasha mosque-zaviye, Amasya: portico

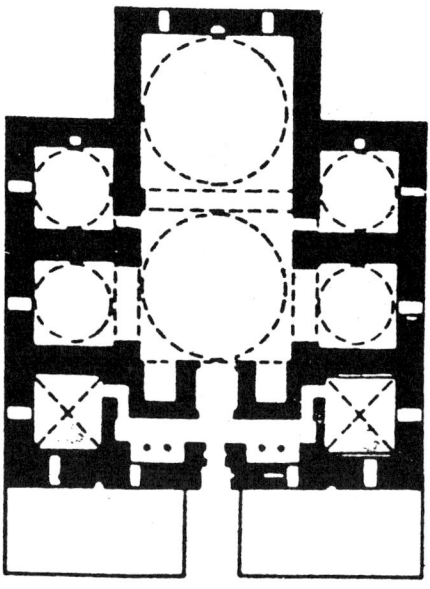

11. Green Mosque (Yeşil Cami), Bursa: plan

Before Sinan

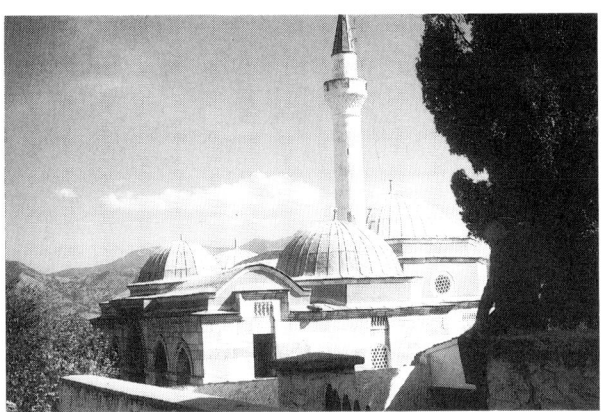

12. *Firuz Agha mosque-zaviye, Milas. The minaret is correctly at the mosque corner.*

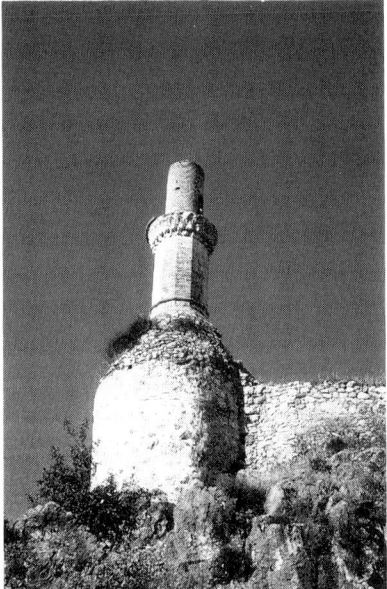

13. *Orhaniye minaret, Bilecik*

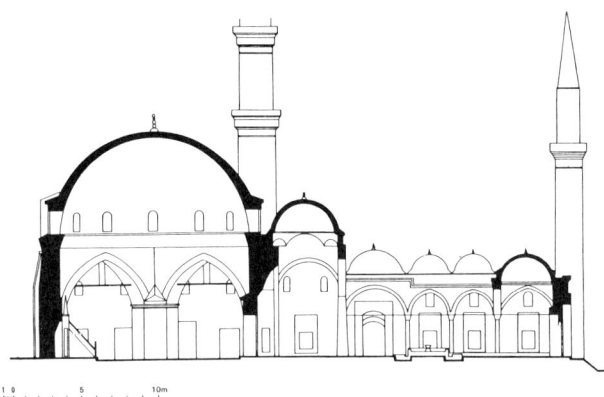

14. *Üç Şerefeli (Three Balconies) mosque, Edirne: elevation*

seven arches with domes above. Variations on this theme were numerous and fascinating including the Bayazid Pasha zaviye at Amasya (1419). At the royal chapels at Bursa such as the Yeşil *Cami* or Green Mosque (1424) royal rooms were built above the vestibule—which should not be read as a narthex for it preceded the court and not the prayer hall. At the Firuz Agha mosque at Milas the minaret was placed against the mosque within the court instead of at the north-west corner of the portico where it was at last coming to rest. This was exceptional if logical but not visually satisfactory. The first Ottoman minarets were of uncertain location due to the functional logic of placing them in the most advantageous position from which to make the call to prayer. Thus that of the Orhaniye mosque at Bilecik was perched on a crag above the mosque itself. Prior to Sinan, the slim stone minarets so typical of Ottoman architecture had been evolved and teams of specialist masons trained to build them. The heavy brick predecessors were abandoned.

With the decline of dervish and Ahi power, due in part to the hostility of the *ulema* (the orthodox religious and judicial intelligentsia), zaviye rooms lost importance while that of colleges for Koranic and legal instruction grew. The rooms either became extensions of the mosque or separate buildings albeit attached to the flanks of the prayer hall with important doorways into them. The lateral development of the mosques precipitated the establishment of forecourts which became spectacular elements in mosque architecture. They had also emerged logically where porticoed colleges were placed opposite the mosque front. It was not long before the muddy space in between was paved and tamed and the rival porticoes united.

A new emphasis which became obsessive was placed on the central mosque dome until the 24-metre giant of the Üç Şerefeli mosque (the mosque of the Three Balconies) in Edirne was achieved by the mid-fifteenth century: the side areas were roofed by pairs of domes a quarter of its size. The central prayer hall could also be roofed by the twin domes over a rectangle as at the Mahmud Pasha mosque (1467) in Istanbul or the Bayazid II mosque in Amasya (1486). This was partly because the Ottoman eye was accustomed to the double domes of mosque and closed courtyard. It was also because those untrained in aesthetics were undisturbed by dissected interior space above wall level.

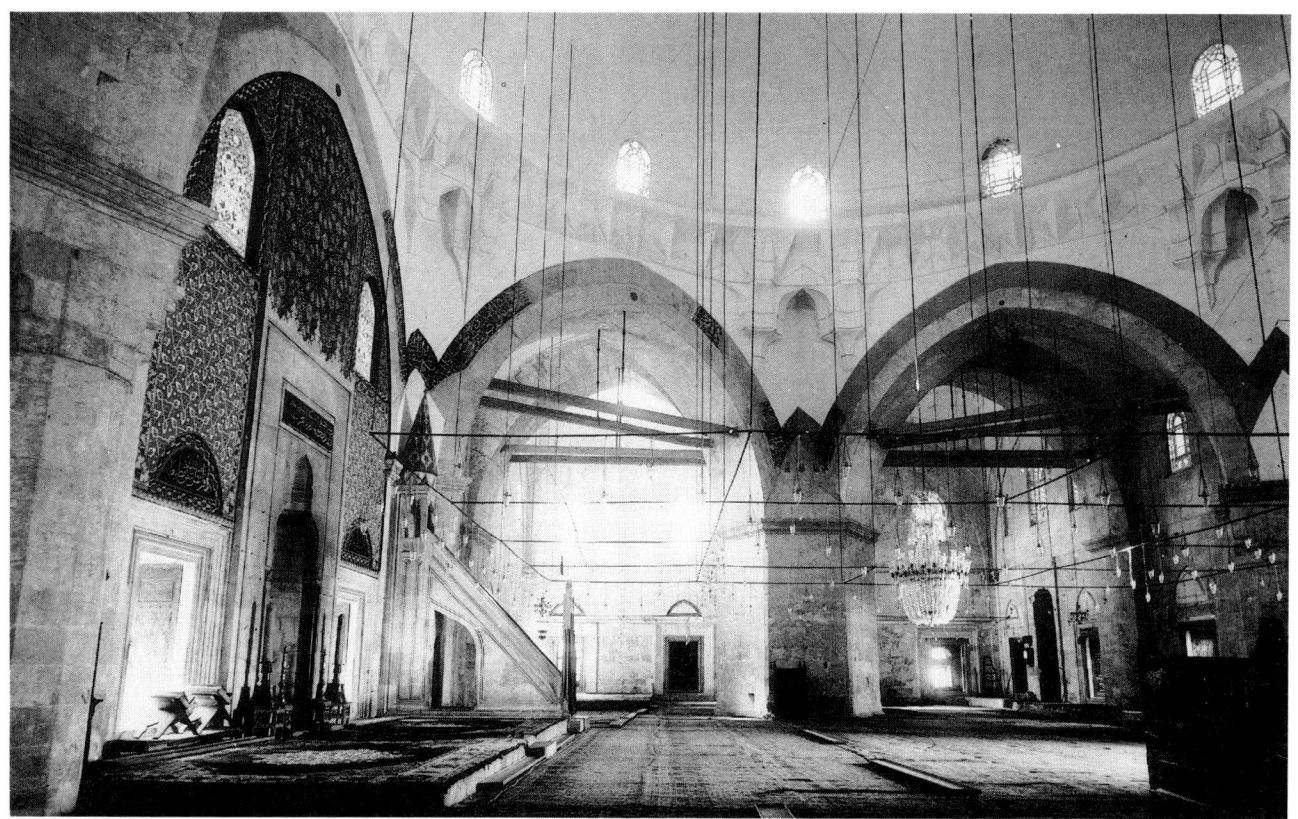

15. Üç Şerefeli (Three Balconies) mosque, Edirne: interior (Graeme Gardiner)

There had been master masons and emergent engineers of great inventiveness but in Edirne and Amasya during the fifteenth century two real architects appear, that is to say builders who broke with tradition. An anonymous forerunner of Sinan created the pier-supported dome of the Üç Şerefeli mosque at the former and Hayreddin is believed to have built the twice-domed prayer-hall mosque of Bayazid II at the latter.

Great piers are not a problem in churches because Christian ceremonial requires a nave and aisles. There are no processions in Islam but prayer only. Thus the four huge piers of the Üç Şerefeli mosque mask the *mihrab* from many of the devout at prayer. Hayreddin reduced the amount of masonry inside his mosque by extending these piers as external towers at the four quarters of the dome so that the weight of masonry remained the same and was sufficient to take the thrusts of the dome. There are usually four of these towers but, exceptionally, there can be eight as at the mosque of Selim II at Edirne. With Sinan's mosques they are perpetual sentinels whereas with St Peter's in Rome, St Paul's in London or the Consolazione at Todi there is no need for such guardians. The thrust is absorbed by

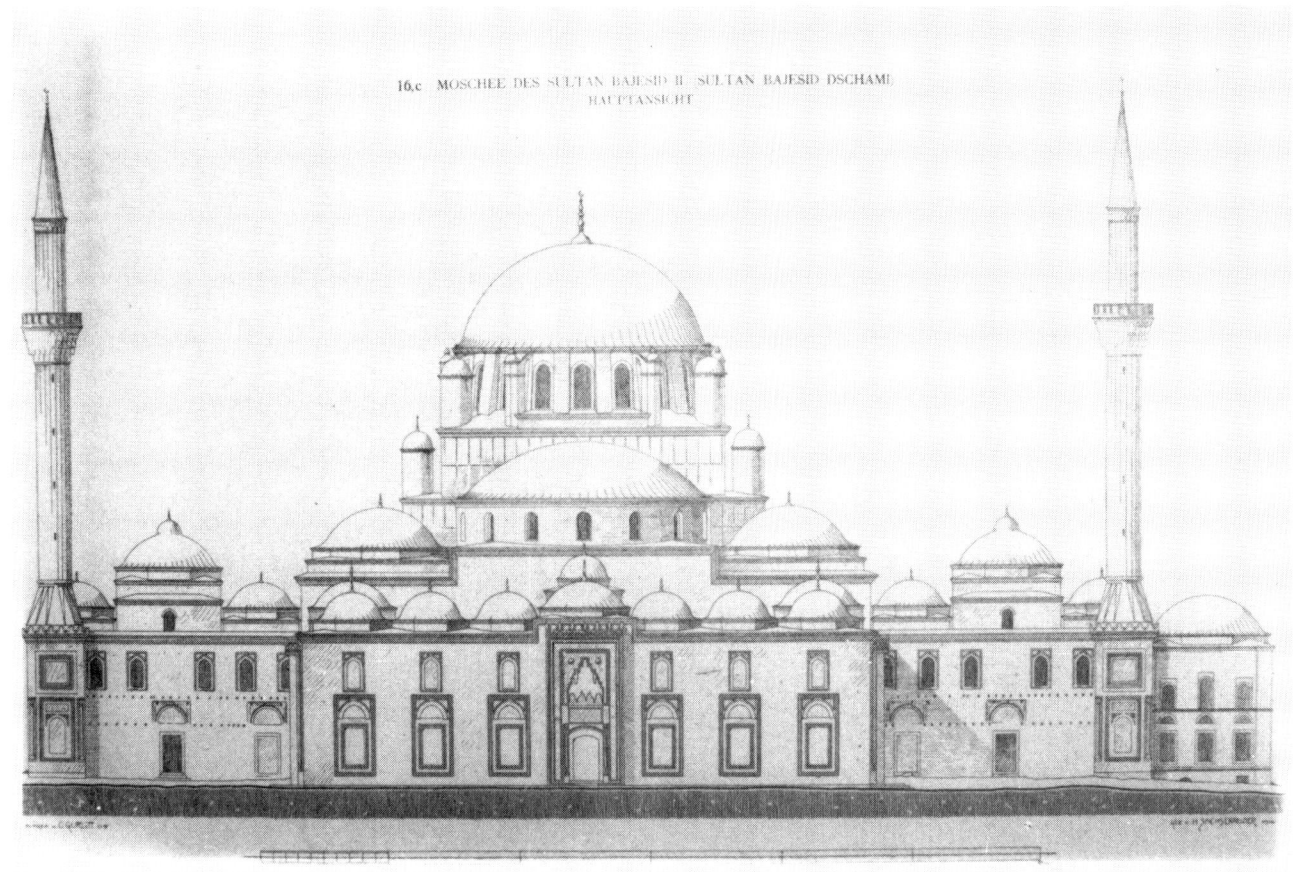

16. Bayazidiye mosque, Istanbul: elevation (Gurlitt)

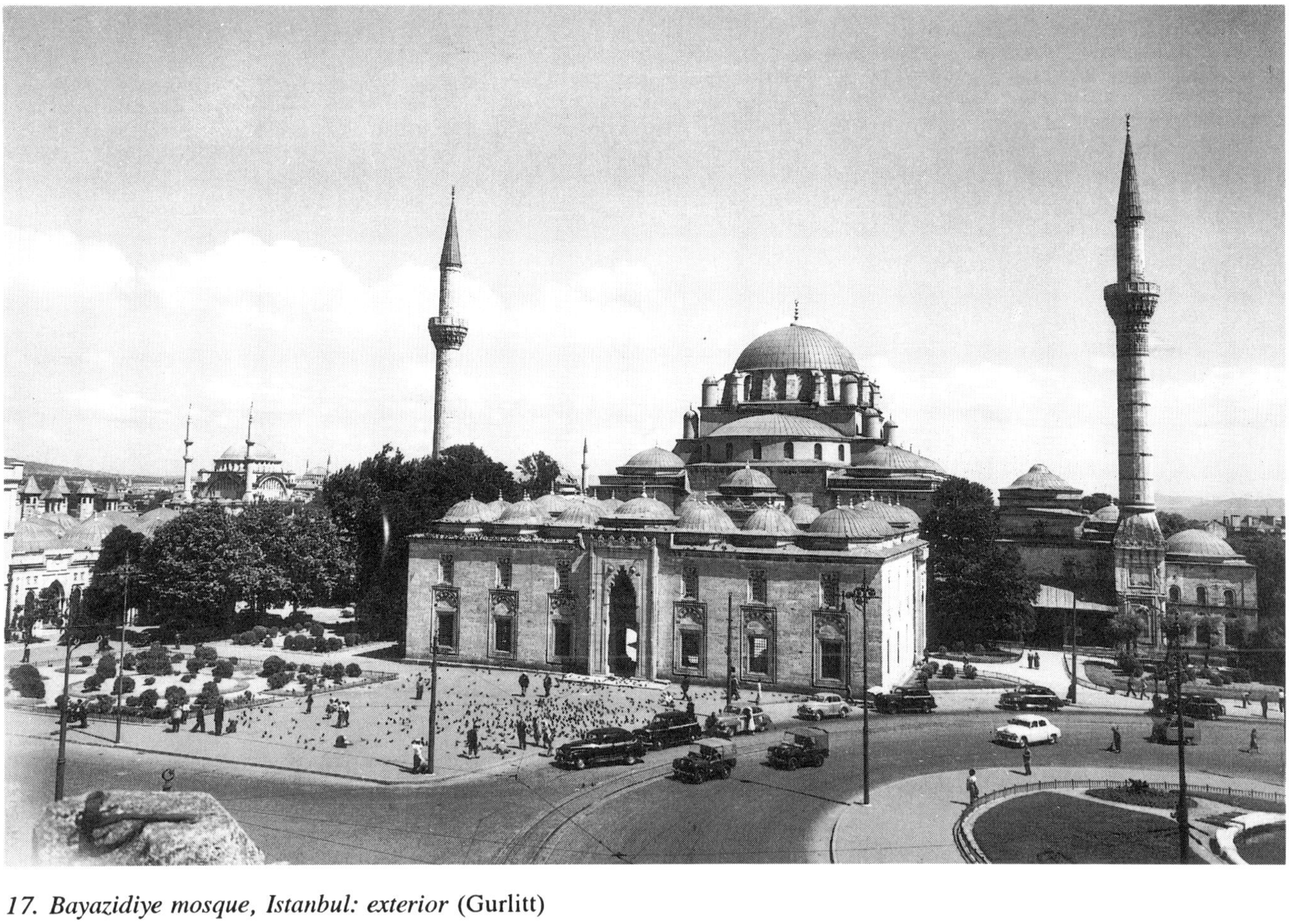

17. Bayazidiye mosque, Istanbul: exterior (Gurlitt)

mammoth piers or, at Todi, into the strengthened corners of the central cube.

The Ottoman style in the fifteenth century achieved that poetic interplay of shaded and sunlit interiors which pleased Le Corbusier[12] when he visited Bursa. But all Ottoman buildings conformed to the basic principle of units welded together to form a whole in which each element is clearly defined.

When he came to break down distinct forms, which had worked ideally with the small mosques of fourteenth- and fifteenth-century Anatolia, Sinan freed both interior space and exterior form and thus saved Ottoman architecture from rigor mortis. He was not the first builder to have been influenced by Haghia Sophia: that leap forward in spatial terms was accomplished at the mosque of Bayazid II (1506) in Istanbul. The cathedral was acknowledged as incomparable for it was established as the first mosque of the empire by Mehmed II on the day of the conquest of the Byzantine capital. Attempts to emulate its size continued until the seventeenth century. The Bayazidiye falters because the half-domes do not merge with the central dome while each side aisle has four similar small domes in the established Ottoman manner. The architect worked as best he could but without the experience or awareness of how to liberate space by using exedras.

The Ottomans used all available materials in their buildings: brick, good limestone and spoglia. Until the seventeenth century the columns which were so important for Ottoman architecture were all re-used Byzantine monoliths while the multi-drummed columns of the Hellenistic period were scorned or used in foundations. Roofing tiles were replaced by lead once the Balkan mines had been captured. The need for economy with stone resulted in mixed courses of stone and brick in the Byzantine manner and Greek mathematics infiltrated Ottoman building because the height and width of columns predetermine the span of arches.[13]

Sinan inherited a formal approach to space imprisoned in rigid units. He had to employ teams drilled in past traditions. A result of this was Hayreddin's hospital (1488), built for Bayazid II at Edirne, which is a noble complex. Here the hostel annexes flanking the mosque collide with the minarets and yet windows were constructed as if they would be unobstructed. This is to work by rote. Sinan could only build logically, eschewing fantasy, and express structure clearly and absolutely— at least, to begin with. Past errors were to be eradicated, a scattering of new ones made. But eventually there was to be something else, which is the subject of this book.

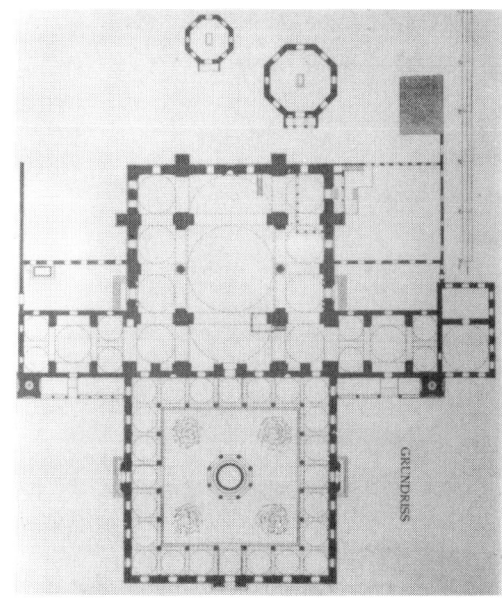

18. *Bayazidiye mosque, Istanbul: plan* (Gurlitt)

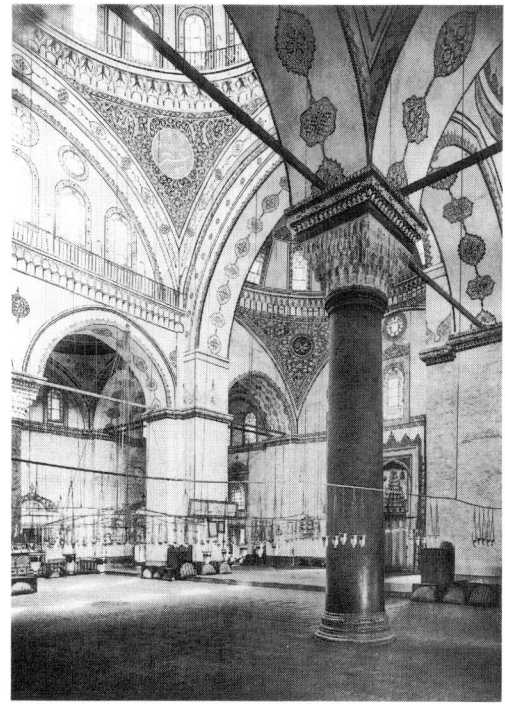

19. *Bayazidiye mosque, Istanbul: interior* (Gurlitt)

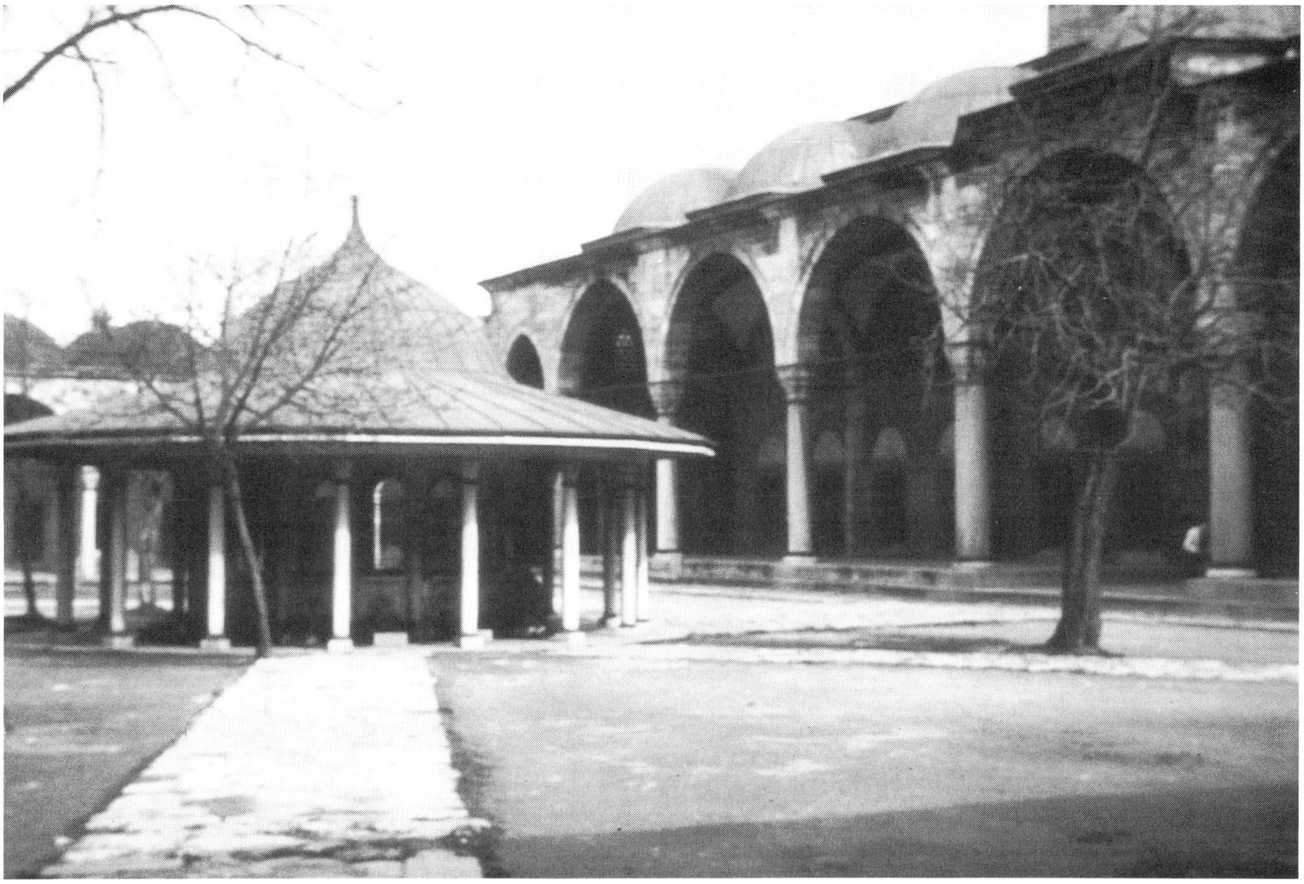

20. Mihrimah mosque, Istanbul: portico

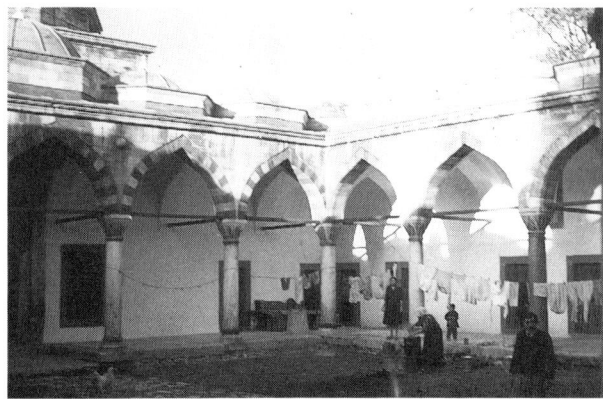

21. Haseki Hürrem complex, Istanbul: court of medical college (tip medrese). A rare use of ogee arches

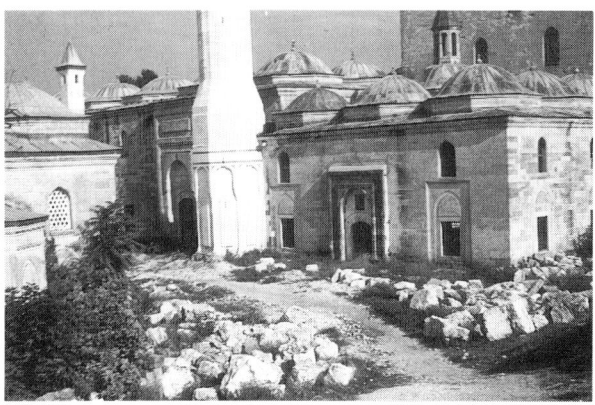

22. Bayazidiye hospital, Edirne: dervish hospice (tabhane) and minaret collide.

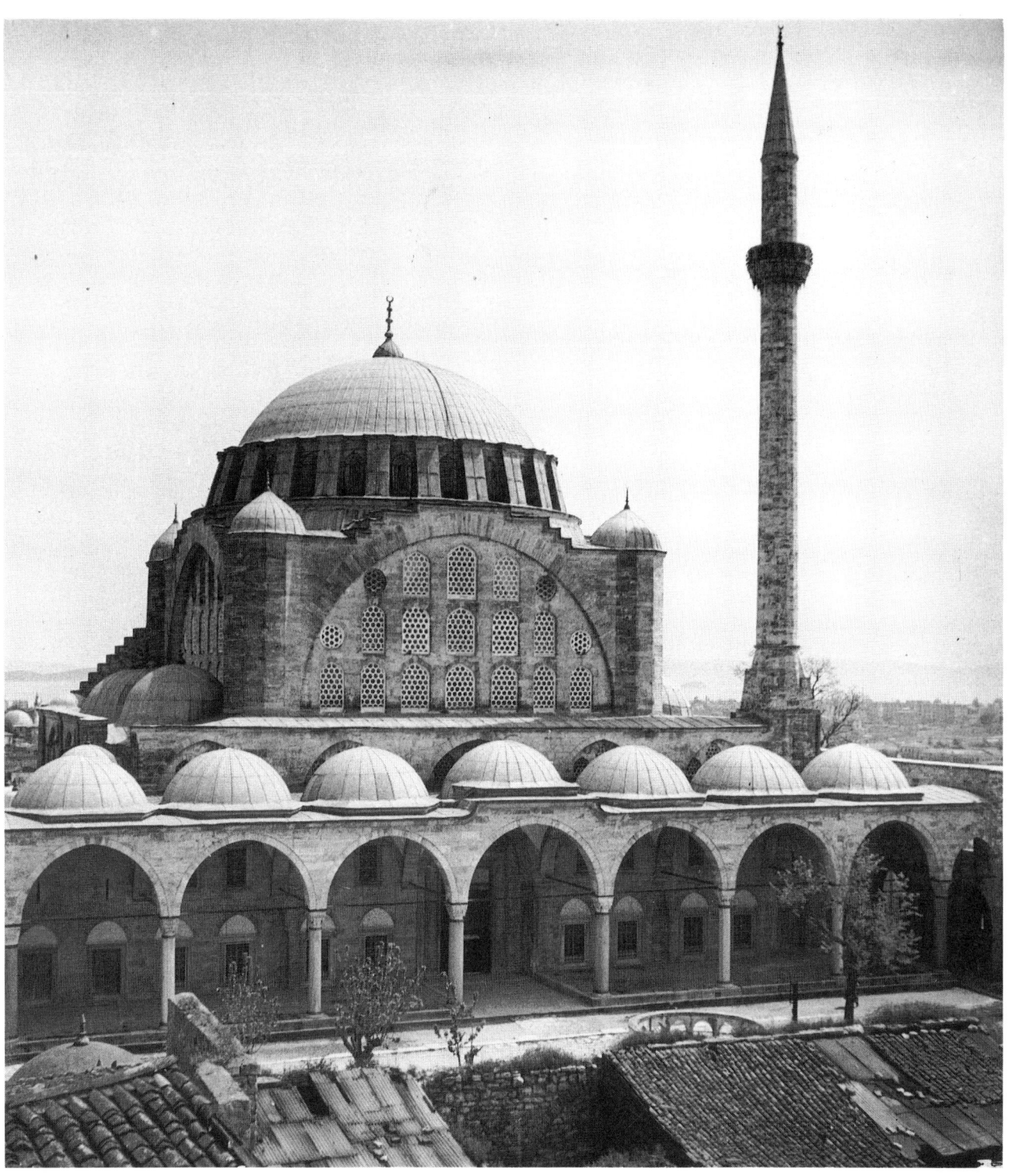

23. Mihrimah mosque, Istanbul: below Theodosian walls (Graeme Gardiner)

Patronage and Sites

An architect's vision is tempered by the exigencies of the site, the money available and the instructions of the patron. Since the size of the mosque was in most cases the measure for the rest of the buildings of a complex, this decision was the most important in Ottoman architecture. It could lead to inelegant cramping as at the complex of Haseki Hürrem or to deformation of the college cells as at the foundations of Zal Mahmud Pasha or of Mihrimah Sultan at Edirnekapı. In these cases, it was impossible for the architect to overcome the difficulties of the terrain. By the sixteenth century there was a shortage of land in the centre of the capital and under Islamic law there could be no question of compulsory purchase let alone confiscation. If with Timur laws were overridden without remorse, the remarkably temperate Ottoman sultans were restrained. It was only the decision to leave the old palace at Bayazid and to make the New Palace or Yeni Saray (now known as Topkapısaray) the residence of the harem as well as the seat of government that made the vast complex of the Süleymaniye possible. There the old palace grounds already belonged to the sultan.

So it was that most vezirial mosques—like those of Kara Ahmad Pasha or of Hadım (Eunuch) Ibrahim Pasha near the Theodosian walls—were built some way from the centre of the city, as was the immensely wealthy Mihrimah's major foundation. In addition, the Mihrimah complex was built on an awkward site too close to the walls. The land in the area was mostly market garden or even waste. Sokollu Mehmed Pasha built beneath the Hippodrome but even with his boundless wealth the site was restricted. In the provinces where land was relatively cheap, Rüstem Pasha and other rich vezirs built lavishly. He left a large *kervansaray* at Edirne and a mosque at Tekirdağ in Thrace.

For a Royal Architect all other work was secondary to that of his sultan whose huge foundations could not be met from the privy purse alone. Subscription lists must have demanded prestigious gifts from the royal family and household and from vezirs and lesser officials according to their degree. The populace also subscribed, as we know from the legend of the poor widow who donated her two pigeons towards the building of the mosque of Bayazid II in Istanbul. Kılıç Ali Pasha received subscriptions from the Guild of Butchers, among others, because one and all were glad to save their souls by acts of benevolence which won merit in the eye of the Almighty.

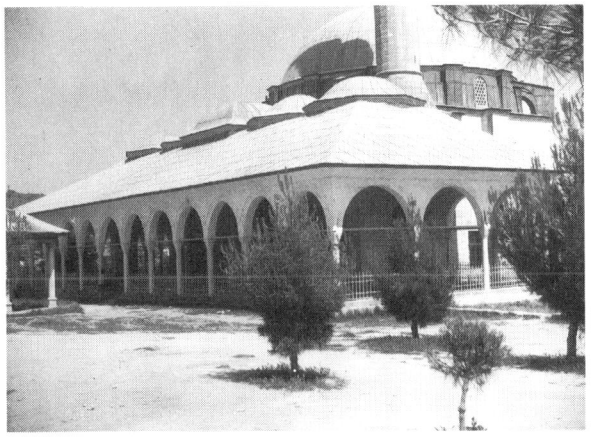

24. *Rüstem Pasha mosque, Tekirdağ: portico*

Sinan

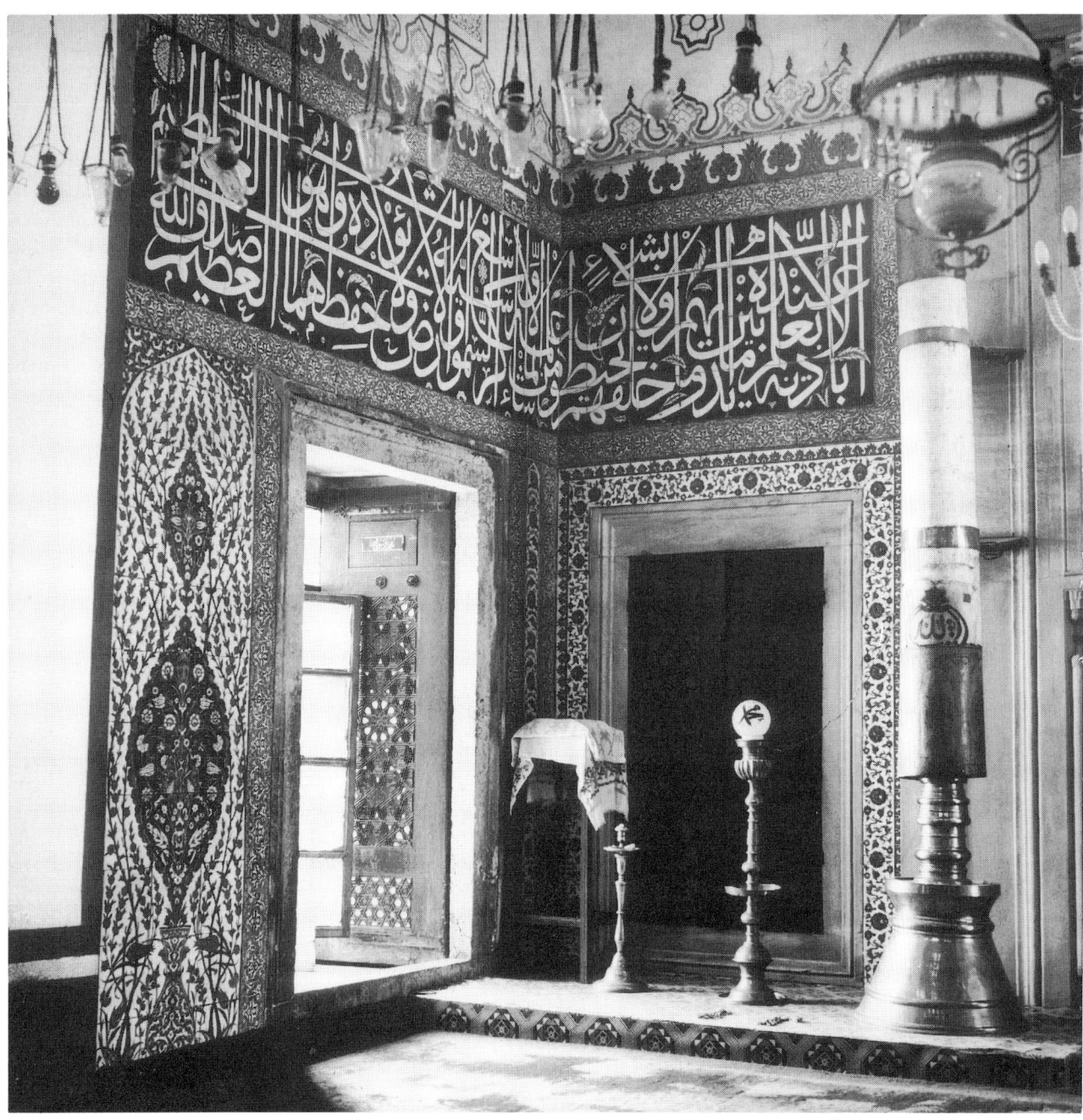

25. *Atık Valide mosque, Üsküdar: panel of Iznik tiles*

Not only did Sinan build for his sultan and the senior vezirs, he also built for lesser men who were his friends. The mosque of the *tekke* (dervish convent) which he built for Ramazan Efendi is modest yet it possesses a glamorous interior with panels of Iznik tiles of unsurpassed beauty.[14] It is unlikely that a friend could make specific demands on an architect so eminent but the braver royalty could. It can only have been at Mihrimah Sultan's[15] command that Sinan used the phalanxes of tiles in the memorial mosque of Rüstem Pasha. Certain

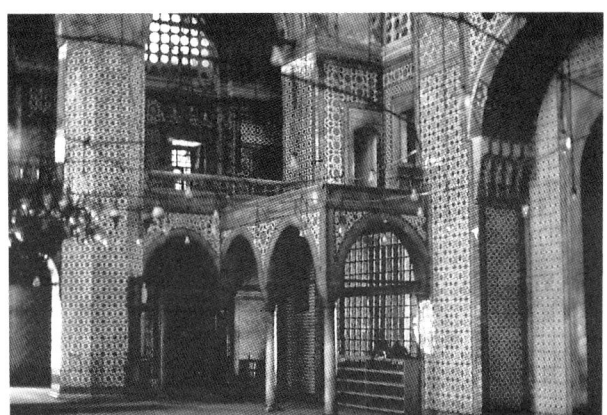

26. Rüstem Pasha mosque, Istanbul: interior (Graeme Gardiner)

details like the magical central fountain of the Selimiye mosque in Edirne may have been requested by that sultan, who was a poet of some merit and likely to have enjoyed discussing aesthetics with Sinan.

Royal and vezirial patrons were alike in their preference for conservative and heaven-ordained coventionality. This underlay all Ottoman building. It is therefore interesting that Süleyman, Mihrimah and Selim II were to support Sinan throughout his revolution and many vezirs were equally acquiescent. This was a tribute to the liberal and Renaissance spirit which briefly abounded in the mid-sixteenth century. It was inconceivable for a sultan not to take an interest in the building of his tribute to God, if not to the degree that was to obsess Ahmad I (1603–17).[16]

There are elements in Sinan's architecture which may be his response to a patron, including the grand portal of the courtyard of the Süleymaniye mosque and the slenderness of the minaret of the Mihrimah mosque at Edirnekapı (the Edirne Gate). There are no letters or other private papers and so such thoughts can only be speculative. Nor is the situation eased by the surviving Orders-in-Council, since they are couched as requests to be approved by the sultan even if they may originally have been his own ideas.[17]

The Royal Architect

Devotees of Ottoman architecture are indebted to Kuran's patient research into the earliest mosques attributed to Sinan which were built before he became Royal Architect.[18] These modest buildings have been so repaired and rebuilt, however, that they have only an esoteric interest. Nor is it important to join in the controversy over which buildings of the Haseki Hürrem complex (1538–40) at Avretpazar in Istanbul were built before Sinan or added later. The square mosque, which was to be doubled in size, is trim. The college with the ogee arches of its arcades, now stripped of their Iznik tile soffits, the very practical public kitchen and the other jostling buildings of a restricted plot may have been added to by degrees. Yet they are all good examples of traditional workmanship, shipshape and proper. The hospital, with its bent entrance in aid of modesty, has a plan said to be more Persian than Ottoman. As an intelligent response to the cramped space the courtyard is cropped at the corners and is not a rectangle or an

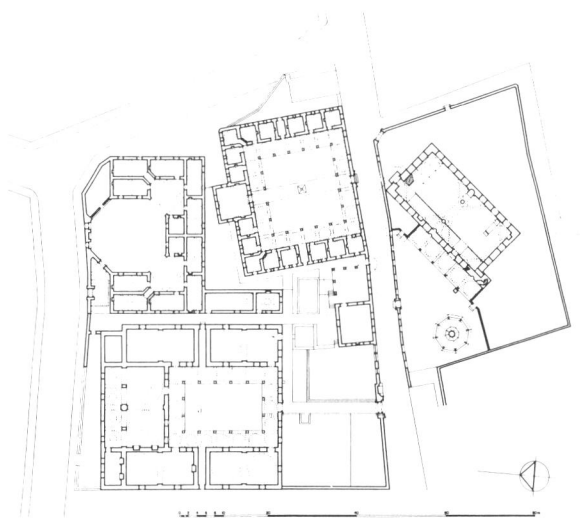

27. Haseki Hürrem complex, Istanbul: plan

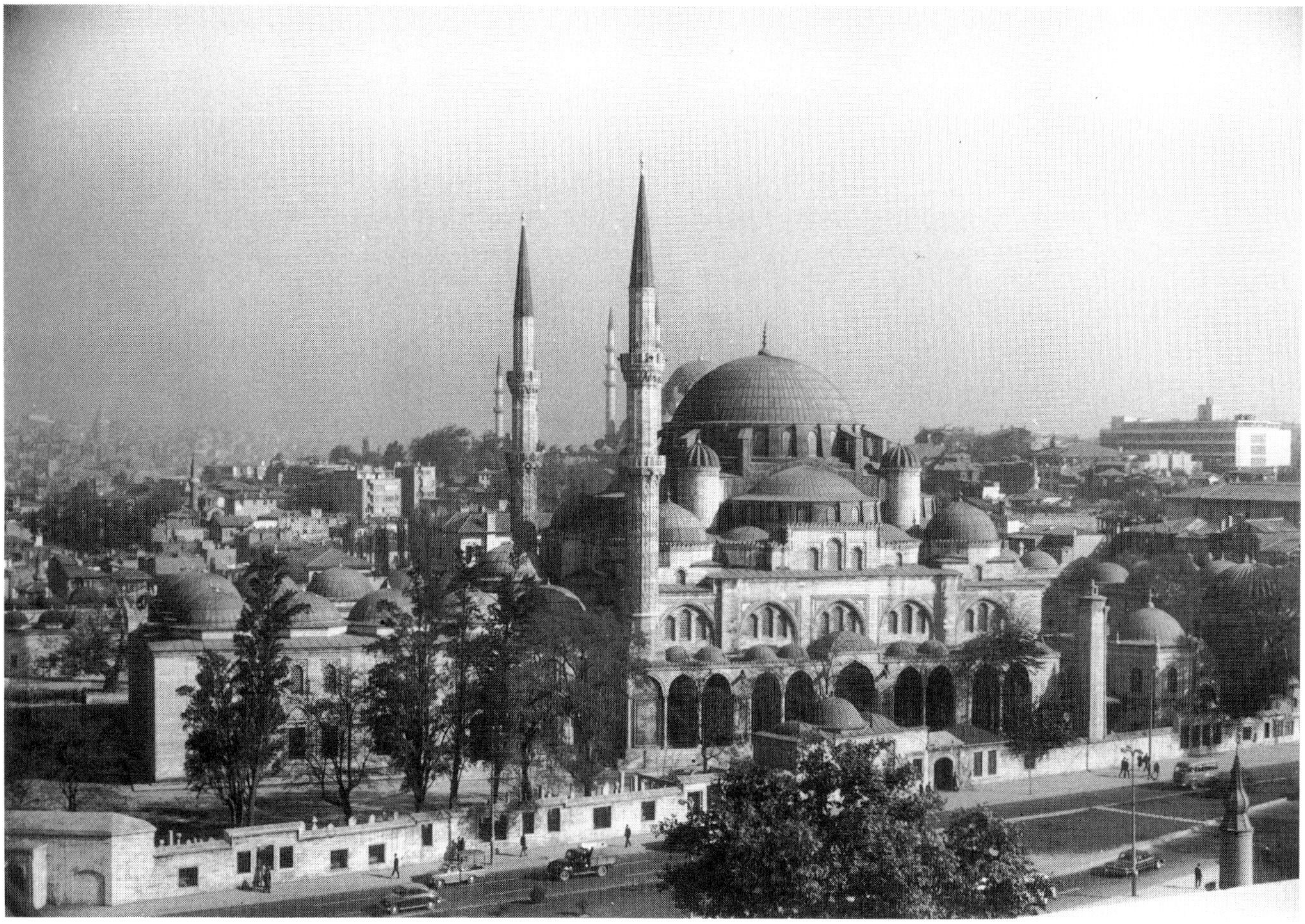

Sinan

![Şehzade mosque exterior]

28. Şehzade mosque, Istanbul: exterior

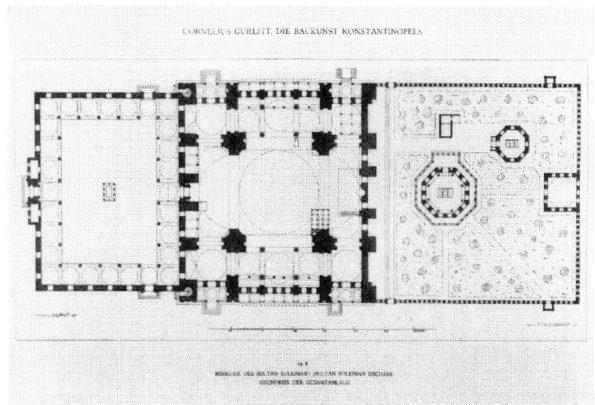

29. Şehzade mosque, Istanbul: plan (Gurlitt)

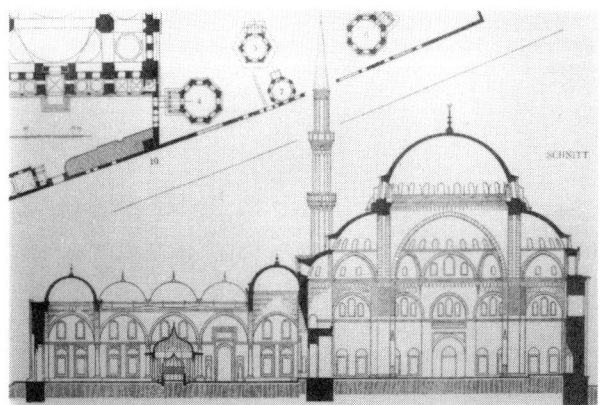

30. Şehzade mosque, Istanbul: elevation (Gurlitt)

octagon while, exceptionally, two major rooms on either side sit flank by flank. Little inner courts or recesses add notes of harmony and the former wards are spacious and well lit. Here we are assured, as Süleyman the Magnificent must have been, that Sinan was trained as a capable builder with potential ideas. Whether he inherited plans from the former Royal Architect Acemi Agha or not, his was the execution. Acemi Agha is a shadowy figure who was probably responsible for the highly derivative major complex of Selim I, the Grim or the Implacable according to taste, and father of Süleyman.

The first important complex undoubtedly built by Sinan was that in honour of the eldest and most loved son of the sultan, Şehzade Mehmed, for whom Süleyman desired a grand mosque and splendid mausoleum.[19] The mosque has been popular with architectural historians because it is the epitome of the Ottoman concept of centripetality, that is the single dome as a core however much enlarged by lesser domes and half-domes. Centripetality implies that the parts are drawn towards the middle whereas they only come to life if seen as radiating from the central dome, as indeed the forces within the structure do. In this sense, the dome descends by means of half-domes towards the four outer walls. This so-called centripetality was not new. As Sinan himself was aware, his fourfoil mosque was the remarkable achievement of an apprentice and apprentices base their work on the tried structures of predecessors.[20] At Dıyarbekir, which Sinan knew for it was the south-eastern headquarters of armies campaigning against Iran, there is the fourfoil mosque of Fatih Pasha (1517) which could claim to be the first example of this Ottoman form. But many Byzantine churches were fourfoil except that economy usually reduced the arms of the cross to barrel vaults with the dome or navel of the design being reserved for the centre of the building. There was the remarkable Armenian example of the church of the Holy Apostles at Ani, for example.

The Şehzade mosque continued the conservative balance for courtyard and mosque, both having the same measurements at ground level. The courtyard was cramped by the exceptionally large domes of the arcading and the portico even before Murad IV hooded the fountain for ablutions in its middle. Sinan also introduced a decorative profusion with the cresting of domes and portals and with the seemingly appliqué decoration on the trunks of the minarets. This may have been due to the availability of craftsmen brought back

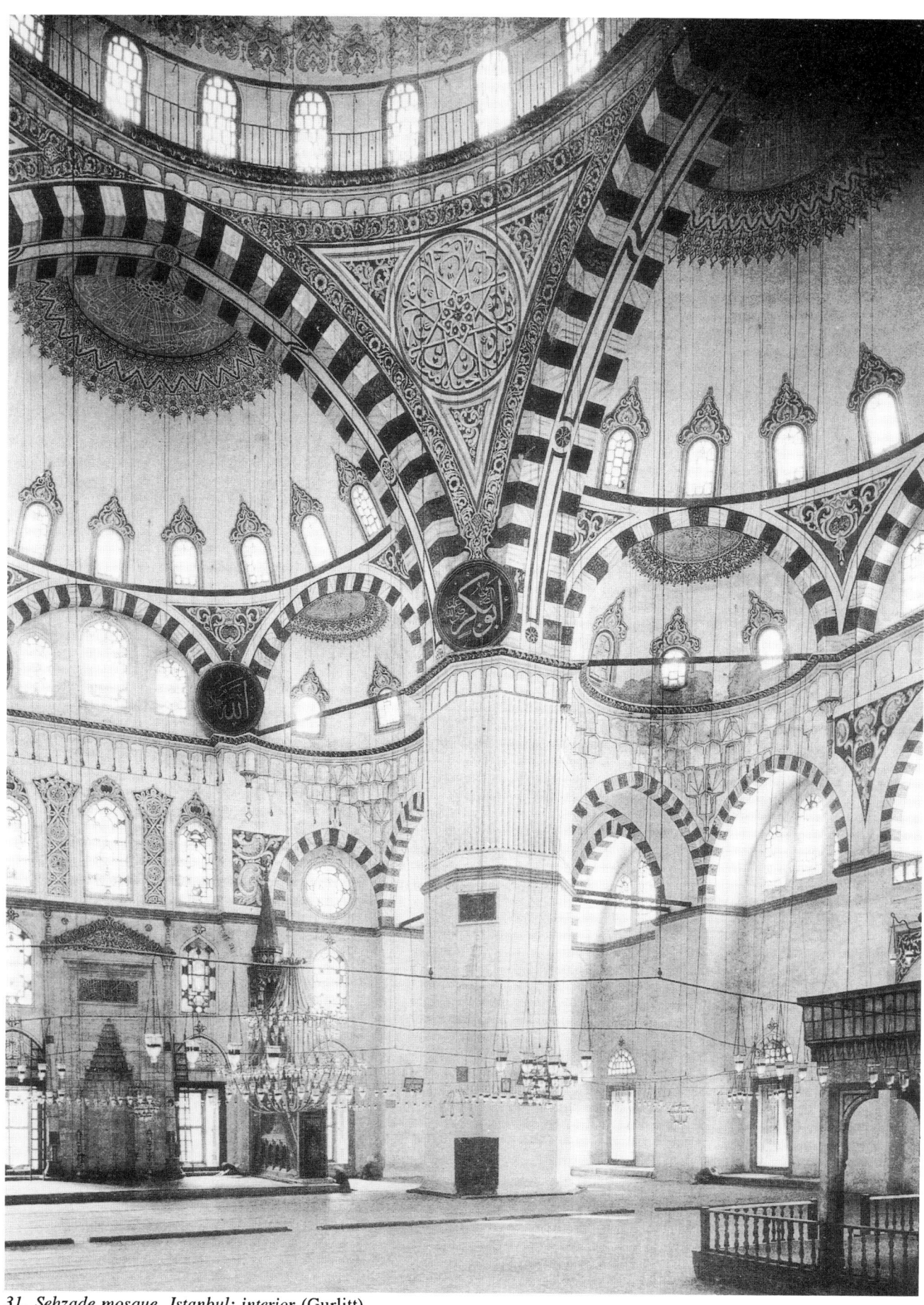
31. Şehzade mosque, Istanbul: *interior* (Gurlitt)

The Royal Architect

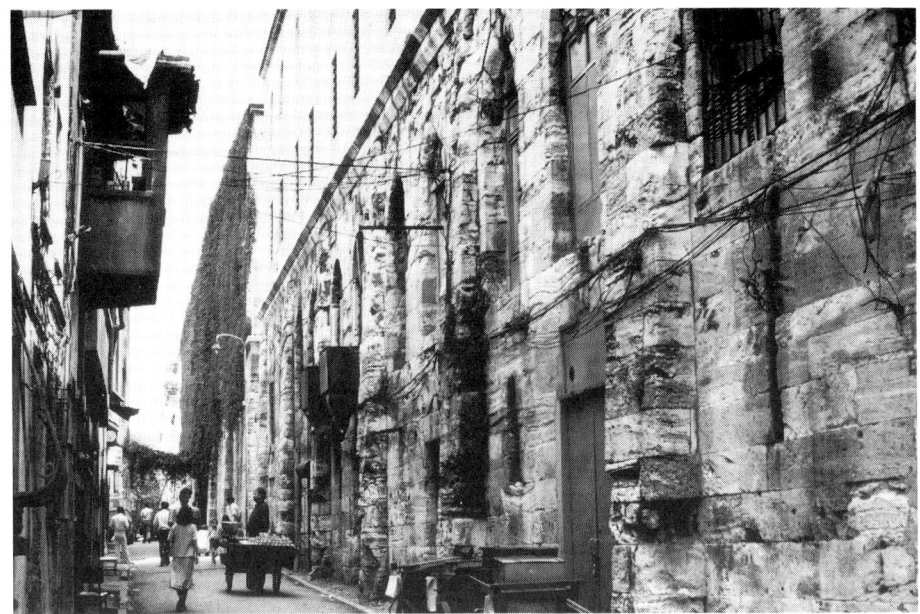

32. Süleymaniye complex, Istanbul: vaults

from Tabriz but it is significant that Sinan eschewed such luxuries after this one example. The Şehzade has creative elements, however, and the seeds of future ideas are plain to see.

Sinan introduced the exedra, learnt from Haghia Sophia, and turned it into an intricate synthesis of dome and half-dome. It adds life to the flow of the major dome into the subordinate roofing level as it stretches at its ease. The interior is a totally balanced and disciplined statement of space that is an engineering achievement but overly formal. What had been lacking in earlier Ottoman architecture were the splendid façades of the Western Renaissance and before. Now these appear in embryo along the sides of the mosque in the form of large arcades with a rhythm of flanking arches at each side of their central entrances: central because this was a building where all was subordinate to rigid rules of balance as if the architect had read Alberti[21] and was afraid that his building might not otherwise stand up. When he found that it did, he was able to break free of the rules. The dome, after all, was 37 metres high and 19 metres in diameter and so somewhat more than a puppy. The lesser buildings of the complex are loosely grouped along the south and east sides of a large outer precinct with trees which is still the scene of a pre-Ottoman fertility rite on Fridays.

Sinan could now feel secure with his ratio of masonry[22] to void which should withstand all but the most devastating earthquake and his imagination could range well outside the palisade of Ottoman orthodoxy.

Süleymaniye Complex (1551-8)

The Şehzade complex was only just completed when the sultan ordered Sinan to build his remarkable foundation.[23] A year was spent creating its podium, an indication of the size and complexity of the vaults and drainage systems quite apart from the need to shift at least 2 million cubic metres of earth. The level stage that was achieved is the setting for a prima donna among mosques which dominates, and is meant to dominate, both its complex and the city.

The plans of all major Ottoman mosques were based on a square divided into sixteen equal squares. Four of these came under the central dome and at the Süleymaniye they were extended by two more squares under each half-dome. These eight domes can be seen as a nave with two aisles, each of four single squares long. Exceptionally, the Şehzade fourfoil plan incorporated three-quarters of the ground area into the central space but left the four corners as detached areas of their own. The longitudinal plan of the mosque of Süleyman, as with the Şehzade, increased the sense of integration between central space and the half-domes by the use of exedras. The aisles were given a new rhythm by varying the size of their five domes, not four (nor were there lateral half-domes), in the proportion of three large to two lesser domes. The space beneath them was revealed beyond the high arches between the great piers which support the main dome. Moreover, lateral galleries were moved back against the side walls and then extended beyond them into the open so that, externally, they ride between the two pairs of outer buttresses. These

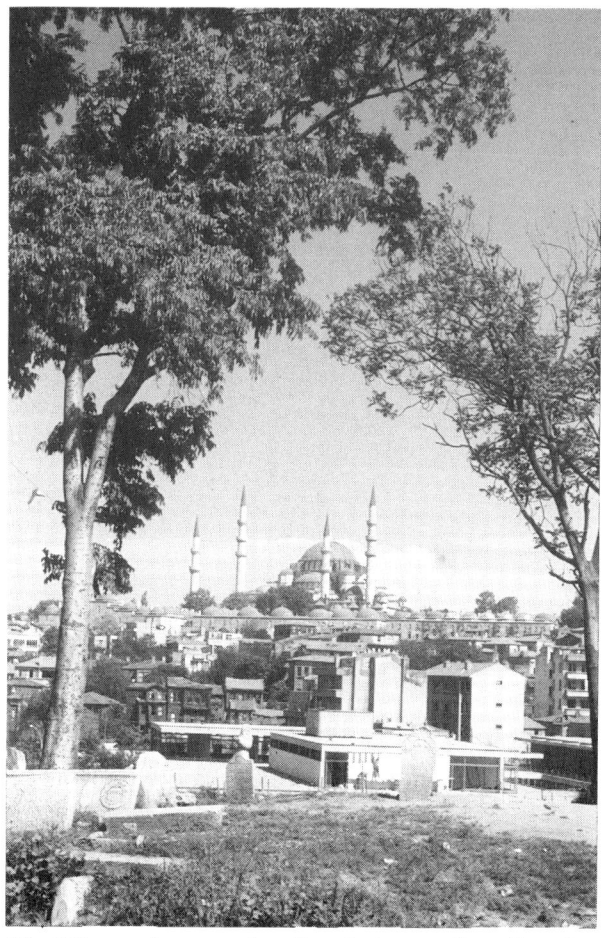

33. *Süleymaniye complex, Istanbul: seen from Zeyrek mosque (Pantocrator)*

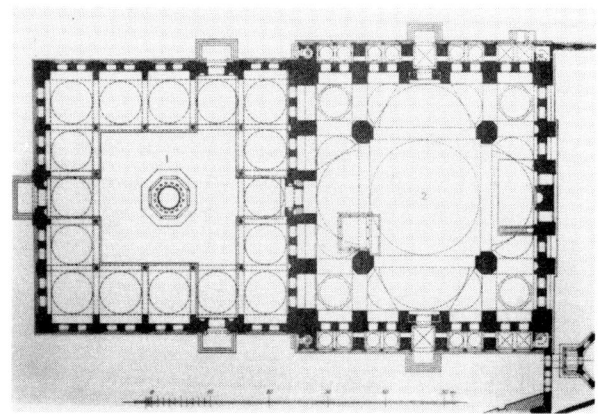

34. *Şehzade mosque, Istanbul: plan* (Gurlitt)

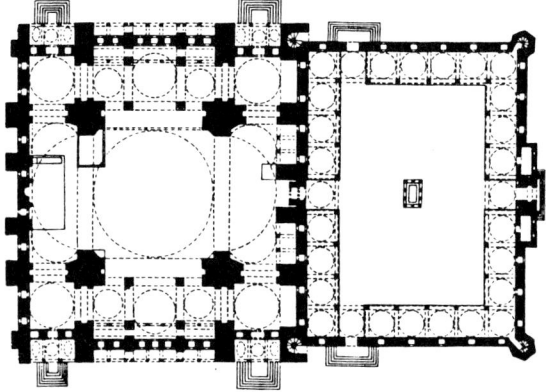

35. *Süleymaniye mosque, Istanbul: plan*

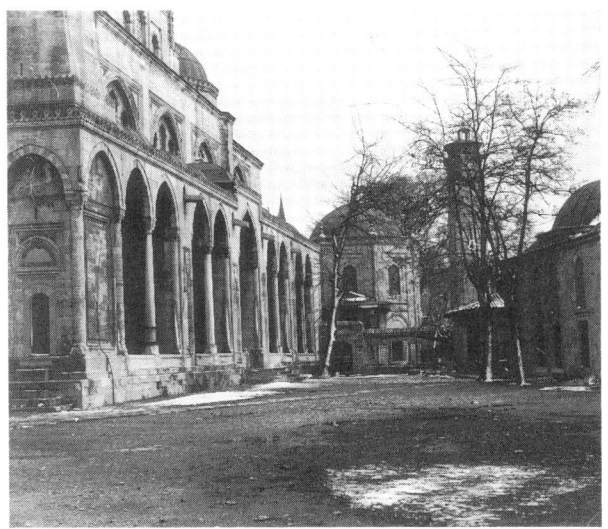

36. Şehzade mosque, Istanbul: lateral arcades

Right:
37. Süleymaniye mosque, Istanbul: lateral arcades

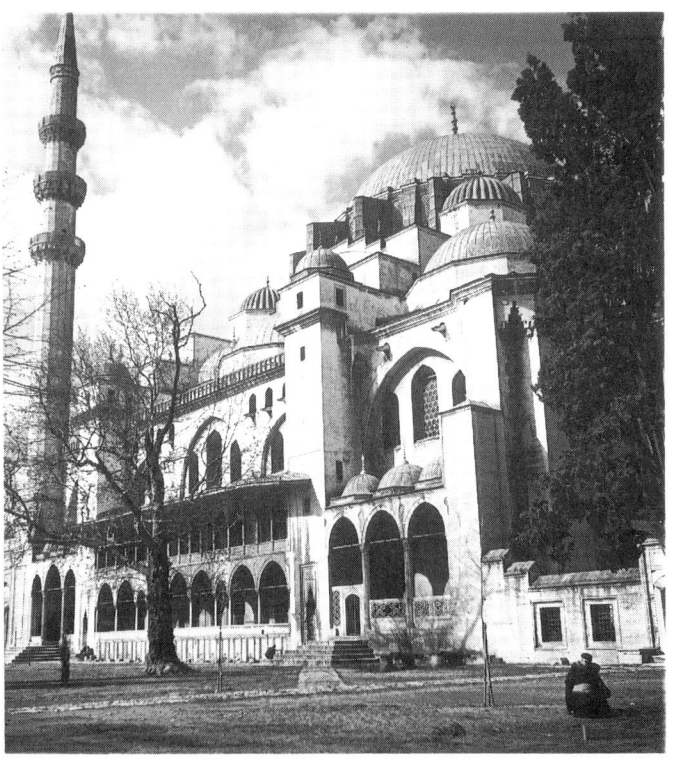

buttresses respond to the forces of the four main piers taking the thrust of the central dome. This meant that aisles were unencumbered and, by extending outside the mosque, enlarged it.

The creation of loggias in the Italian Renaissance manner gave the sides of the mosque a new importance which was enhanced by the use of two storeys, each with its own rhythm to its arches. These richly structured mosque flanks were set between the main doors at each end which, with their triple-domed porches, acted as anchors to these embryonic façades. The porches were recessed into the mosque and so gave life and purpose to the previously aloof corner areas, such as at the Şehzade mosque. The loggias, ensconced between their buttresses and above the taps for ritual washing, were also, in a sense, one-sided courtyards which can be seen as a definition of a façade. These loggias, however, do not mask the domical structure of the roof where lesser domes rise to the climax of the main dome. We have also seen that the galleries were half inside and half outside the mosque at first-floor level: thus they achieve an ideal of Ottoman architecture in that interior and exterior architecture should not just be complementary to each other but one and the same.

Sinan

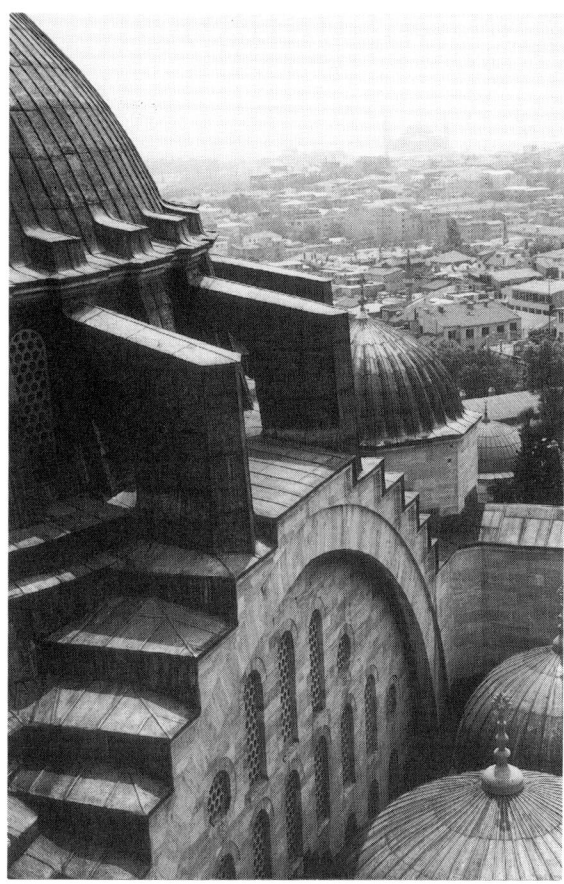 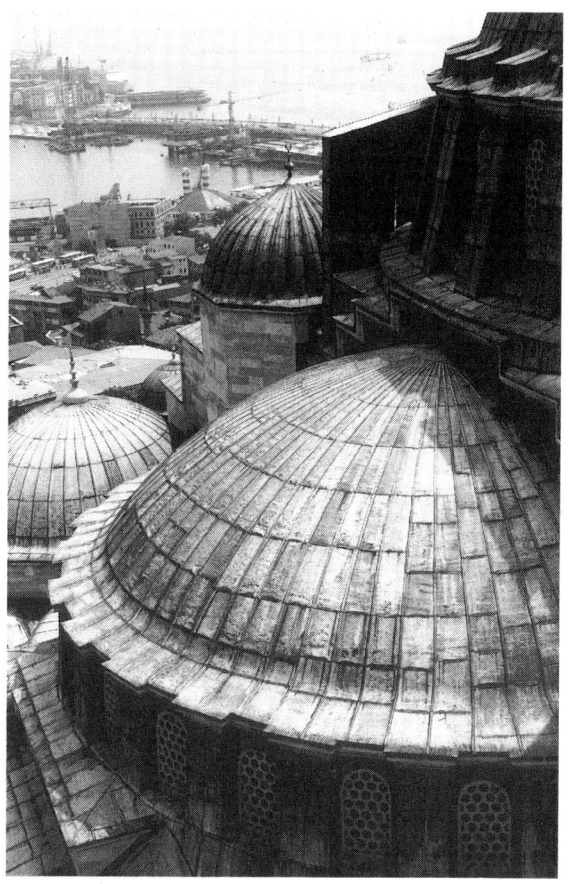

39. Süleymaniye mosque, Istanbul: roof level

Left:
38. Süleymaniye mosque, Istanbul: roof level

Four minarets were built, the two at the far corners of the courtyard being calculatedly lower than the pair at each side of the mosque itself with the result that they imply the silhouette of a triangle, as many writers have remarked. It is difficult to accept that it is imaginary, for the force of the image of security is so strong that it could be the flank of a pyramid. It is a development of the triangular effect of the minarets of such mosques as those of Mihrimah, Üsküdar and Rüstem Pasha, Istanbul. Their dimensions are determined by these triangles. The contrast of convexity and concavity is the architect's response to a nature made up of hill and dale, foreground and background—the swelling and sinking of landscape so well expressed by Robert and James Adam.

Briefly, each structural element of the mosque was used to enhance it yet the proportions vary only within the limits of the square ground plan imposed by custom—although not on the rectangular courtyard. The building is the sum of its parts aesthetically as well as structurally and expresses that freedom from inward conflict which is the aspiration of the great religions.[24]

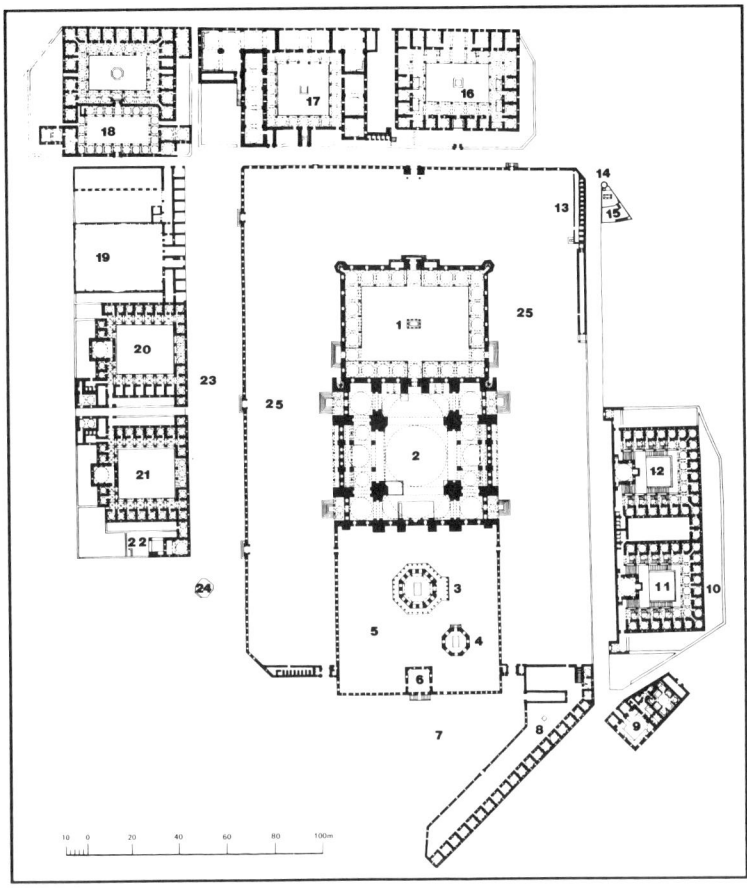

40. Süleymaniye complex, Istanbul: plan

Key

1. *Avlu* (courtyard)
2. *Cami* (mosque)
3. *Süleyman türbesi* (Süleyman's tomb)
4. *Haseki Hürrem türbesi* (Roxelane's tomb)
5. *Mezarlik* (cemetery)
6. *Türbedar odasi* (tomb-keeper's chantry)
7. Wrestling ground
8. *Darül-hadis* (graduate college with shops beneath)
9. *Hamam* (Turkish bath)
10. Apprentice college (basement)
11. *Rabi medrese* (fourth college)
12. *Salis medrese* (third college)
13. Latrines
14. Sinan's fountain *(sebil)*
15. *Sinan türbesi* (Sinan's tomb)
16. *Tabhane* (dervish hospice with stables and kervansaray in vaults beneath)
17. *Imaret* (kitchen and refectory over vaults as above)
18. *Darüşşifa* (hospital and asylum with metal workshops in vaults below)
19. Site of *tiphane* (medical college)
20. *Sani medrese* (second college)
21. *Evvel medrese* (first college)
22. *Sibyan mektebi* (primary school)
23. *Meydan* (piazza)
24. *Taksim* (water cistern)
25. Mosque precinct with metal workshops in vaults on east side

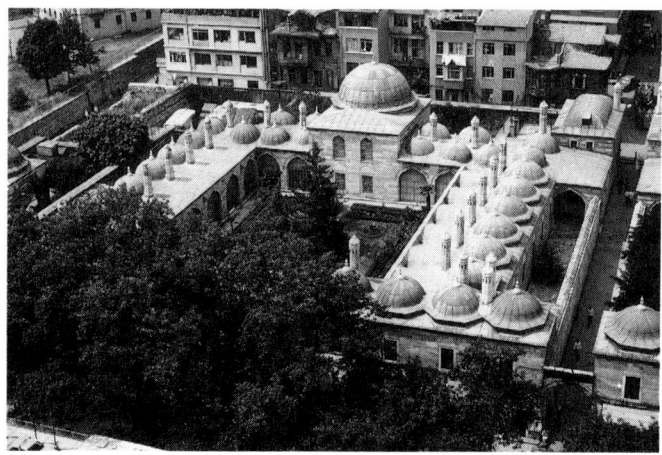

41. *Süleymaniye complex, Istanbul: first and second colleges (evvel and sani medreseler)*

The mosque is the centre of a highly organized complex in the way that the vast university of Mehmed II, Fatih (the Conqueror) in Istanbul in the 1470s had been. At the Süleymaniye the design is more compact and the plaza between mosque garden, colleges and the public kitchen is meaningful whereas the immense esplanade at Fatih is too diffuse. Moreover, the walling of the park in which the mosque is set wards it off as a spiritual sanctuary. Down the west flank is a small but domed Koran school, attached to the first of the two law colleges on the site. These are divided by a passage with their entrances facing each other and each with a small residence of two storeys for the master of the college: they are the only houses built by Sinan in existence and are commodious inside. The next-door medical school has been demolished on all but the side onto the plaza, where it more or less survives, as does the postern gate opposite the hospital. The latter stands on the towering vaults which support all the buildings along this side of the complex, and is divided into the medical section and the asylum. Across the sweeping stairway down to the lane, where there was room for stables and kervansaray in the vaults, is the public kitchen with its garden courtyard and then the hospice for dervishes: and others as time went by.[25] This possesses the most beautiful of all Sinan's courtyards due to its austerity and perfect proportions. Cells and open halls alternate behind the arcades and look onto the central pool. It is the continuous flow of the arches, which do not change at the corners but continue to flow over columns of equal size, that gives the sense of unbroken movement round the rectangle as if turning into an oval.

On the side facing the Golden Horn a row of tinsmith shops run in the vaults under the podium. These face the

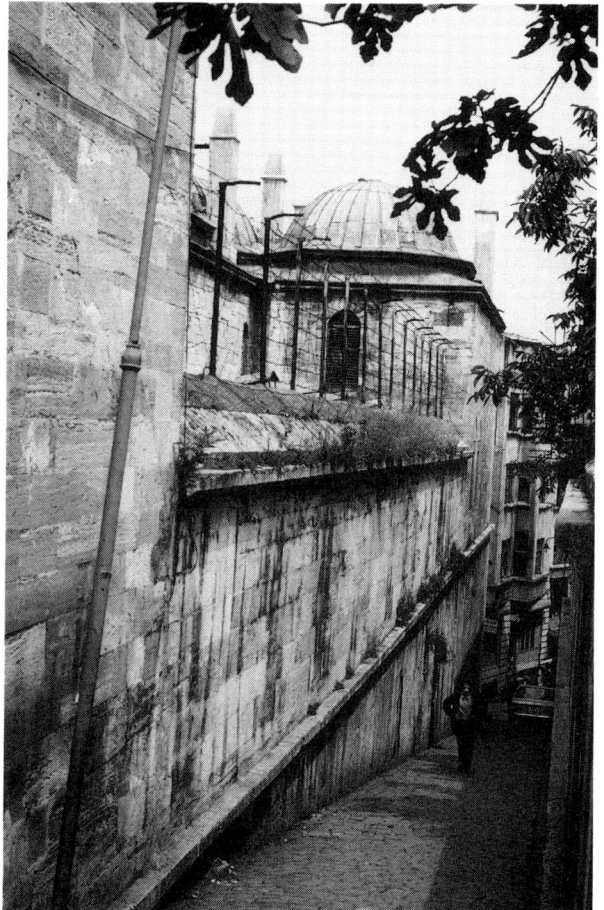

42. *Süleymaniye complex, Istanbul: lane of steps to vaults*

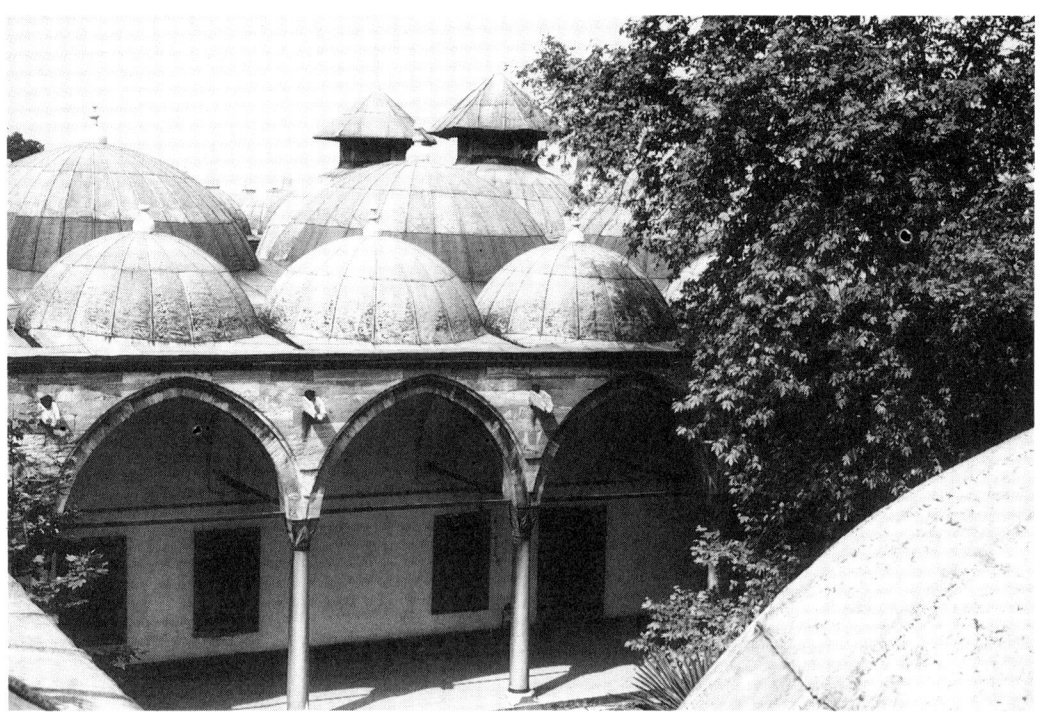

43. Süleymaniye complex, Istanbul: kitchen (imaret) court

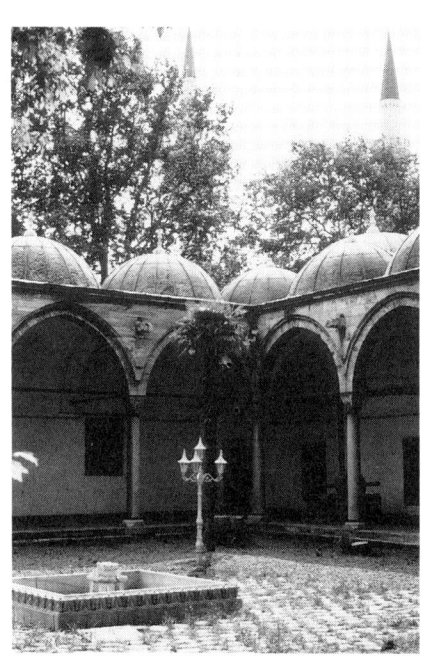

44. Süleymaniye complex, Istanbul: kitchen (imaret) court (Graeme Gardiner)

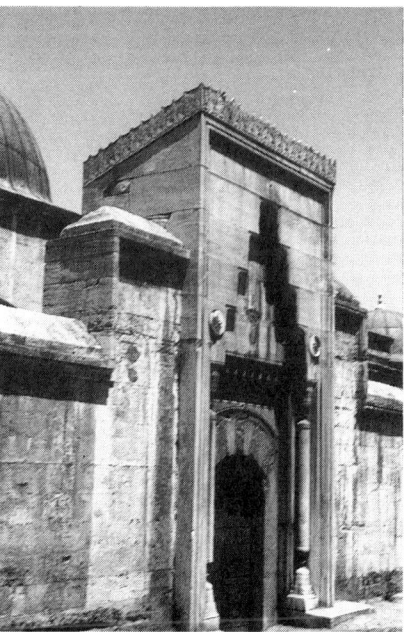

45. Süleymaniye complex, Istanbul: gate of dervish hospice (tabhane)

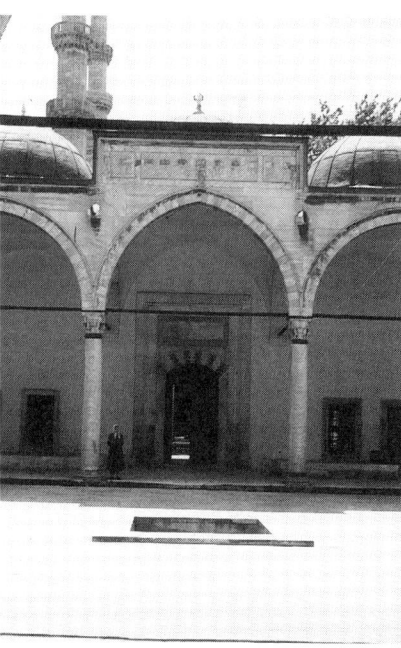

46. Süleymaniye complex, Istanbul: court of dervish hospice (tabhane)

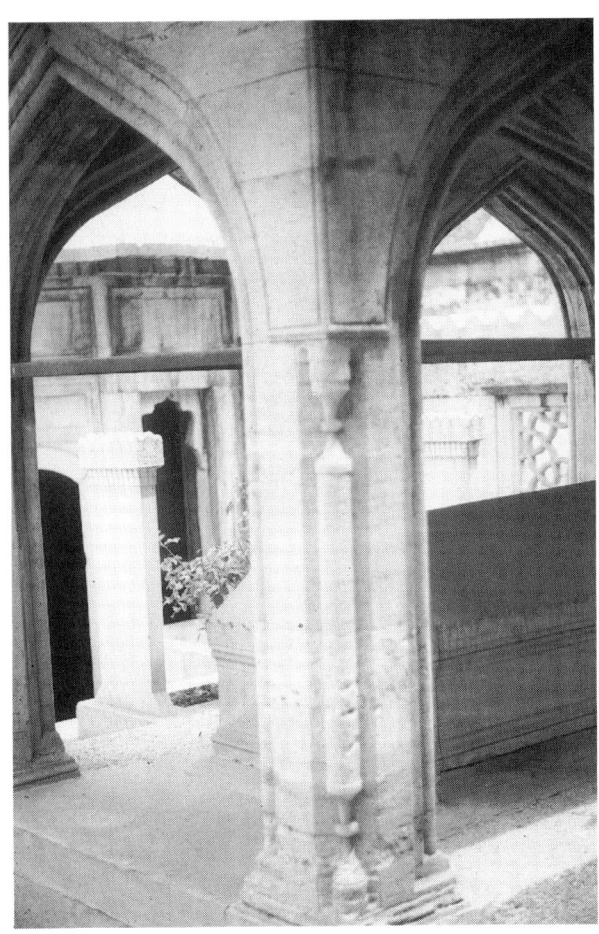

47. Süleymaniye complex, Istanbul: Sinan's tomb

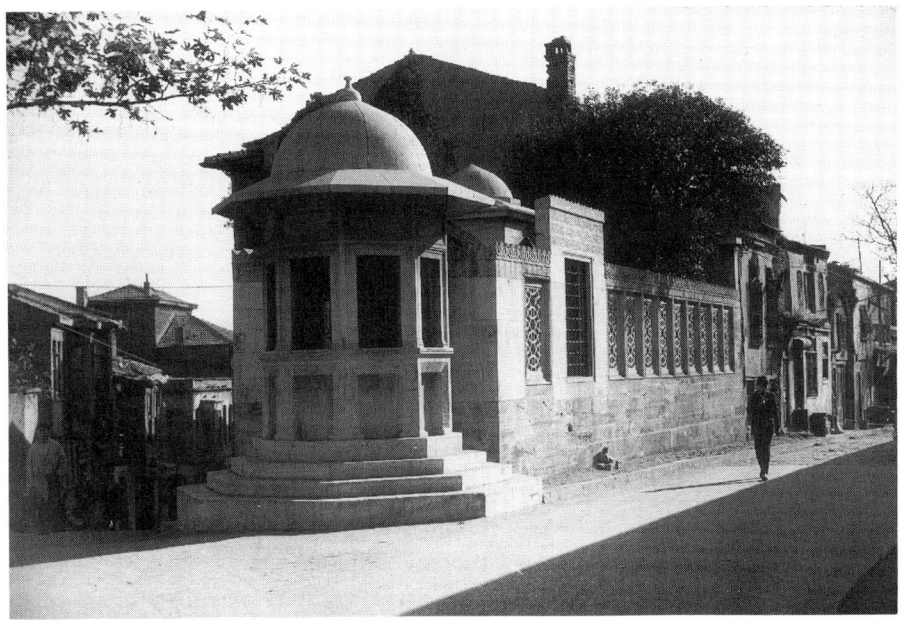

48. Süleymaniye complex, Istanbul: Sinan's fountain (sebil)

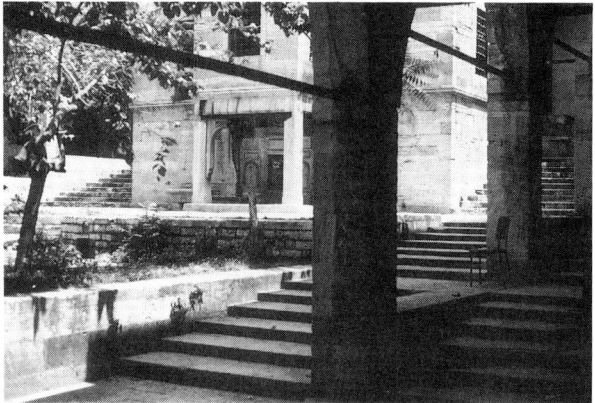

50. Süleymaniye complex, Istanbul: court of fourth college (rabi medrese)

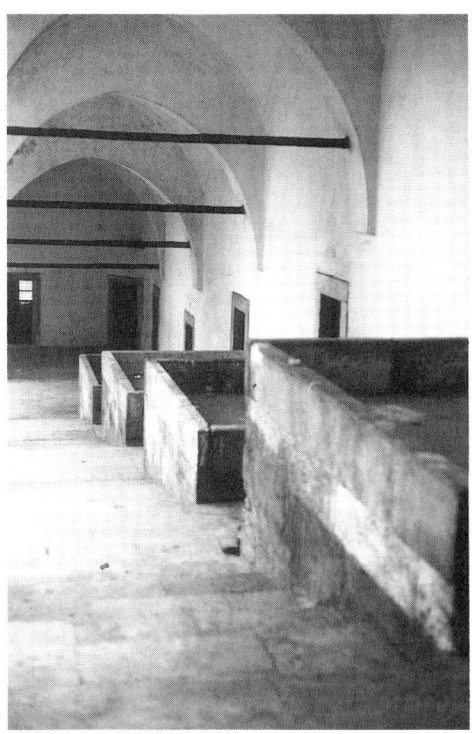

49. Süleymaniye complex, Istanbul: court of fourth college (rabi medrese)

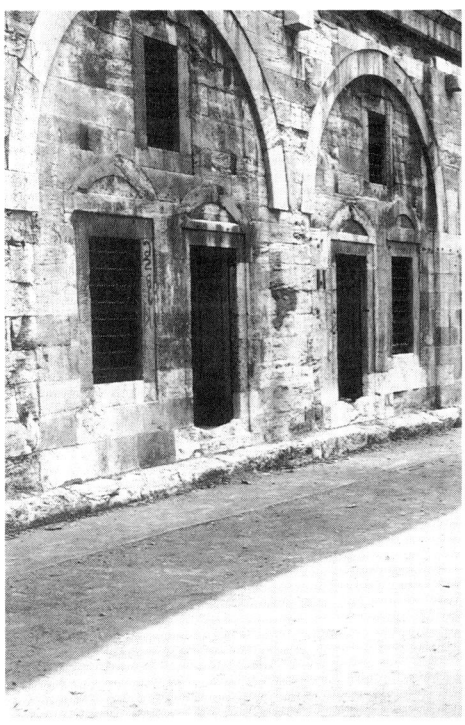

51. Süleymaniye complex, Istanbul: apprentice college

fountain and grave of Sinan at the corner of his garden but his home and offices have vanished. Then come two more colleges which descend the hillside so as not to obscure the view of the mosque from Galata. In fact, and it is important, they ascend the hill from their rows of cells up separate low stairways under and outside the arcades to the lecture hall over lofty arches inset with fountains, central but detached. They are unique and a tribute to Sinan's solution of the problem that would have existed had he extended the podium: the view would have been blocked and the authority of the mosque by that much diminished. The unique quality of these two buildings is enhanced by their lyrical gardens and contrasting stairways. The lower range of cells of these colleges is supported on a line of cells which form a college for apprentices at a lower level. A stair in one cell leads down to them but the apprentices were detached from the colleges above them. Their cells face a wall across a narrow open space. This has latrines curiously inset into the buttresses.

Detached from the complex is a relatively small *hamam* (ritual bath-house) which is finely decorated with plasterwork and marble mosaics. It was used only by poets, students and mosque personnel for there is a major hamam at the foot of the hill in the open market for the public. The sultan's entry has both stairs and a ramp up which the monarch could ride, a ramp that Mehmed Agha[26] and other successors of Sinan were to transform into the entry of a lofty pavilion beside a mosque which served as royal retiring room and which had a private door into the sultans' rostrum.

Behind the mihrab wall of the Süleymaniye was the future garden of the dead where the first traditional but

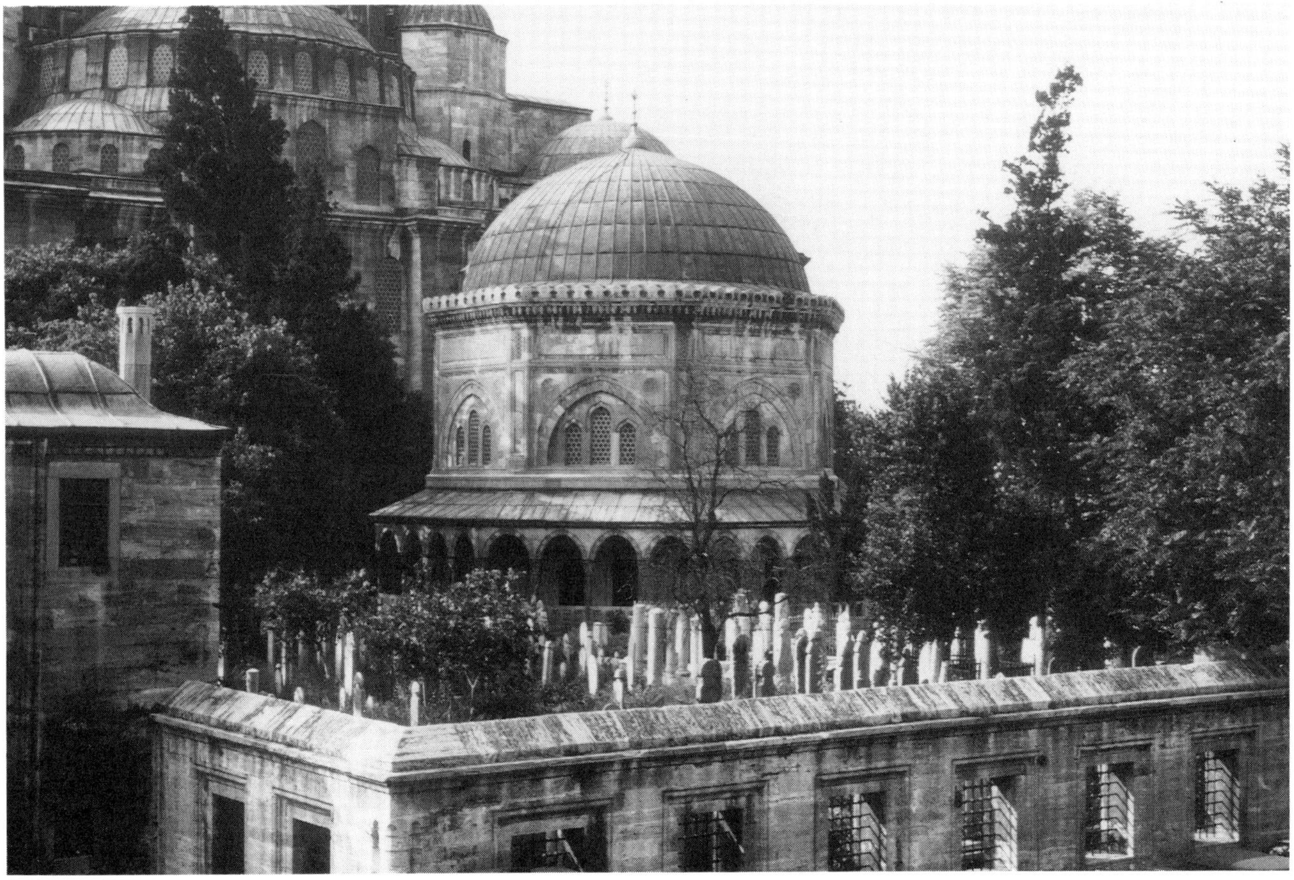

Sinan

52. *Tomb (türbe) of Süleyman the Magnificent and cemetery*

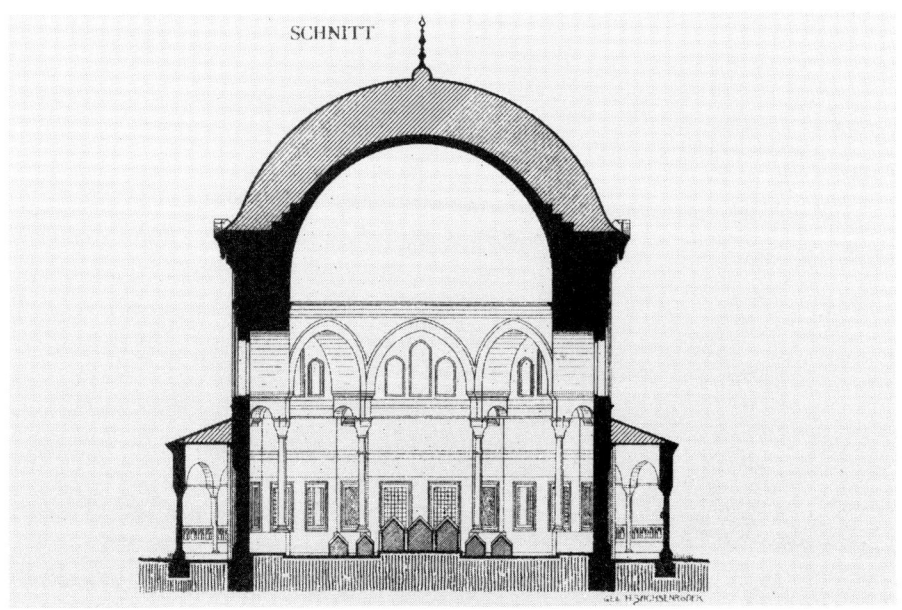

53. *Tomb (türbe) of Süleyman the Magnificent: elevation* (Gurlitt)

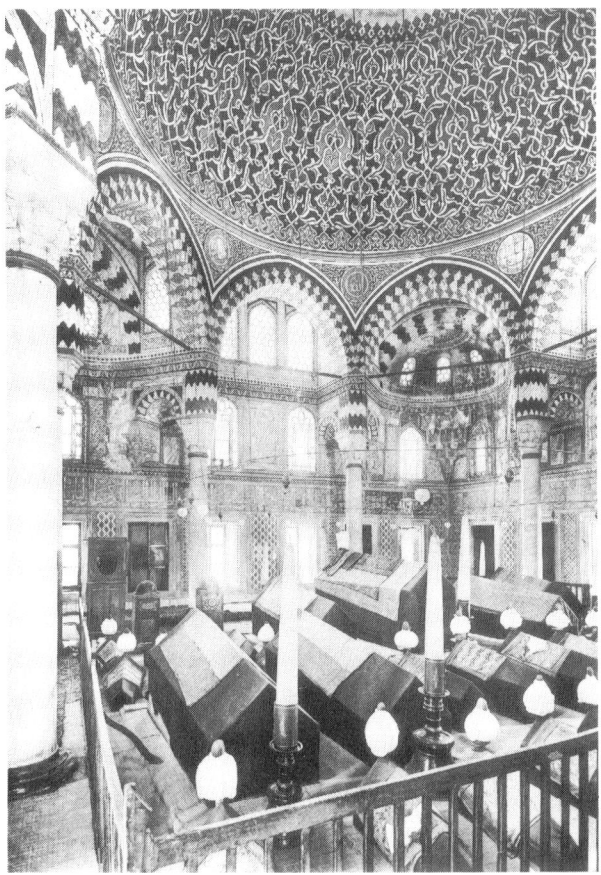

54. *Tomb (türbe) of Süleyman the Magnificent: interior* (Gurlitt)

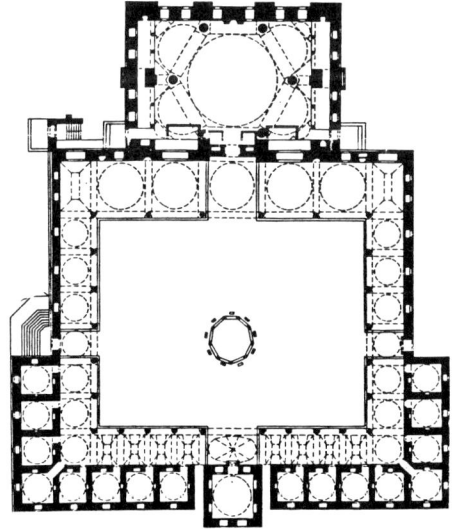

55. *Hadım (eunuch) Ibrahim Pasha mosque, Istanbul: plan*

large *türbe* (tomb) was to be that of the sultan's much-loved wife, Haseki Hürrem, the Roxelane of Europe, who died in 1558. The porch has re-used *cuerda seca* tiles[27] as decoration. The interior enjoys perpetual spring for the walls are brilliant with contemporary panels of almond blossom. Roxelane, Süleyman declared, was the springtime of his life and she died, appropriately, in April.

In 1566 Sinan was to add the mausoleum of Süleyman the Magnificent in a very grand manner which he excelled only with that of Selim II at Haghia Sophia. Standing immediately on the axis of the mihrab in the middle of the garden, it is strictly against the canon, for no tomb should profane this path to Mecca. It is girt with a fine colonnade under a shed roof which serves to soften the light of the interior. This is reached through a porch and thick walls in which is the staircase that leads up between the outer and inner dome, a concept completely new to Ottoman builders and which reflected Sinan's perception of the proportion of interior height to exterior. Thus he abandoned structural truth in favour of effect. Inside, the burial hall has fine and colourful Iznik floral tiles, with a tile inscription above them to turn the high octagon into a garden. The ceiling has been repainted but retains the crystal roses that give glitter to the starscape. Recent claims have been made that the tomb of Süleyman is based on the plan of the Dome of the Rock in Jerusalem but no one who has seen and understood both buildings could possibly be deceived.

Other Buildings

It is remarkable that while supervising the construction of two great complexes Sinan had time to build smaller foundations for vezirs: much of the work could only have been in the hands of his *kalfas* (assistant architects), of whom there were seventy at one time. The mosque of the Grand Vezir Hadım Ibrahim Pasha,[28] completed in 1551, under the city walls, is a square ashlar building with the one minaret permitted subjects. There is a fine portico but no courtyard for there is no college opposite. The great door is alive with stalactites only rivalled by the forest over the entry to the Süleymaniye mosque. The octagonal interior space is created by the use of shells in each corner thus adding a Western note to a strictly Islamic building. In the garden is the elegant but relatively humble open tomb of the Grand Vezir.

Kara Ahmad Pasha Complex (1561-2)

Much grander is the complex of the Grand Vezir Kara Ahmad Pasha[29] near the Topkapı Gate, in the walls, including his detached and inelegantly tall mausoleum. Kara Ahmad's complex was built posthumously at the same period as that of his rival, Rüstem Pasha, and both have exceptionally large windows flanking the main entry. It is as if the trustees could not build Ahmad Pasha's complex while his executioner was still alive. The foundation has a large garden court and at each side of the mosque door are remarkably large grilled windows as there were in the mosque of Rüstem Pasha. Lower windows were for air and had shutters to keep out the wind and rain, and grilles as a defence against birds and animals and impish little boys. Only upper windows were glazed, usually with bottle glass, and were there only for light. If expensive Venetian stained glass was used then a second outer window of bottle glass served as protection.

The relatively small mosque is built of ashlar but the college has alternating courses of brick and stone. It was surely an economy measure but the brick softens the appearance of the usual C-shaped college, usual except that it blocks the way to the mosque so slypes, or tunnels, divide the main line of cells. This goes well with what was a rural setting, which is emphasized by the extension of the courtyard wall each side of the mosque and its own large windows from which to survey the city. Because Sinan was not cramped for space, it would seem that he kept the buildings of this complex low and becoming to the setting. The mosque is prominent

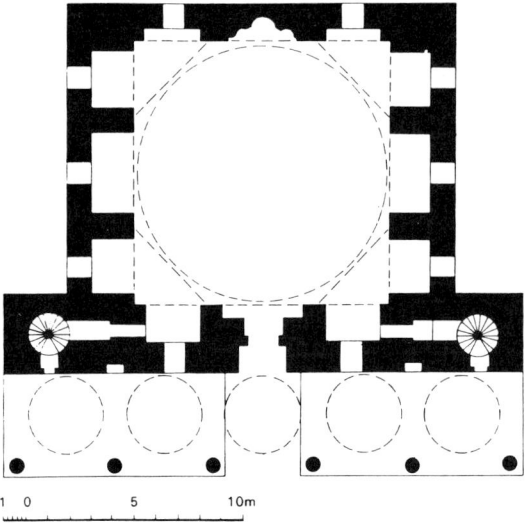
56. *Kara Ahmad Pasha complex, Istanbul: plan* (Gurlitt)

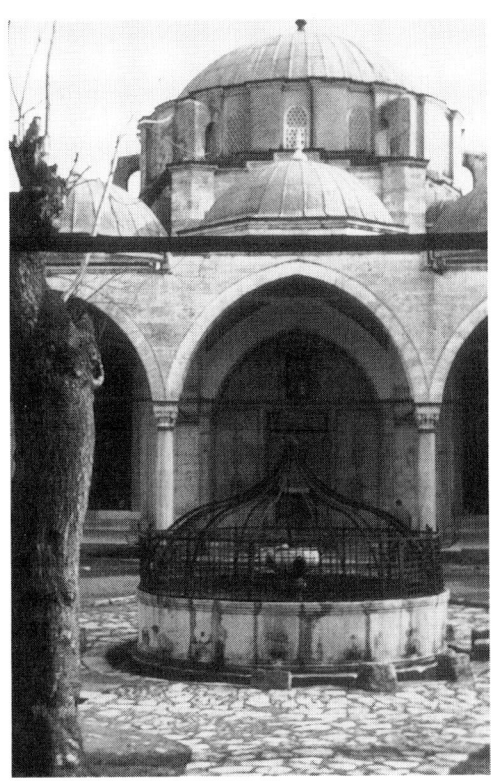
58. *Kara Ahmad Pasha complex, Istanbul: court and portico (large windows flanking door)*

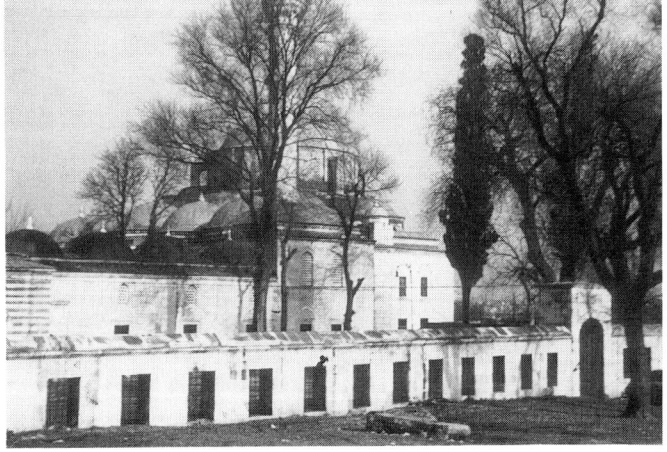
57. *Kara Ahmad Pasha complex, Istanbul*

Other Buildings

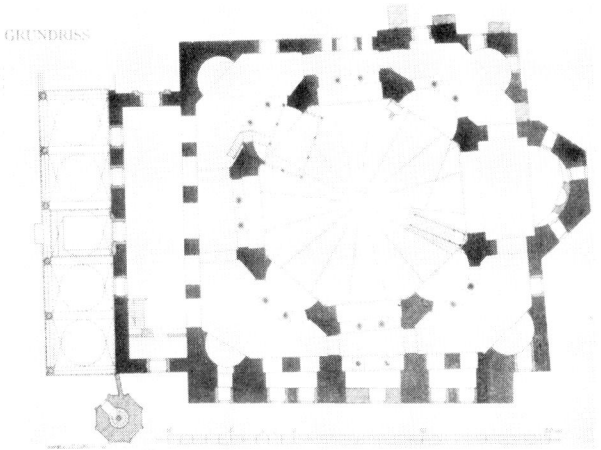

59. SS Sergius and Bacchus church (Küçük Aya Sofya mosque), Istanbul: plan (Gurlitt)

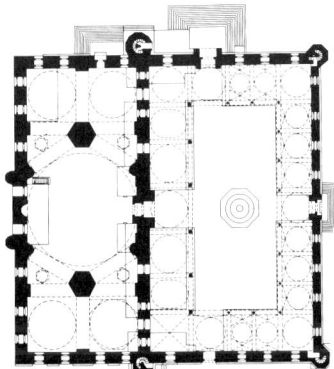

60. Üç Şerefeli mosque, Edirne: plan

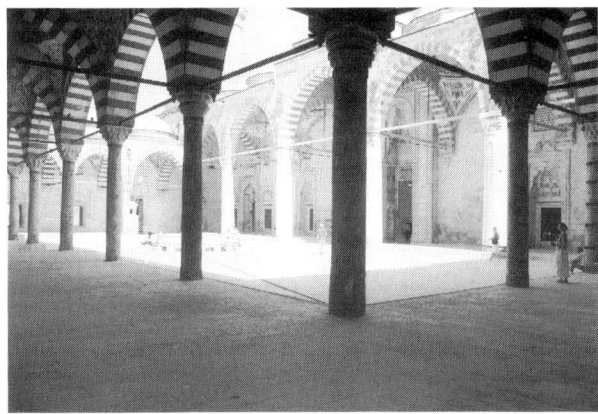

61. Üç Şerefeli mosque, Edirne: court

because it stands on a modest height but not at the top of the hill which obscures it.

In the creative period of his career, Sinan abandoned the simple domed square for rectangular mosques with only the central space square, the two wing areas often marked by wide galleries. There were two realistic methods of supporting the dome. In both cases four supporting piers were embedded in the walls on the entry and on the mihrab sides. Then there was either one free-standing pier, central on each side to make a hexagon, or two which divided the sides into three and created an octagon. These approaches made for a surprising number of permutations in the design of interiors. The concept of the octagon was not new to Istanbul because the church of SS Sergius and Bacchus, now Küçük Aya Sofya mosque, was built as an octagon in 527. That this building is also an elaborate and sophisticated *mise-en-scène*[30] is not relevant to the Ottoman design.

Üç Şerefeli Mosque, Edirne (c. 1450)

Fifty years before Sinan, but very influential, is Murad II's mosque of the Three Balconies, Üç Şerefeli, in Edirne. Here it had evolved the hexagonal form of support but used massive piers in the walls and the two free-standing piers effectively divide the mosque from its wings. These wings had until then been rooms for dervishes who must still have frequented the mosque. The size of the piers simply reflects the architect's caution since he was building what was then the largest Ottoman dome, 24 metres in diameter.[31] It was not to be excelled until that of the Süleymaniye, which was 26.2 metres across and 49.5 metres high. Üç Şerefeli is a majestic mosque in the way that a castle can be majestic. Sinan would refine and therefore transform this solidity.

When Sinan adopted the hexagonal form of mosque, he developed several ways of roofing the lateral spaces. Quarter-domes or even half-domes at angles of 45° across each corner were the most sympathetic because then the galleries which usually spanned the side areas were drawn towards the central dome and the square space under it. This gave a sense of protection and also unity to the whole in the Italian Renaissance manner of using the symbol of a shell.

Sinan

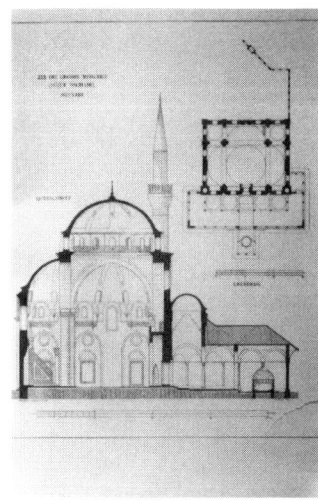

62. Mihrimah mosque, Üsküdar: elevation and plan (Gurlitt)

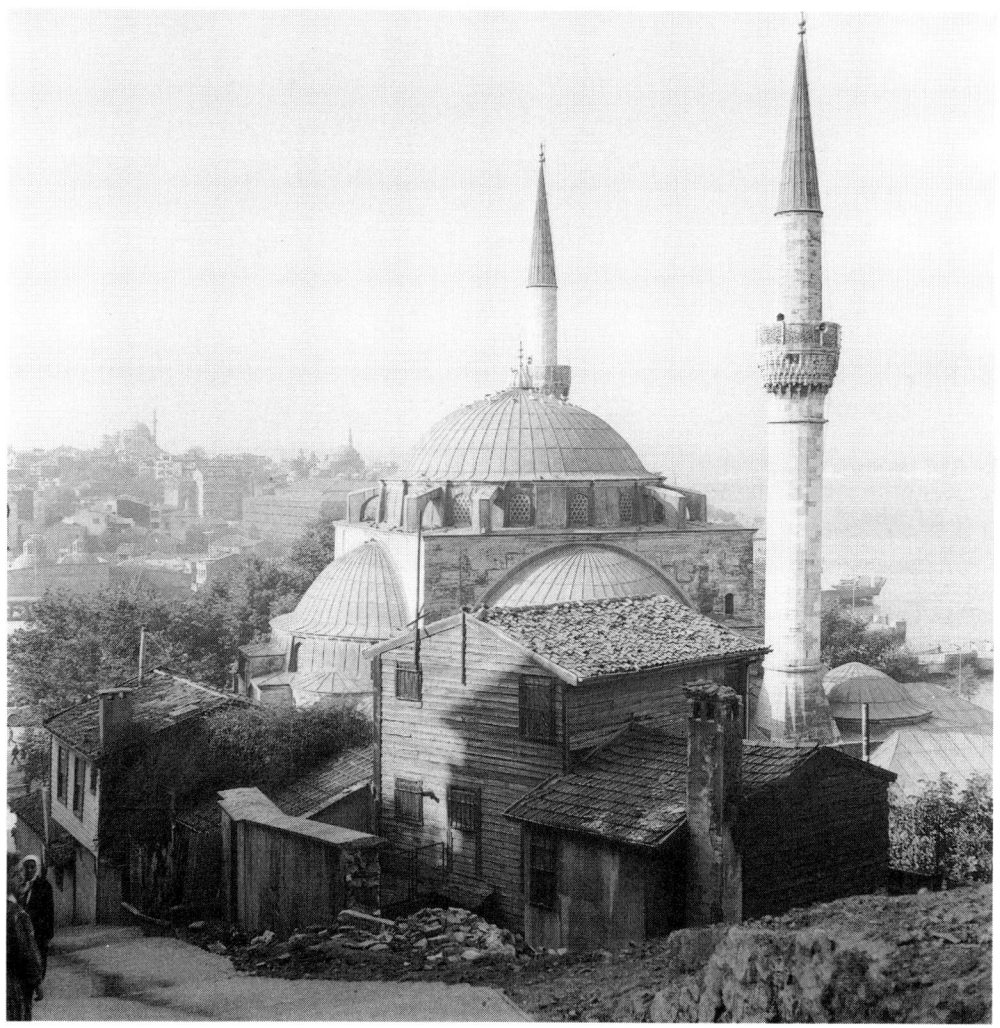

63. Mihrimah mosque, Üsküdar: view from south

Mosques of Mihrimah Sultan, Üsküdar (1547–8) and Edirnekapı (c. 1565–70)

Mihrimah Sultan was responsible for the early Sinan complex at Üsküdar[32] where the site, once again, enforced a double portico made attractive by the use of a projecting belvedere in which to place the *şadırvan* (fountain) looking out onto the Sea of Marmara. An extension of the second portico leads to the formidable college, which presents a flank like that of a fortress to the sea. The interior of the mosque disappoints because the central dome is flanked by half-domes with a further half-dome over the mihrab. The result is that, on entering, a visitor is brought up short to stand in the central space without a pause. It is this plan, imposed by lack of space because of the hillside, which must have confronted the Conqueror, Mehmed II, when he entered his now rebuilt mosque and it is this that may have led to the execution of the architect—Atık Sinan, who was no relation to the great master and far too conservative for the royal aesthete who admired Haghia Sophia.

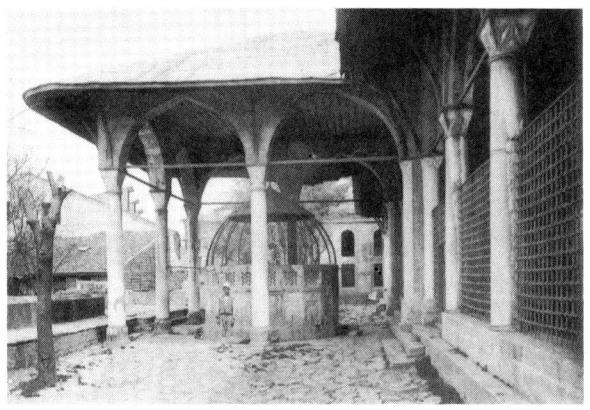

64. *Mihrimah mosque, Üsküdar: ritual fountain (şadırvan)* (Gurlitt)

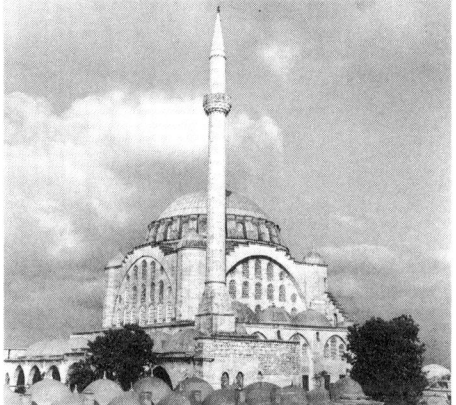

65. *Mihrimah mosque, Istanbul: exterior*

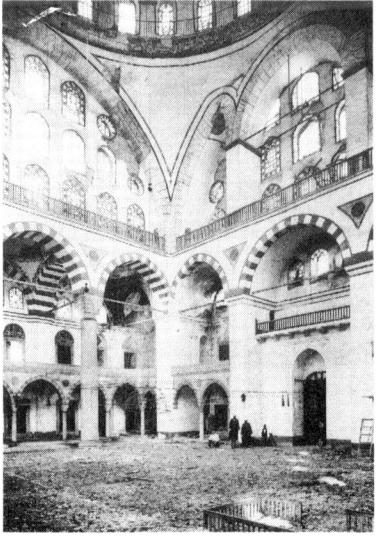

66. *Mihrimah mosque, Istanbul: interior after 1894 earthquake* (Gurlitt)

The mosque of Mihrimah was built in the lifetime of her father and he must have given a special dispensation for his well-loved daughter to be able to frame it with two minarets, to which only sultans were entitled. The mothers of sultans, however, were also granted the privilege partly because their mosques were built, theoretically, by their sons in their name. The immediate suspension of work on the Yeni Valide mosque of Safiye Valide on the death of Mehmed III supports this contention. Yet after the death of Süleyman, when Mihrimah acted as *valide sultan* (Queen Mother and ruler of the palace) for her orphan brother, Selim II, she was permitted only one minaret for her vastly more important complex at Edirnekapı. But what a minaret: slender as a gazelle![33]

The second Mihrimah complex suffered from its site, too hard against the city wall. Thus the broad open court has college cells only on two sides because they are shaved away under the wall for lack of space although there is a second college behind. Space there had to be because the effect of this mosque is monumental in a manner which needs to be seen from a distance. It is unique because four corner towers rather than turrets take the main stresses of the structure although two of these only partially reach the ground.[34] The four walls are stretched between them, lending minimal support. There is as much window space as there is wall, thus taking voids in the masonry to the limit of structural

Sinan

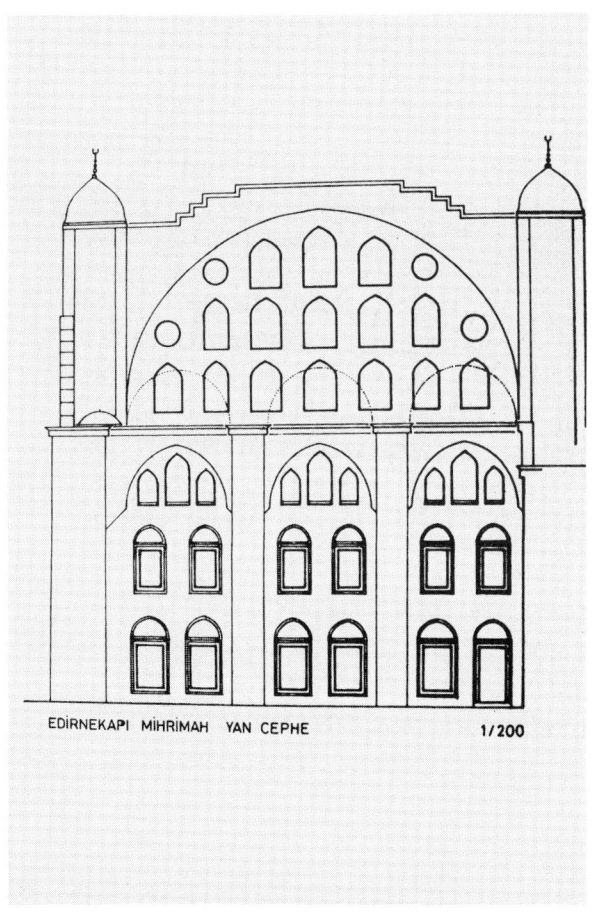

67. Mihrimah mosque, Istanbul: elevation

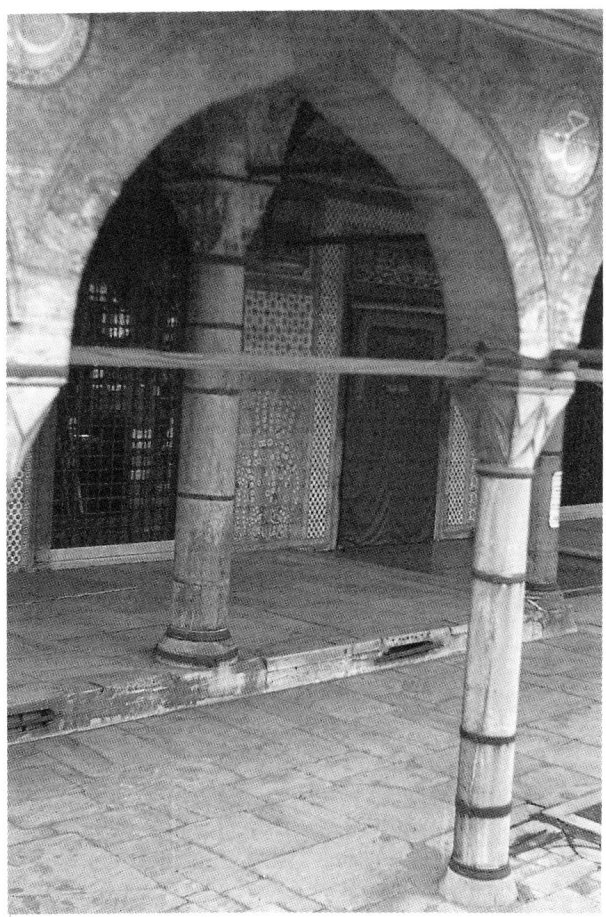

68. Rüstem Pasha mosque, Istanbul: interior

possibility. This means that the interior is alive with light all day. Other Islamic masonry buildings matched but could not excel this achievement which would only be surpassed in the eighteenth and twentieth centuries.[35] And when the walls of glass were possible, they presented the same aesthetic problem that Sinan faced. The feat was not repeated because light in itself is not enough. It must be given form and when light has form it also has mystery. His rejection of the wall of windows on this scale suggests that Sinan had that divine discontent with his own achievements which differentiates great artists from the rest.

Rüstem Pasha Mosque (1561-2)

It was the same with the multiple use of Iznik panels on the walls and piers of Rüstem Pasha mosque[36] both inside and out. The tiles are of the finest quality,

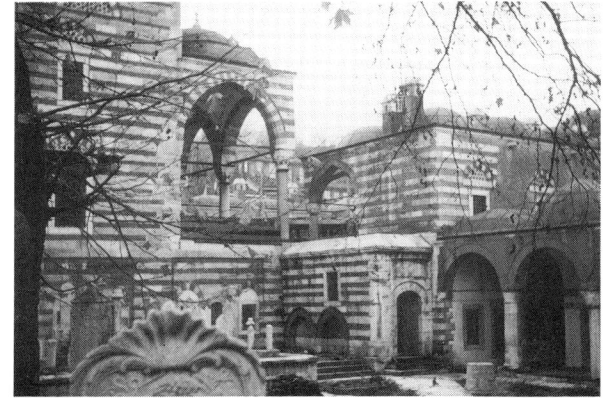

69. Zal Mahmud Pasha complex, Istanbul

Other Buildings

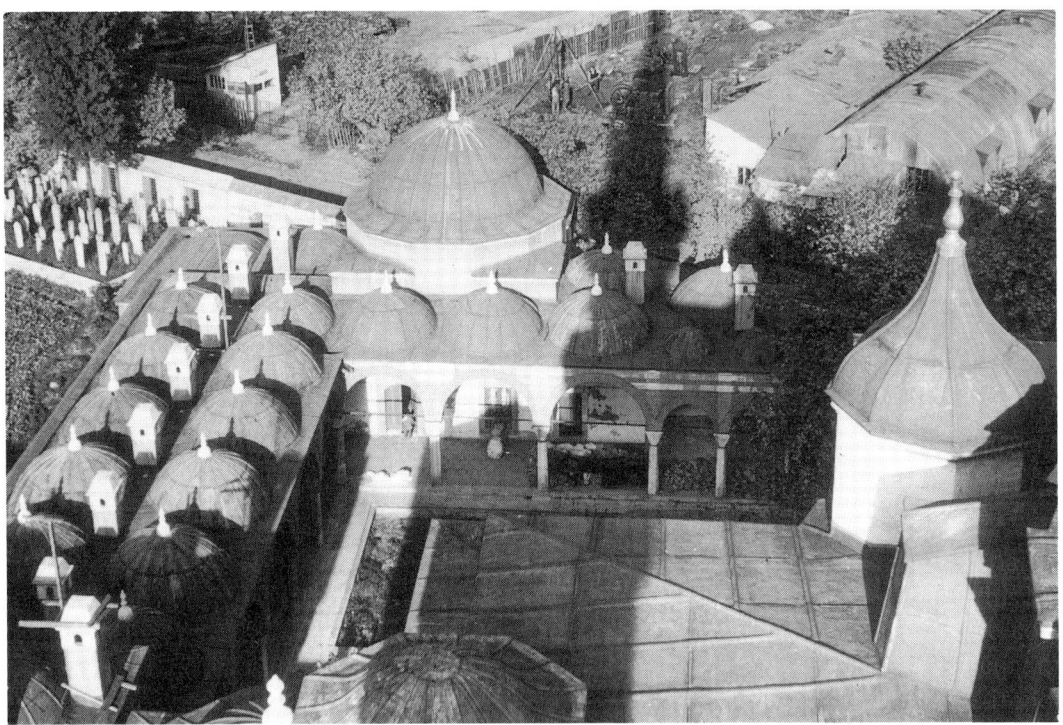

70. Zal Mahmud Pasha complex, Istanbul: mosque court

although dominated by reds, white and blues, yet their sheer number detracts from their importance. Not that they are not splendid. The use of large windows each side of the entry suggests that they are there because of the shadow cast by the double portico—the mosque stands above the market and so has no courtyard but only a terrace—when the tiles require the maximum light for their tulips to bud and flower.

Zal Mahmud Pasha Mosque (c. 1580)

There is fascination in the way that each of the vezirial mosques varies in important details, but the most fortunate pasha was the one who purchased an awkward site or a stretch of hillside for he could not have it levelled without the resources of a sultan. The braggadocio of the vaults under the Süleymaniye complex was not for him. Because Sinan had to make sense of a disorderly site, his mind was brought into full play in order to create levels of purpose and importance. So these vezirs were rewarded with complexes which, even if small, were of an interest of which the huddled complex of Haseki Hürrem gave no hint.

Of such mosques, that of Zal Mahmud Pasha is a good example. Superficially, the site was divided into a lower and an upper area united by stairs and by the east flank of the mosque itself. Sinan was required to build a commodious mosque, two colleges and the very large tomb that the pasha and his royal wife demanded in their vanity. The catafalques stand side by side.[37] The mausoleum commands the ground level with its paved walks and strips of garden and graveyard. It faces a modest college built of alternating courses of brick and stone. The higher ground has been cut like a disciplined cliff and a handsome staircase ascends to the small but well-defined gatehouse into the upper court. On the left is the astonishing and monumental flank of the mosque, which rises from dervish cells in its open basement, while the flat wall of alternating courses soars up to roof level pierced with row upon row of windows, as if a mansion block, but with two enormous waterspouts projecting at the corners of the eaves. Inside, the court, the portico and the mosque itself are characteristic of Sinan's style but the college round the court is perforce odd because of lack of space. The lecture hall had to be tucked in a corner and loses its emphasis and the cells, which start square beside the gatehouse, become broad and shallow as the space withers. In this, Sinan might only do what he could once the dimensions of the mosque itself were determined, just as with the mosque of Mihrimah Sultan. The mosque and its minaret fill the rest of the space with comfort and escape the exigencies of the terrain.

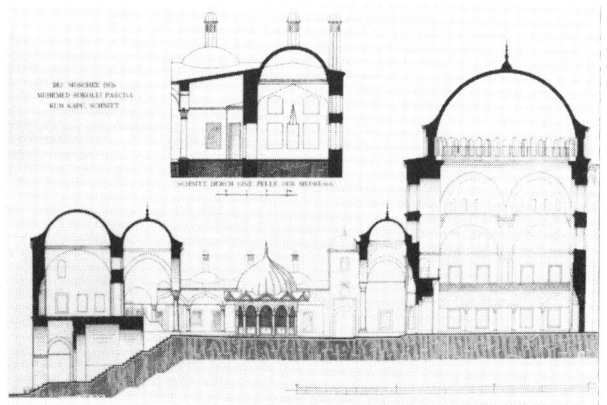

71. *Sokollu Mehmed Pasha complex, Kadırga (Istanbul): elevation* (Gurlitt)

Sokollu Mehmed Pasha Mosque, Kadırga (1571–2)

But when Sinan came to build the mosque of the Grand Vezir Sokollu Mehmed Pasha[38] at Kadırga, in a sense, he did more than he could be expected to do. He cleared a podium but had to cope with the precipitous slope that led up to it from the road below. There was just room for the rectangular mosque without an apse back to back with the tekke, which was a different foundation. There were problems here of a major kind because the teaching hall ought to be central to the college as should be the main door facing the mosque entry across the fountain. The disinterested observer takes Sinan's solution for granted for it has the simplicity of any equation once it has been solved. It was not simple at the time. The mosque itself is finely proportioned inside and all the workmanship is excellent. It is by no means small and its portico stretches to seven domes due to the placing of the minaret and by use of a compensating room on the other

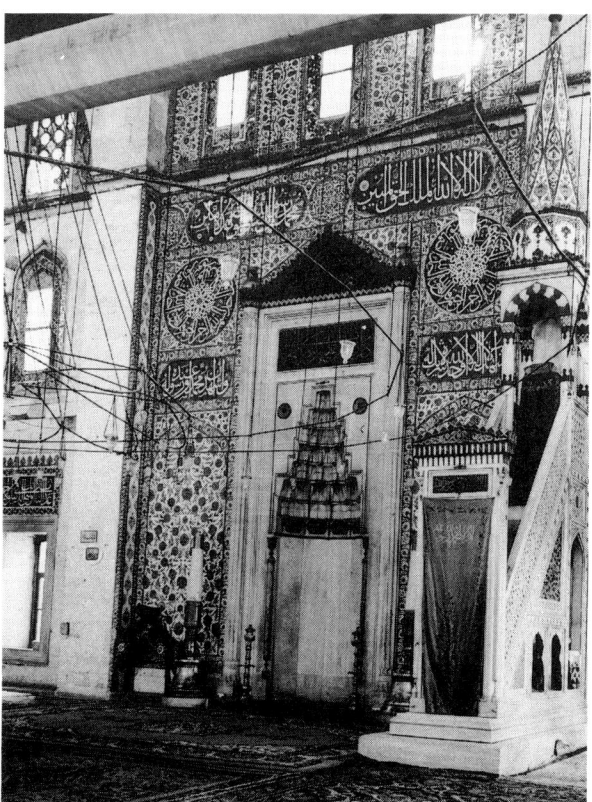

72. *Sokollu Mehmed Pasha mosque, Kadırga (Istanbul): interior*

Other Buildings

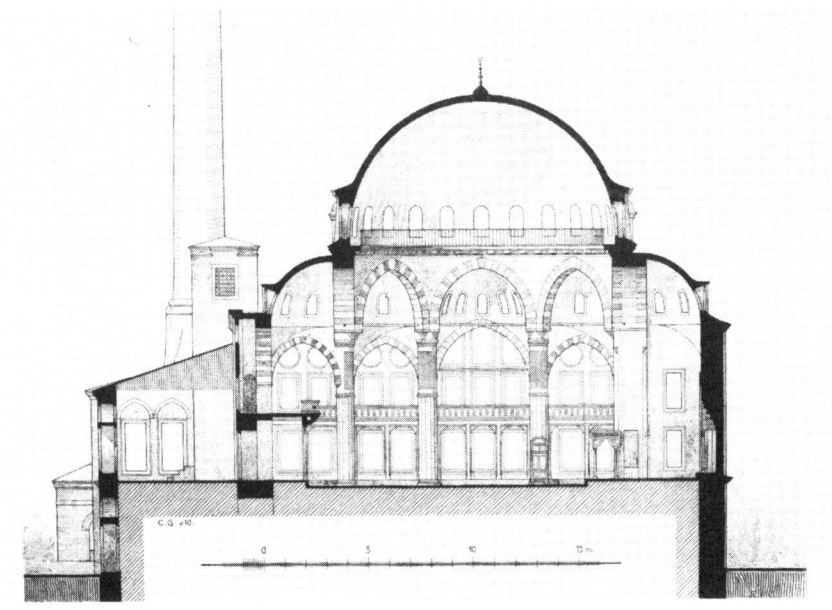

73. Sokollu Mehmed Pasha mosque, Azapkapı (Istanbul): elevation (Gurlitt)

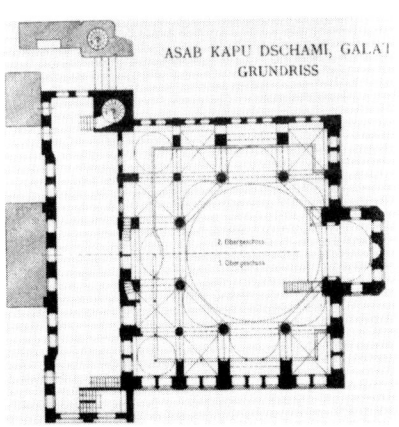

74. Sokollu Mehmed Pasha mosque, Azapkapı (Istanbul): plan (Gurlitt)

side. Two gatehouses divide mosque and college with its ogee arched arcades, now sadly glassed in. What is unique is the large stair which drives up the hillside and passes underneath the teaching hall to lead the faithful into the court. The hall is raised up with a balcony reached by stairs on either side to achieve a lofty majesty that other colleges did not possess. Inside the mosque, the tiled mihrab wall is without rival as is the tiled hood of the *mimber* (pulpit). These can distract from an appreciation of the lofty proportions and the refined details.

Sokollu Mehmed Pasha Mosque, Azapkapı (1577–8)

In 1577 when old and honoured, Sinan started work on another mosque for Sokollu Mehmed, that ever-ready patron of the arts, between Galata and the Arsenal. This was a market mosque like that of Rüstem Pasha and so raised up above the turmoil.[39] Because space was tight, there was no double portico but a roofed gallery reached by means of broad stairs at either end. There was no room for a minaret on the mosque side of the lane on the east side, so it was built across the street to be reached by a bridge from the outer gallery. The undercroft of this mosque was used for shops with a warehouse in the centre. Inside, the dome is supported on four small and four larger semi-domes, which results in a sense of space unrestricted by the side galleries.

Sinan

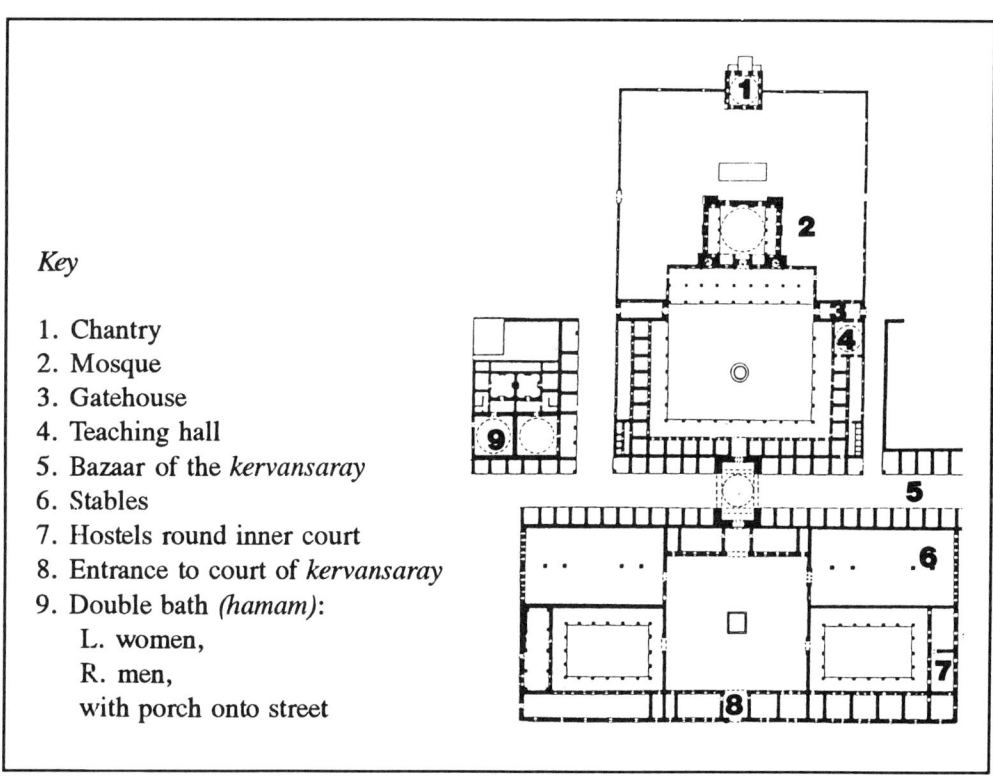

Key

1. Chantry
2. Mosque
3. Gatehouse
4. Teaching hall
5. Bazaar of the *kervansaray*
6. Stables
7. Hostels round inner court
8. Entrance to court of *kervansaray*
9. Double bath *(hamam)*:
    L. women,
    R. men,
    with porch onto street

75. *Sokollu Mehmed Pasha complex, Lüleburgaz: plan*

Sokollu Mehmed Pasha Mosque, Lüleburgaz (1569–70)[40]

Some years previously, Sinan had built the same vezir a complex at Lüleburgaz on the road to Edirne. (Lüleburgaz was an important staging post.) He had no problems with space and he built a large kervansaray, divided into two courts by the central entrance on the axis of the distant mihrab and with a long *arasta* (parade of shops) running from end to end. Those on the mosque side lie back to back with the cells of the college, which embraces the commodious court in the traditional manner except that the central gate in this instance has driven the teaching hall off down the western side. The mosque is compact rather than large but given an appearance of size because of the splendid columns of its main portico and second portico. There was no lack of space: this use of two porticoes can only have been intended to aggrandize. Behind the mosque is a garden with a pool and a little domed room used as a library. Beside it was a very necessary double hamam for travellers.

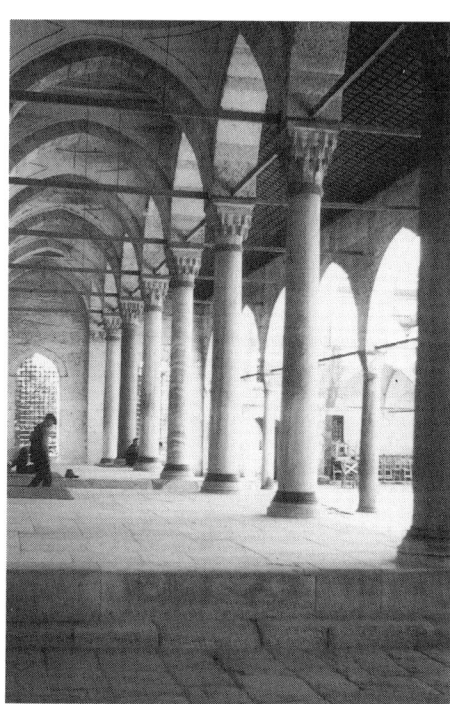

76. *Sokollu Mehmed Pasha complex, Lüleburgaz: portico*

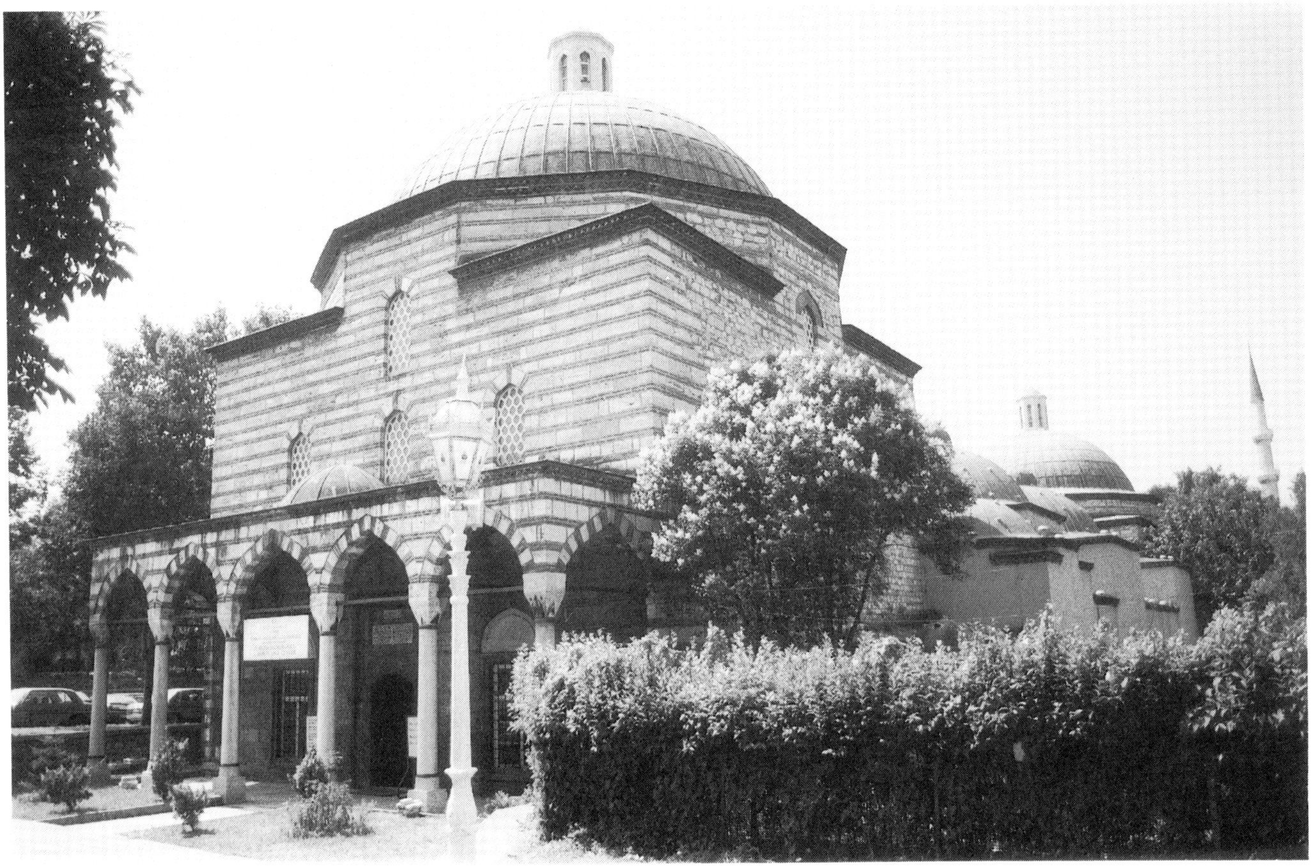

77. Haseki Hürrem hamam, Istanbul
   (Graeme Gardiner)

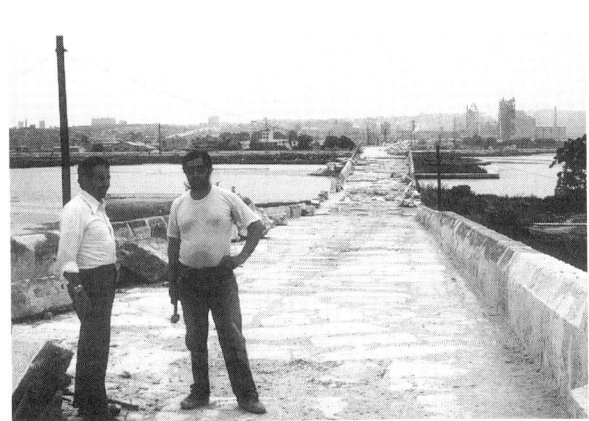
78. Bridge at Büyükçekmece

Civil Buildings

There were civil buildings by Sinan but the palaces of the great vezirs beside the Hippodrome have gone and we are left with his work of rebuilding after the fire at Topkapısaray in 1574. Exactly how much of the palace can be attributed to him is uncertain apart from the tall kitchen chimneys, which look as if on parade when seen from Marmara, and perhaps the great chamber with its superb dome which is the pavilion of Murad III. Here the vaults below were transformed into a pool for winter pleasure since boilers supplied hot water. Sinan also built hamams at the saray for the sultan and valide sultan but these were so altered in the eighteenth century that his work has been obscured. The best surviving example of his baths is that of Haseki Hürrem, completed in 1557 opposite Haghia Sophia, where the workmanship is impeccable. The majestic disrobing rooms are simple square halls with lofty domes rising from

Sinan

pendentives. The best example of the use of a semi-dome in a hamam dates from 100 years before. It is in the cool room of the still-frequented hamam of Mehmed II's unfortunate Chief Vezir Mahmud Pasha.

Bridge at Büyükçekmece (1566–8)

The one monument recorded on Sinan's tomb, and therefore the one on which he prided himself above all others, one would assume, is the causeway of four bridges over the marsh at Büyükçekmece on the road to Edirne. It is unusually broad and springs from island to island with the road rising and falling like a switchback. This feat of engineering was undertaken because Süleyman had been cut off by floods while out hunting. It is still beautiful, although the setting has been destroyed by the monstrous encroachment of the city. The structure of this bridge reflects how much architecture in the sixteenth century depended on undervaulting. Now that the Kilim Museum is open inside the vaults of the mosque of Sultan Ahmad in Istanbul it is possible to walk about in these and understand the sheer grandeur of pure engineering.

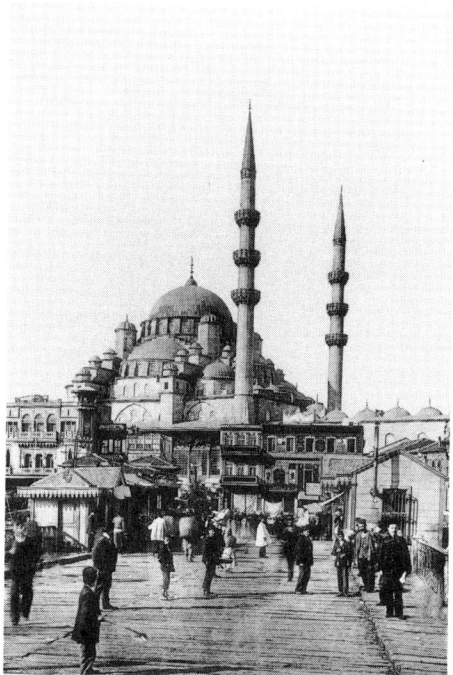

79. Yeni Valide mosque, Istanbul (Gurlitt)

Students and Disciples

During his fifty years as Royal Architect, Sinan trained many subordinates. Some of their names are known but most of their lives have not been researched. There was a large staff in Sinan's offices below the Süleymaniye complex with as many as seventy kalfas.[41] Of these many were engineers, capable of carrying out instructions concerning structure, but only a few are likely to have been architects in the modern meaning of the term. Of those who were, Davud Agha, Dalgıç (the Diver) Ahmad Agha and Mehmed Agha are pre-eminent since there are important buildings extant that are attributed to them. Davud Agha built the mausoleum of Murad III, Dalgıç began the Valide mosque at Eminönü and Mehmed was to be the last of the grand old men whom Sinan trained to achieve immaculate exactitude. It was he who built the remarkable mosque of Sultan Ahmad on the site of the vezirial palaces which had replaced the Great Palace of the Byzantines beside the Hippodrome. Other names like that of Mustafa, who died while building the mosque of Murad III at Manisa, have no other known building which can be attributed to them.

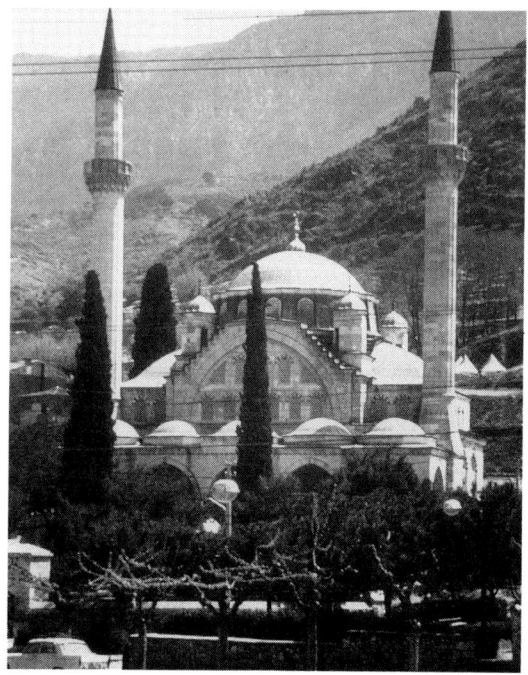

80. Muradiye mosque, Manisa

Students and Disciples

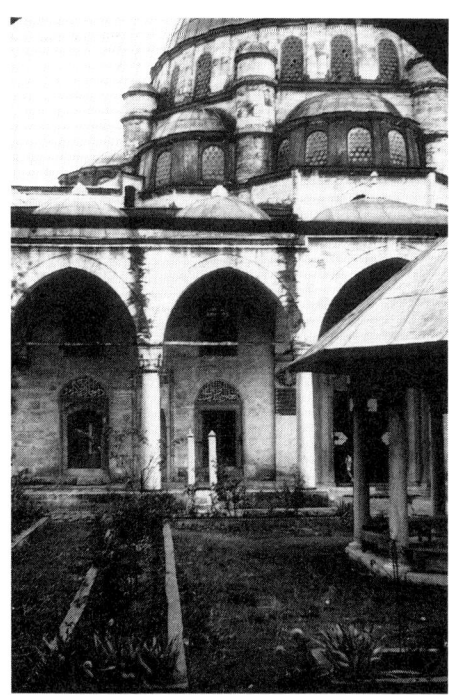

81. Nişancı Mehmed Pasha mosque, Istanbul

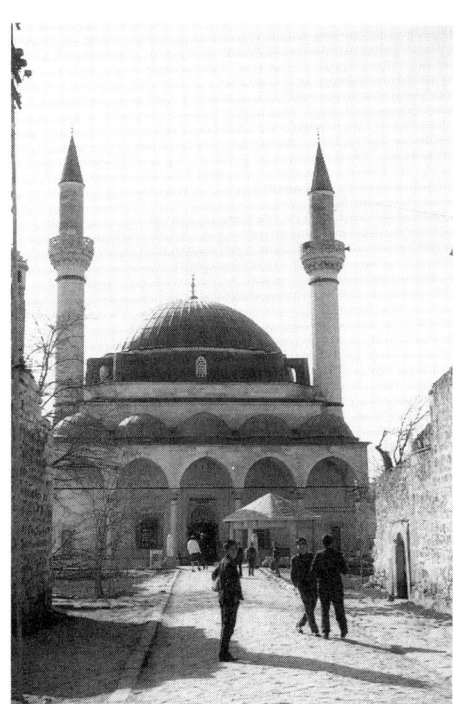

82. Selim II mosque, Karapınar

Yet more architects than these must have gone out into Anatolia and Thrace to build many of the mosques now attributed to Sinan. The many signs of individual caprice in structural details bear witness to their numbers. Any important mosque in the provinces must have required at least two or three years in which to collect the materials, dig the foundations, lay the drainage system and build and decorate the mosque itself: and then only if labour were plentiful and artisans available. Moreover, Mehmed Agha was for long in charge of the capital's waterways. He may, however, have been the Mehmed who succeeded Mustafa as architect of the Muradiye at Manisa. The record is complicated by Mehmed being sent to assist in provincial government on occasion. Moreover, most senior architects received government appointments, although it is difficult to discover whether the posts were honorary and simply a means by which to augment a modest salary.

Sinan's office was responsible for the building of mosques and major dependencies all over the empire including the Holy Cities. Many of these buildings were finely achieved, others were of good workmanship and even the least happy examples, like the mosque of Sokollu Mehmed Pasha at Bor, were so clearly Ottoman in style that it has been natural to append Sinan's name to one and all in order to enhance local prestige.

Selim II Mosque, Karapınar (1563–4)

There can be no doubt that the mosque of Selim II, at Karapınar,[42] has proportions so excellent that one would dearly like to think that Sinan was totally responsible for it. This is, unfortunately, nonsense for the town is well beyond Konya and built when Sinan was particularly busy in the capital and at Edirne. The fine proportions of this small mosque, enhanced by twin royal minarets, give it an august grace from the moment it is framed in the gateway to the dilapidated complex. The basic plans and elevations could have been drawn, or at least approved, by Sinan but they would have been very simple working drawings for use on the site and no one would have thought of preserving them. There is evidence that models were made, yet the simplicity of the forms of this mosque make that appear to have been unnecessary.[43] In any event, the proportions would have been worked out beforehand in order to determine the size of the columns needed for the portico. These would have been sufficiently simple for a well-trained architect to transfer into structure on the site. A register of all known Byzantine monolithic columns, their whereabouts and their dimensions was maintained in the Royal Architect's office.

If one considers how far afield works were executed, the position becomes clearer.

Süleyman Mosque, Damascus (1554–5)

The fine complex of Süleyman the Magnificent was added to the initial dervish centre founded by his father, Selim I, at Damascus. This assembly point for the pilgrimage to Mecca has Ottoman and Syrian characteristics entangled. The garden court and the tiles are Syrian, although the latter are closely related to those of Iznik in style and are perhaps pounced (patterns pricked through paper to effect a transfer). The patterns might have been sent from Topkapısaray's studios. The spacious court, with its pool, has no more to do with Ottoman traditions than has the earlier example of the Hüsrev Pasha complex at Aleppo (1545–6).

It is the plan and elevation of the mosque, together with its minarets, that are distinctively Ottoman even though the alternating courses of black and white stone do not belong to an Istanbul tradition but to the availability of basalt in the area. What is certain is that the accounts passed through the Royal Architect's office since the commission emanated from that department and the scale of the work was royally decreed. The secret of the building surely indicates how well Sinan trained his subordinates, intolerant as he was of less than excellence. This excellence included a training in the proportion and the mathematics of structure. Moreover, any students of this master had been able to study his mosques and thus had achieved a sound grounding in how each was individually built. With such simple rules as that the span of an arch must be justly related to the height and width of the supporting Byzantine columns, if they were to remain vertical, the control of Sinan over his delegate was real enough even if he never saw the building himself.

But proportion was relative to the purpose and to the language which architecture speaks. In the Balkans, and as far away as the eighteenth-century Osmaniye college at Aleppo, the tall, slim minarets soar above all other buildings to assert the lordship of the Ottoman sultan

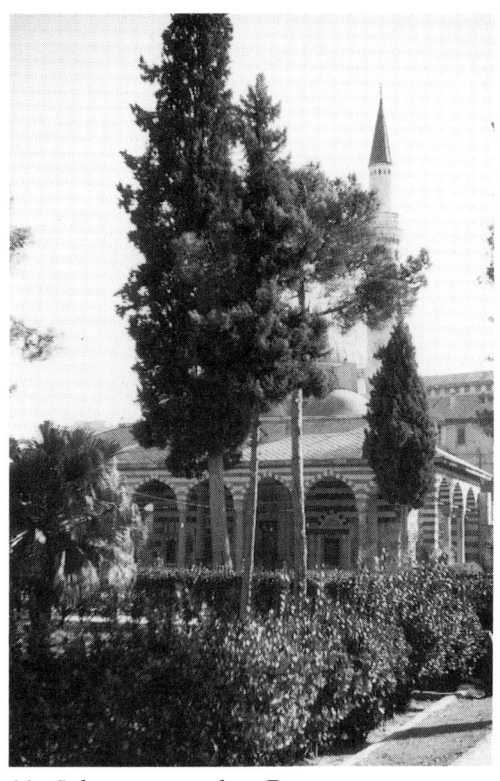

83. Süleyman complex, Damascus: mosque

Students and Disciples

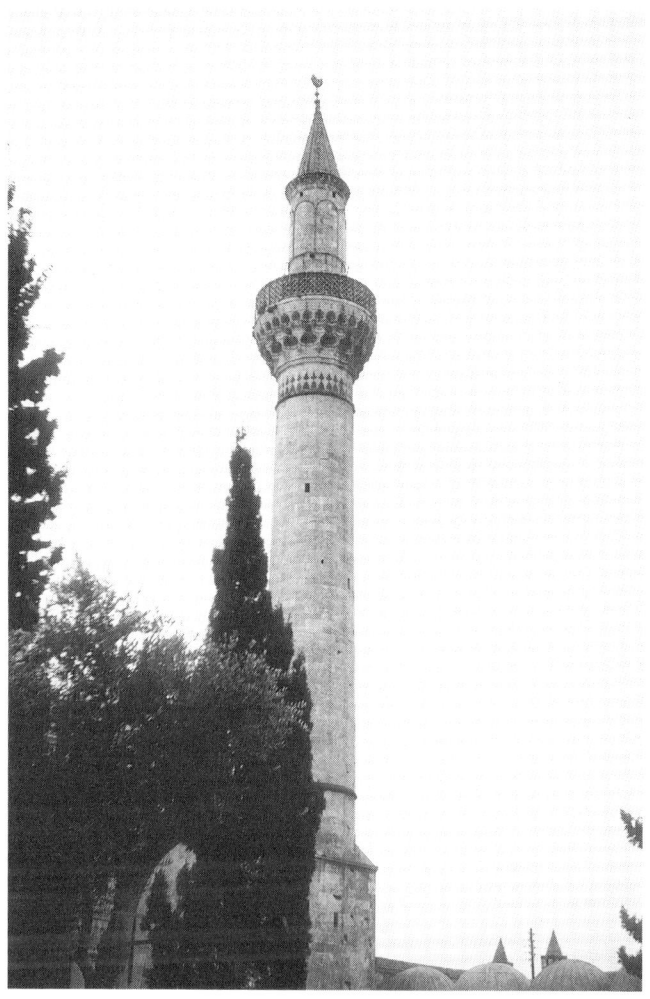

85. *Osmaniye dervish convent (tekke), Aleppo: minaret*

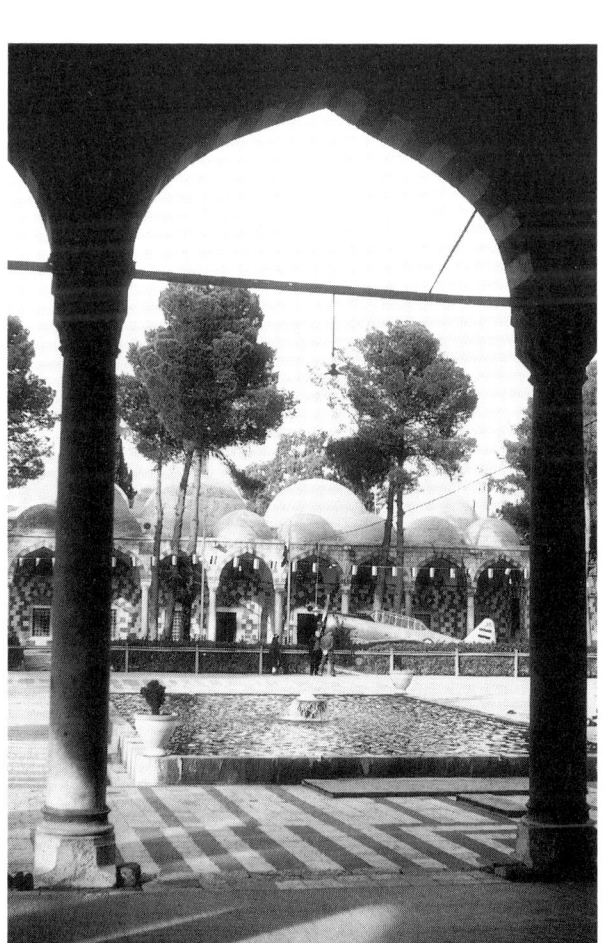

84. *Süleyman complex, Damascus: court*

over the town or city: this was true even of quite modest mosques which seem to cringe beneath their own towers.

Lala Mustafa Pasha Mosque, Erzerum (1562–3)

At Erzerum, the mosque of Lala Mustafa Pasha has astonishingly archaic squinches instead of classical pendentives, let alone exedras, and the stumpy minaret is tucked into a corner of the mosque and portico. It looks as if the architect could not find local masons who were capable of erecting pendentives and so let them build as grandly as they could in the technique that they knew. The stout minaret may have been deemed more rational in an earthquake area, as the ruined mosque at Van bears witness.

Most provincial mosques were little more than domed cubes but of good proportions and endowed with well-built porticoes and double porticoes where there was no

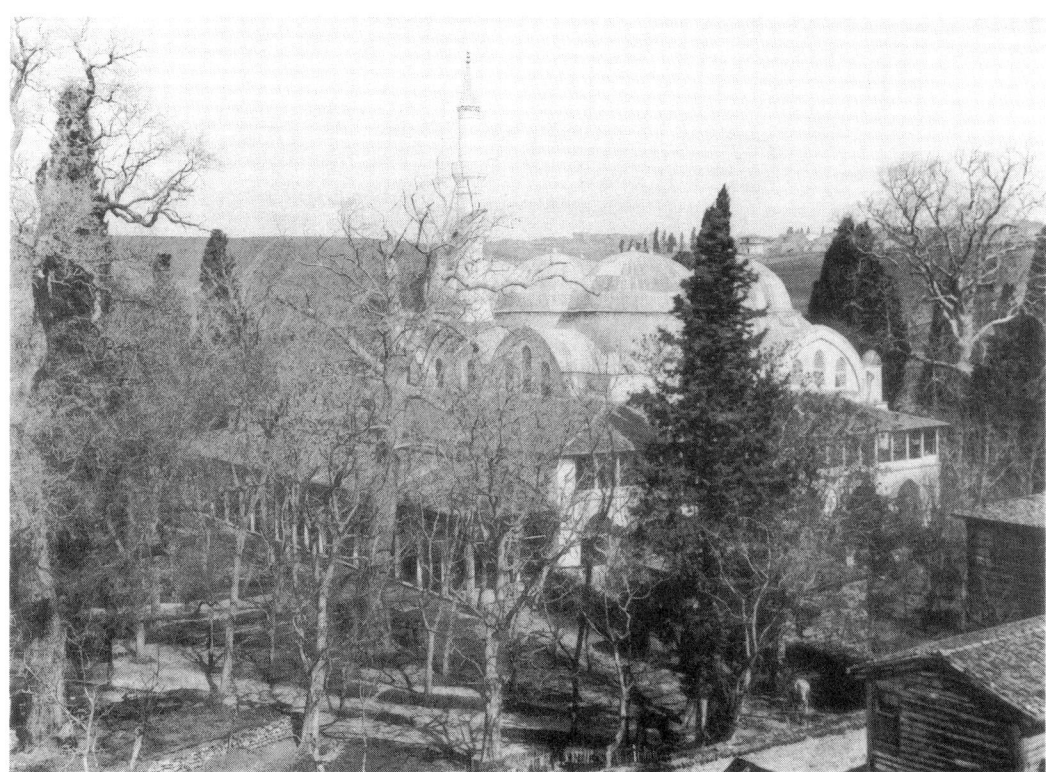

86. *Piyale Pasha mosque, Istanbul*
(Gurlitt)

college. Such was the Ahmad Pasha or Kurşunlu (lead-covered) mosque in Kayseri. The nickname arises because humbler mosques were roofed with tiles. Courtyards were not frequent since the donor could not afford the rich endowment that a college required. When one does appear, with the exception of the Süleyman Pasha mosque in the citadel at Cairo, it is but a rough enclosure. The mosque itself, with its low-springing dome and Mamluk-style slim marble dados, was only half Ottoman in character.

It is true that Sinan experimented with extending porticoes down the sides of mosques without proper courtyards as at that of Rüstem Pasha. But the two mosques in Istanbul where these porticoes appear—those of Piyale Pasha and Hacı Ivaz Efendi, beside the land walls—have never been attributed to him. The latter once had porticoes on three sides and the minaret was drawn back to the corner of the mihrab wall. The use of galleries and lateral porticoes occurs with the Murad III mosque at Manisa and elsewhere. There the architect, unknown as with the other two, was more restrained than the architect of Piyale Pasha, who carried his use of columns to the frontiers of possibility.

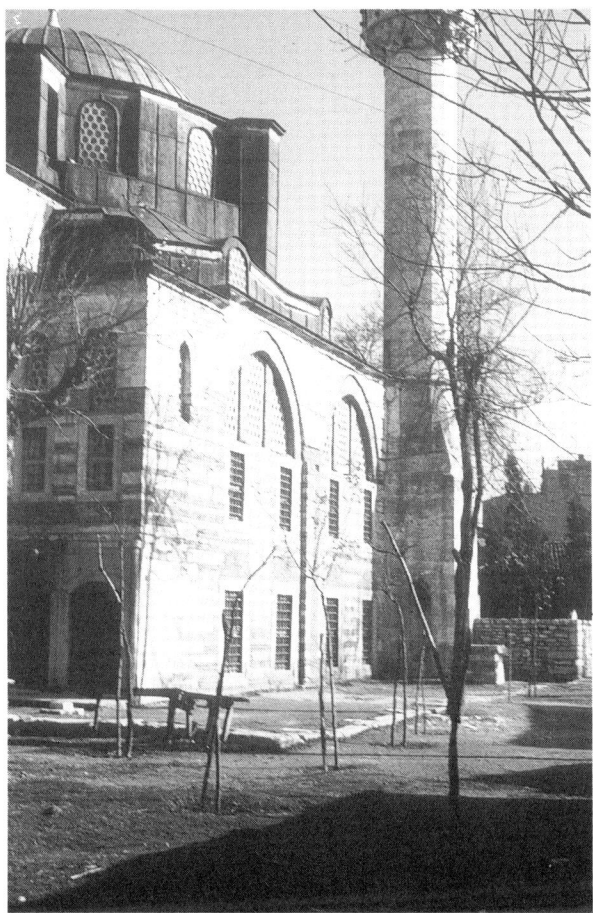

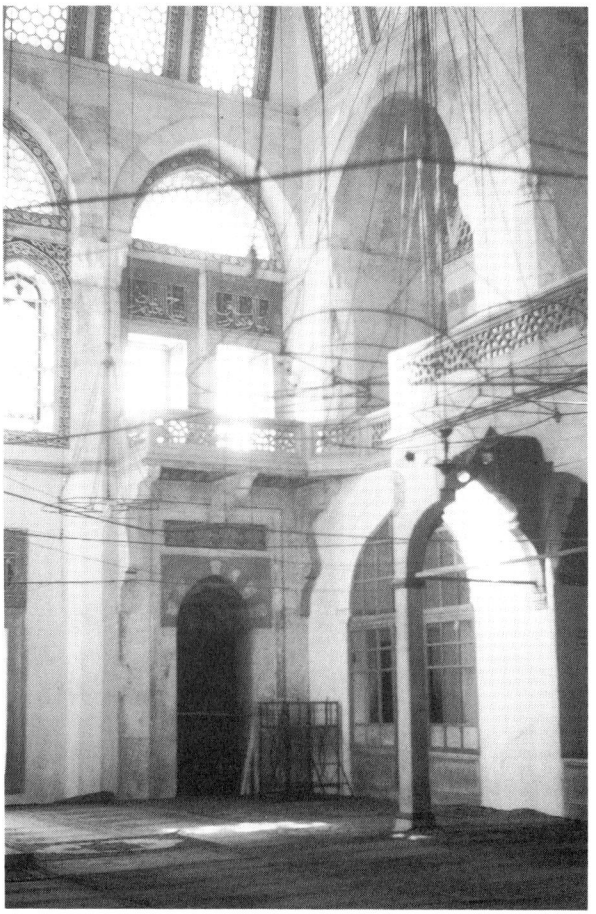

87. Hacı Ivaz Efendi mosque, Istanbul (Graeme Gardiner)

Right:
88. Muradiye mosque, Manisa: interior

Murad III Mosque, Manisa (1586–7)

The Muradiye was built on a hillside, which forced the architect Mustafa, if it were he,[44] to erect a severely rectangular mosque across its slope in order to include a rectangular mihrab apse which is one third the area of the mosque. This means that various galleries dominate the space—or would do if the mihrab were not so rich in fine paintwork and Iznik tile panels bathed in bright light from large windows which lean inwards. It is likely that the mosque is more Mustafa's adaptation of the original plan than any one his master drew. For this was a royal commission and therefore one with which Sinan had to take special pains—the costly tiles bear witness to this—at however far a remove. Yet it is unlikely that Murad III or Sinan ever made an excursion to Manisa to see the building at any stage.

Other Mosques

More difficult problems of attribution arise with the Pertev Pasha complex at Izmit or the Rüstem Pasha mosque at Tekirdağ. Those sites which were near enough to Istanbul to allow an occasional visit, or which are on the road to Edirne that Sinan had frequently to traverse so that he could easily survey work in progress if only for a day or two, present even more difficult examples. Some complexes are fine enough to believe that they were under Sinan's supervision, as with the two building campaigns at Sokollu Mehmed Pasha's complex at Lüleburgaz (1549 and 1569–70); but the Semiz Ali Pasha mosque at Babaeski, for all its noble site, is hard to accept as a building supervised by Sinan. The ill-matched columns of the portico and some clumsiness in the placing of large windows make it improbable that he worked there. The royal commissions for great complexes came one after another: the architect would have needed time for surveying of the site and the meticulous planning of the relationships and positioning of many buildings differing in both size and purpose. The intervals were barely sufficient to work full

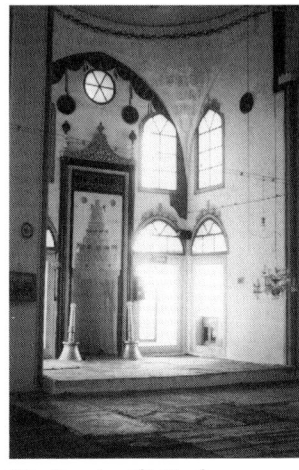

89. *Semiz Ali Pasha mosque, Babaeski: interior*

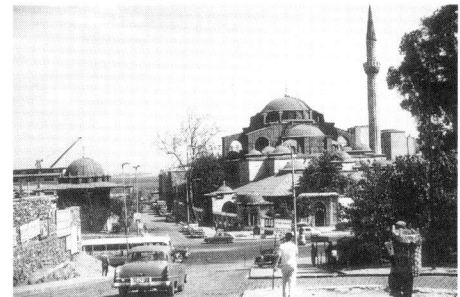

90. *Kılıç Ali Pasha mosque, Istanbul: exterior*

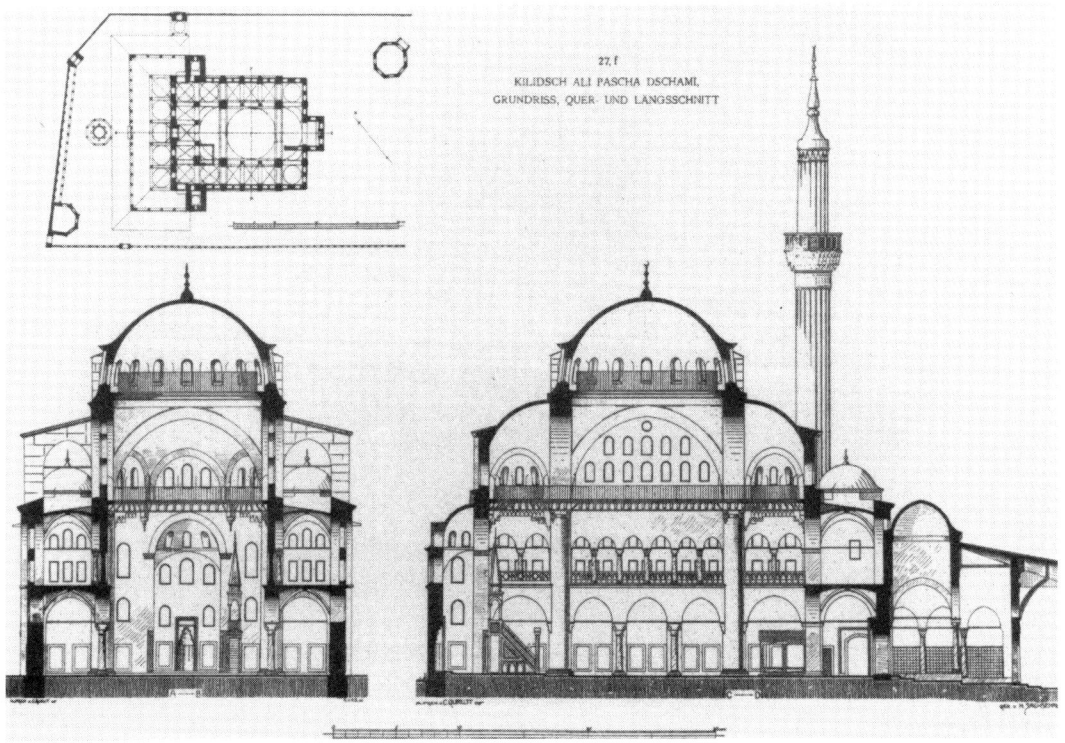

91. *Kılıç Ali Pasha mosque, Istanbul: plan and elevation* (Gurlitt)

Other Mosques

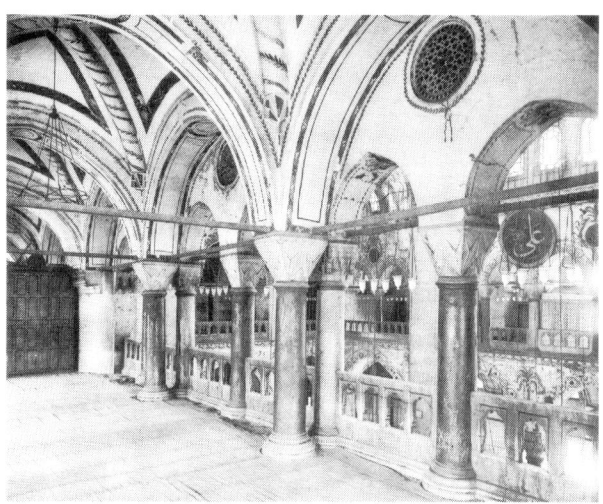

92. *Kılıç Ali Pasha mosque, Istanbul: interior at gallery level* (Gurlitt)

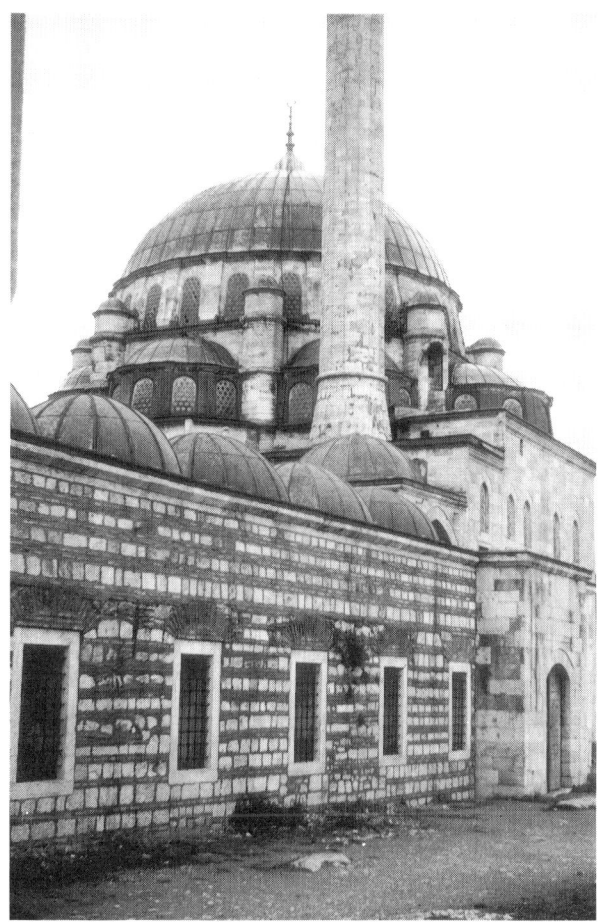

93. *Nışancı Mehmed Pasha mosque, Istanbul: exterior*

time on the major complexes of Grand Vezirs like Rüstem Pasha or, even more, of Sokollu Mehmed Pasha. If there were minutes to spare, such considerable tasks as the rebuilding of Topkapısaray after the fire of 1574, or the new pavilions for the summer palace at Edirne, ate them up.

Sinan did have time to marry and have children (who were all to die young), draw up wills, petition for grants of land for his relations and protect them from the Order-in-Council that sent the Christian peasants and farmers in the Kayseri area to repopulate Cyprus after the conquest of the island in 1572.

He had time, too, for experiments such as the stilted version of the great mosque that was Haghia Sophia and which was built on a reduced scale for Kılıç Ali Pasha, the captor of Cervantes and a Sicilian. It has length and emphasizes Sinan's conversion to the use of an apse. With this mosque, the lead that covered the dome was carried all over the roof area like a shroud. This extended use of lead was to be employed on other mosques of the period such as Hacı Ivaz Efendi. Lead is laid to protect stonework and this doubling of the quantity normally used was due to a fortuitous glut: the result of illegal trafficking by English ships in the 1570s and 1580s, which meant that lead was cheap and no longer a luxury in Istanbul. Such is the nature of chance in the history of architecture, and its effect upon taste and aesthetics should no more be overlooked than patronage and cash.

Until the death of Selim II in 1574, the Ottoman treasury enabled sultans to commission unprecedented numbers of large complexes and important buildings while engaged in extensive military campaigns and the government of vast territories. This abundance could not last and inflation (and economic decline) was well under way before Sinan died. Yet even when wars were lost and not won, it was possible to plan the building of the imposing Valide complex at Eminönü on the shore of the Golden Horn, and the huge Sultan Ahmad complex was not completed by Mehmed Agha until 1616.

Of all the men trained by Sinan, Davud Agha may claim to have been the most interesting. At the mosque he built for Nışancı Mehmed Pasha, for example, he created a central space on an octagon which is vibrant with the experience of the Selimiye at Edirne to a degree which suggests that he worked with Sinan on that

Sinan

building and had listened to his master's intentions. Others of his mosques showed that he was intelligent and it is therefore surprising when he returned to the fourfoil plan of the Şehzade as the plan of the Yeni Valide mosque[45] in 1597. He was to die (perhaps he was executed) in 1599 when Dalgıç Ahmad Agha succeeded him; work on the mosque was suspended in 1603, on the death of Mehmed III, and was left untouched until 1660. Ahmad Pasha, recalled to military service, was given command of the army sent to rid north-west Anatolia of the Celali rebels and was killed in battle. This event serves as a reminder of how much the army and architects were interlinked at this period. Mehmed Agha, the Worker in Mother-of-Pearl as he was known, was the last of Sinan's great students to survive. He had been Master of the Waterways for a long time but must also have had experience of building mosques.

Sultan Ahmad Mosque (1609–16)

The Sultan Ahmad mosque was grand in its conception: too grand, for the monumental supporting piers of the dome had to be clad in scalloped marble in an attempt to reduce the effect of their bulk, thus giving them the nickname of elephant feet. By contrast, the dome itself appears to be even more modest than it is. Yet the interior is breathtakingly large and the mihrab wall is dramatic even though the original Venetian glass has been lost and replaced in the twentieth century by garish substitutes. The arcades of the courtyard are too small in relation to the spaciousness of the courtyard itself and are the same height as the portico. Nor did Mehmed Agha modulate the long march of arches that stretch along the flanks of the court and the mosque. The build-up of semi-domes and turrets, which perfectly expresses the internal structure, reaches a climax with the major dome from all four sides. This is indeed a *tour de force*. That there are six minarets is emotive indeed: even more emotive was the hostility they provoked at a time of increasingly heavy taxation and declining national fortunes.[46]

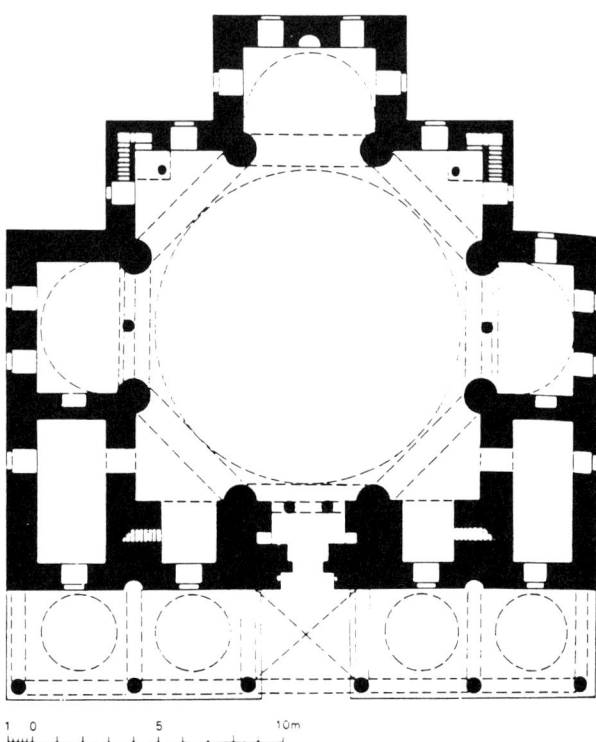

94. Nışancı Mehmed Pasha mosque, Istanbul: plan

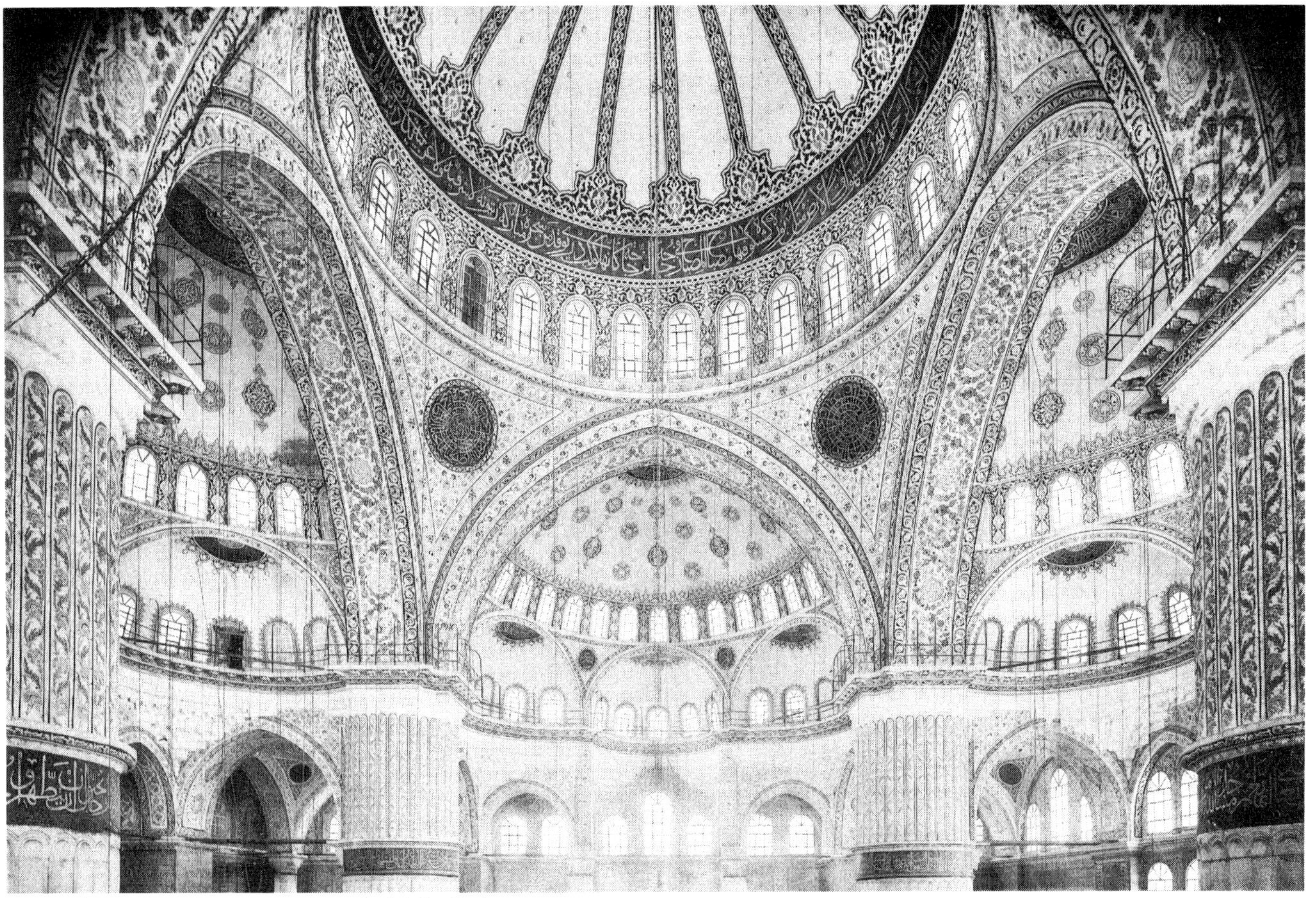

Other Mosques

95. Sultan Ahmad mosque, Istanbul (Gurlitt)

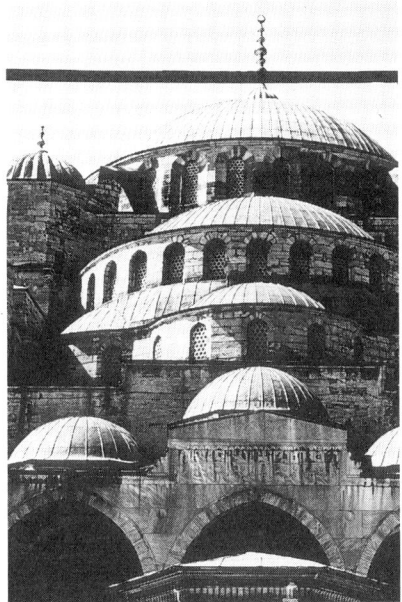

96. Sultan Ahmad mosque, Istanbul: build-up to dome

Such then were Sinan's aides, along with others who as yet have no history. With such a skilled team to carry out his instructions, one can better understand how he was able to make that imaginative leap represented by the mosque of Selim II at Edirne. The elements and ideas which go to make up the concept of this building will be taken one by one and will be seen not simply comparatively but as the climax of Sinan's intellectual evolution towards unsurpassable excellence. It is appropriate, therefore, to begin with the concept of light in the hope of illuminating his final majestic achievement.

The Importance of Light

Sinan took Ottoman architecture to academic perfection ith the mosque of Süleyman and then he crossed that border and set about the achievement of a broader understanding of form, not for the sake of novelty but because he could see beyond the traditional limits of his world. There is nothing surprising in his drive to escape from the established rules which meant that he had to create new ones of his own by deduction. What was apposite was that his evolution can be credited to a fascination with light. He manipulated it intellectually to enhance elements and spaces in a building which gave that structure spiritual force. As we have seen, at ground level windows were for air, deep and grilled against bird and animal intrusion and shuttered against the wind when it blew. Only the upper windows were there precisely to admit light. They were guarded by stone grids of bottle glass which also filtered strong sunlight. The deep recesses of the casements were useful small retreats and their floors at such important mosques as that of Süleyman were patterned with coloured marbles. In his pursuit of light Sinan enlarged the casements onto the porticoes of several mosques, including that of Rüstem Pasha in Istanbul as well as Kara Ahmad Pasha and the very late Atık Valide mosque above Üsküdar. Descending from Byzantine traditions, the most significant windows were those around the base of the dome, all-important symbolically and for lightening the impression of weight a dome otherwise gives. The masonry lost because of these apertures was replaced between them in the form of buttresses, a basic rule in Ottoman design throughout any building.

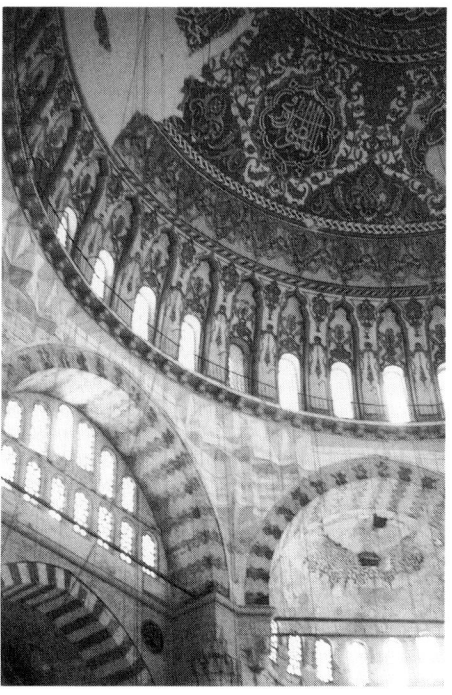

97. Selimiye mosque, Edirne: towards the dome (Graeme Gardiner)

At first Sinan was concerned to achieve the maximum inflow of light possible just as twentieth-century architects like Mies van der Rohe or Neutra removed masonry entirely and substituted glass. Then in his maturation from the simple desire for illumination for its own sake, Sinan rejected light as an intrusion from the outside world into the interior like a river in spate. Retracing the route of this visual journey, it becomes clear how his mind was at work. As we have seen with the mosque of Mihrimah below the walls of Istanbul, he removed every superfluous stone in order to insert the greatest number of windows possible. This was the achievement of a master engineer and with its four impressive corner towers a new form was created for this mosque. Their size is structurally essential to support the wide curtain walls between, while visually they express

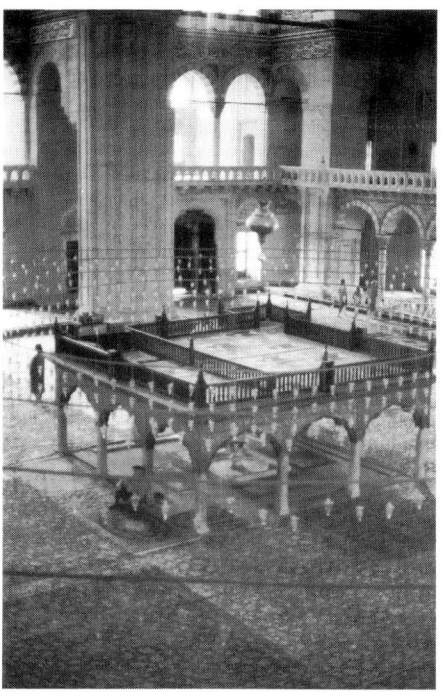

98. Selimiye mosque, Edirne: the centre (Graeme Gardiner)

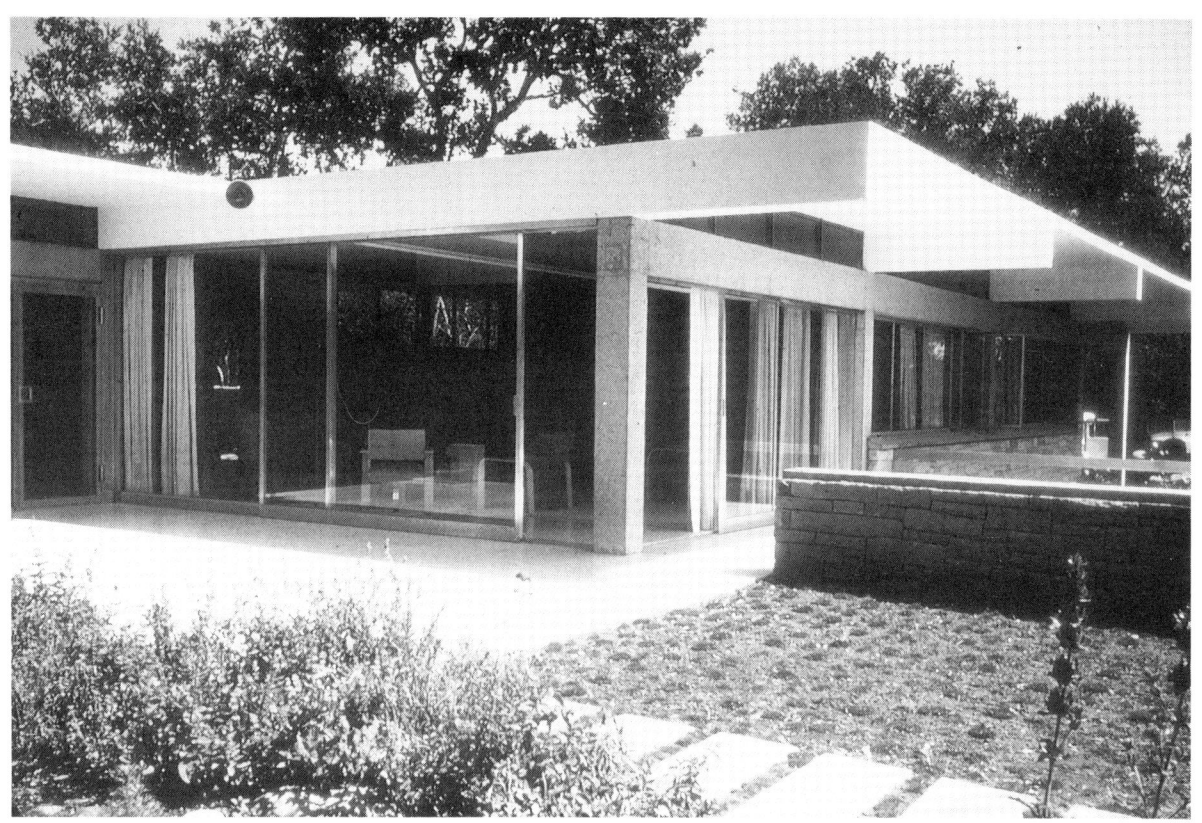

99. House by Richard Neutra, Santa Barbara: glass in the shade of great eaves

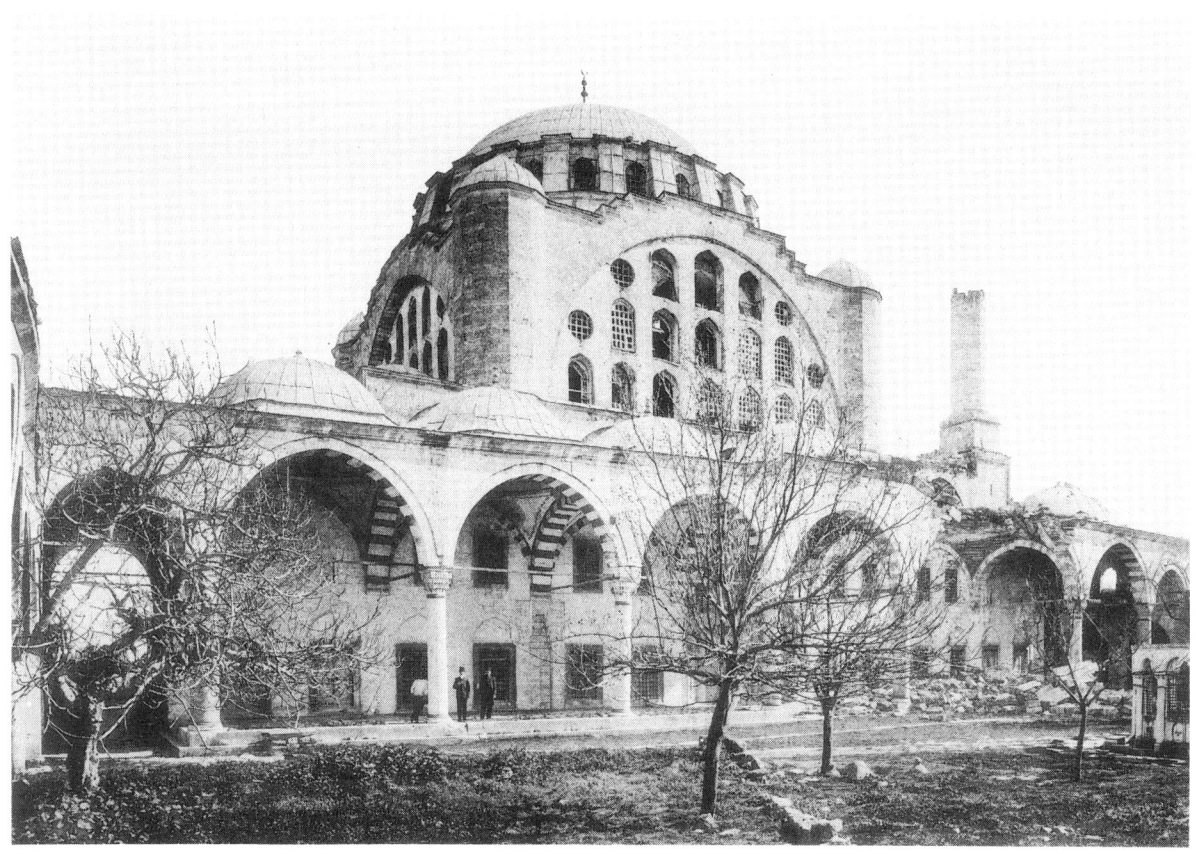

100. Mihrimah mosque, Istanbul: exterior showing damage after 1894 earthquake (Gurlitt)

stability and grandeur. In the creative yet simple sense of power, the engineer and the artist coalesce as architect. Sinan could not and would not wish to repeat this unique building because he had admitted just as much light as any Ottoman masonry structural techniques could hope to achieve. It was not that it was not enough: it was too much.

What developed next was Sinan's recognition of the mystical value of the abstract language of shadows. What he did not turn to was that veritable orchestration of shadow and sunbeam which was, and at times still is, the magic of Haghia Sophia. The fascination of Haghia Sophia lies in the contrast between its deliberately created vistas of interlocking areas of light and shade and the Ottoman exactitude of good mathematics along with the worldly problems of stress and compression which permitted no element which was not structurally essential. This exactitude meant that no element of religious mysticism could be introduced without it weakening structural integrity.[47] As so often when contrasting Ottoman and Byzantine civilization, there is more that is common to both than is not. Moreover, certain driving forces were shared such as the prime duty of charity and the celestial nature of the deity whom Dante described as Light: 'l'amor che muove il sole e l'altre stelle'.

Byzantine architecture was introverted, however, and its truths were interiors of shadow and shafts of light. Ottoman truth was revelation and every effort which the structure would permit was exerted in order to illuminate the darker corners. Anthemius painted with a grey palette: Sinan with a white. It was Sinan who enlarged the windows of the apse of Haghia Sophia, an alteration which was likely to have been proposed to the sultan, his patron and master, and not by the sultan to Sinan.

It was a felicitous chance that Sinan should have tested masonry to its limits at the Mihrimah mosque immediately before Selim II called on him to build his mosque at Edirne. Sinan had little left to learn about the nature of stone and his deputies were all trained by experience. It was not just the Mihrimah's windowscape that was daring but also the minaret, which was as exceptionally slender as it was tall. But this extravagance of glass was not enough. Sinan turned from light for its own sake, free and untrammelled, to modulation and a greater aesthetic perception.

Light in itself has no value. The cloudless skies of a desert prove that it is not life-enhancing. It kills. Great architects trap it and redirect it. They use it as a language

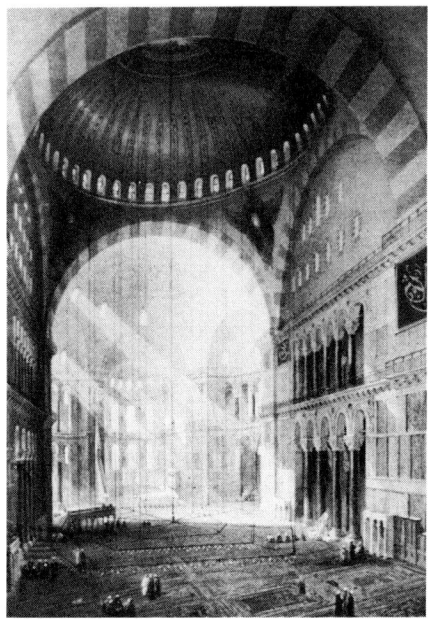

101. *Haghia Sophia (Aya Sofya mosque), Istanbul: interior by Fossati*

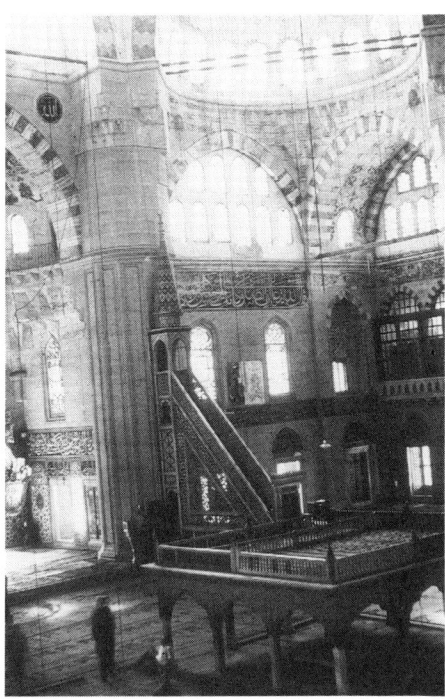

102. *Selimiye mosque, Edirne: interior*

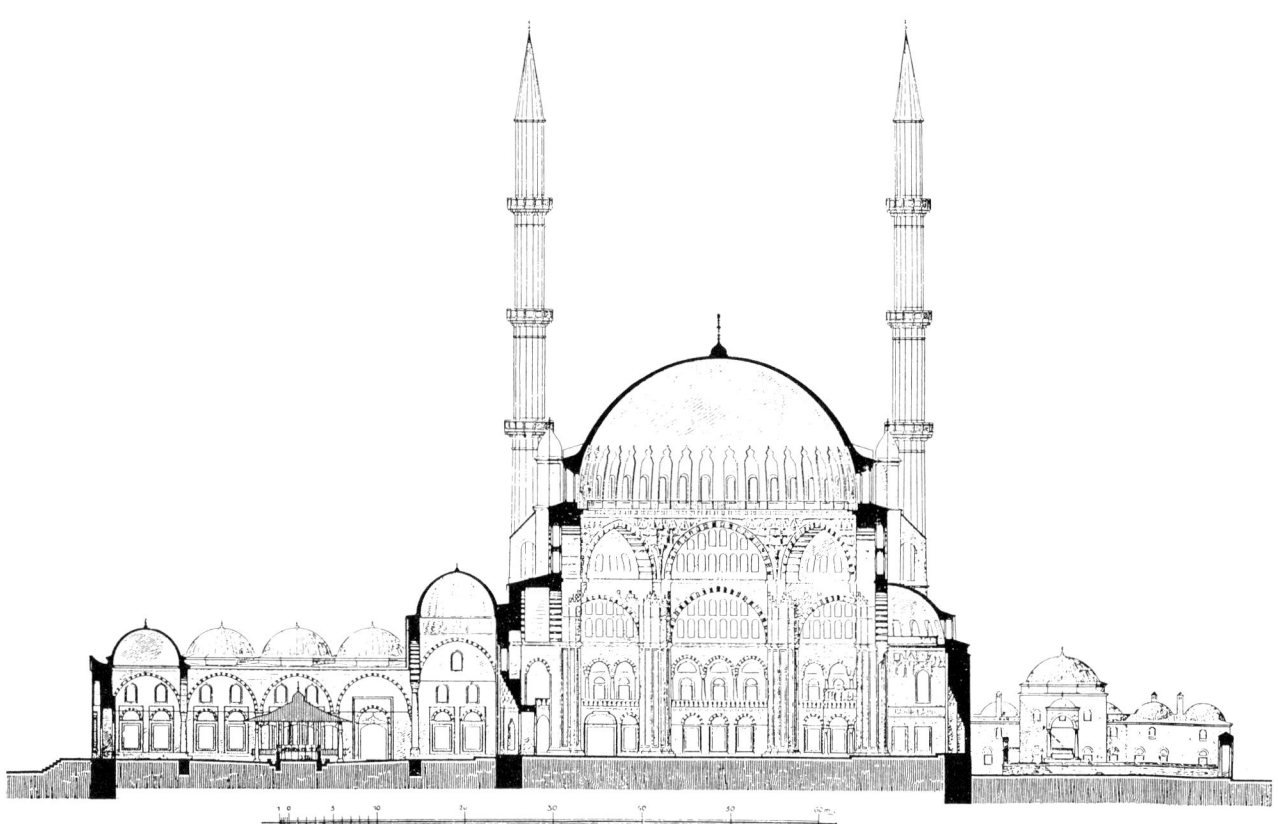

103. *Selimiye mosque, Edirne: cross-section* (Gurlitt)

by means of which sun and moon and interior space intercommunicate. Sinan learnt this language, which Bernini was to perfect, when he had his vision of what was to be the Selimiye mosque.

Light and the Selimiye Mosque (1572–5)

On the drawing-board the mosque of Selim II is a square set in a rectangle cornered by the four loftiest minarets ever built by an Ottoman architect. Inside the building the effect is of a circle beneath a dome which rivals that of Haghia Sophia in its dimensions. In the centre of the circle beneath the crown of the dome is a large, square muezzin's gallery above a marble fountain which serves to define the cylindrical sense of space and to anchor its huge volume. The reason for the dominance of the circle is that the dome springs from eight piers forming an octagon and not four as at the Süleymaniye or other major mosques. Moreover, the tailor-made stalactite capitals, if such the heads of piers can be called, are concave and carry four arches and four exedras which cross the corners of the building. All of this enhances the hemispherical dominance of the dome and the sense of circular movement girding the prayer hall. At ground level, the lateral walls of the mosque are drawn almost to the bases of the piers. This transforms the otherwise undesirable areas of interior space each side into deep porches. These support the broad galleries at upper-floor level which are brilliantly lit by large windows and are a part of the interior and detached from it at one and the same time.

With the north wall, Sinan exploited its blind nature due to the domes of the great portico onto the courtyard on its other side. Apart from the modest pools of light under the galleries from the ground-level windows, its shaded space contrasts with the concentration of light in the heart of the mosque. In addition, the mihrab is set in a broad apse filled with fine floral panels of Iznik tiles and lit by large windows under its own semi-dome. The direction of prayer, accentuated by the paradisaical garden in which the grandiose mihrab is set, is unmistakable yet the central circle and the dome above it do not lose face.

The play of light changes with the seasons and time of day and its qualities vary as well. It must be remembered that unlike Haghia Sophia the Selimiye is to be judged in daytime for it is by day that it functions whereas the greatest solemnities of the Byzantine church took place by night.[48] At the Selimiye, as with most Ottoman mosques, it is at the belt of windows above the springing of the domes and semi-domes that there is the most forceful concentration of light. This brilliance is reflected in the inscription to God as light, the usual Koranic quotation placed in the crown of the dome where once the Byzantine Pantocrator would look down in judgement. At gallery level the light is more diffused yet still bright—on the one side in the morning and on the other in the afternoon. There are few places where the shadows are deep except between the lateral piers and the porch walls and in the deep thresholds of the five great doors into the building when they are closed or masked. The light everywhere is articulated and so articulates the considerable spaces of the interior. Abetted by the winds and clouds of Thrace, it often moves imperceptibly like Dante's great wheel turning.[49]

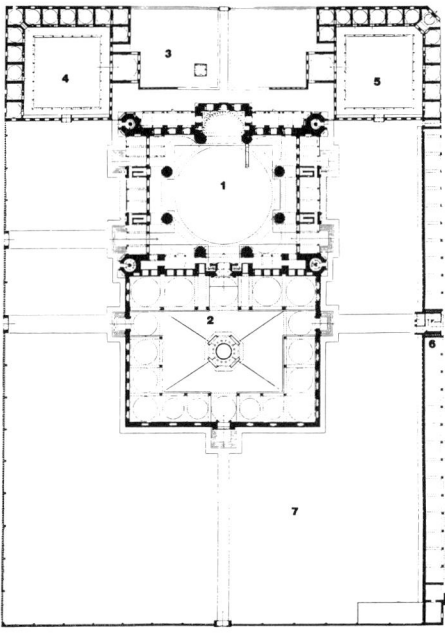

104. Selimiye complex, Edirne: plan

Key
1. Mosque
2. Court
3. Burial ground
4. College
5. Graduate college
6. Boot market
7. Esplanade

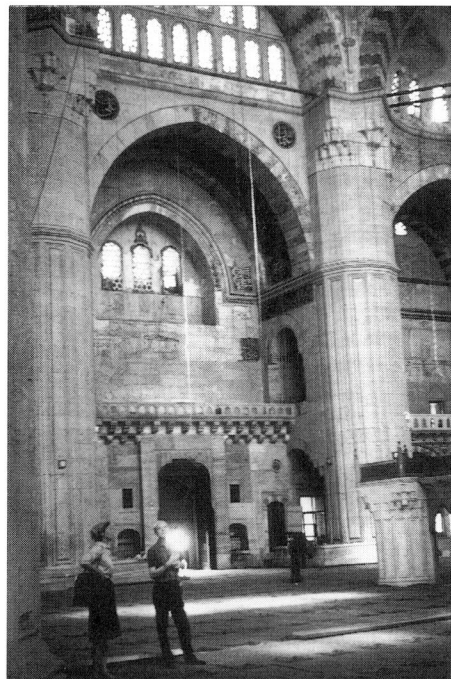

105. Selimiye mosque, Edirne: north wall

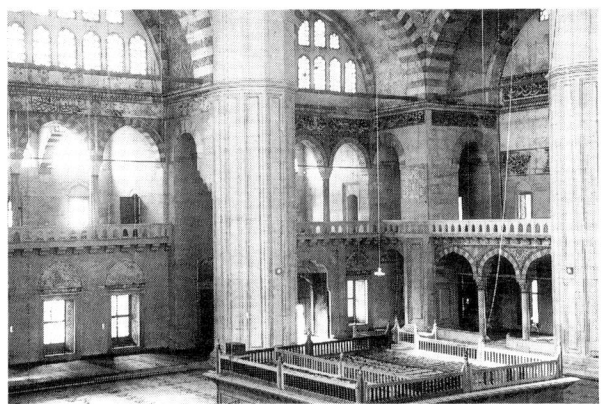

106. Selimiye mosque, Edirne: side galleries

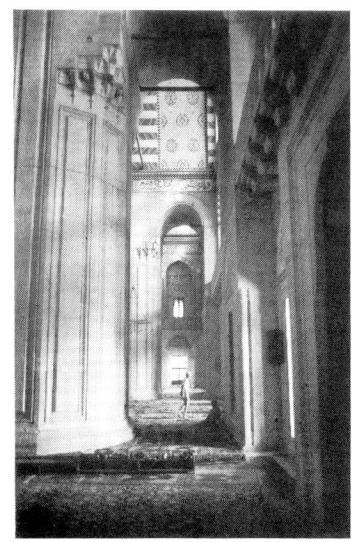

108. Selimiye mosque, Edirne: shadow areas (Graeme Gardiner)

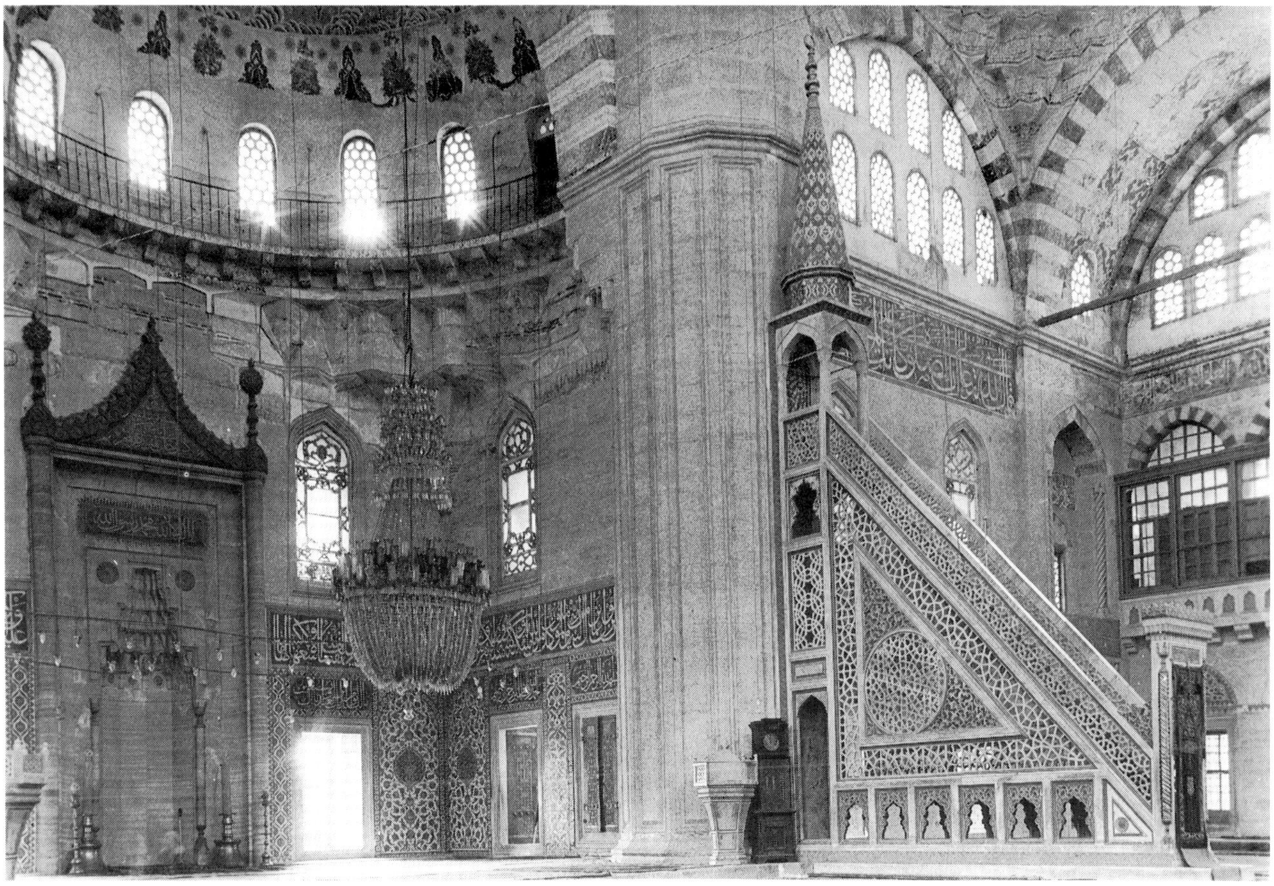

107. Selimiye mosque, Edirne: south wall

Sinan

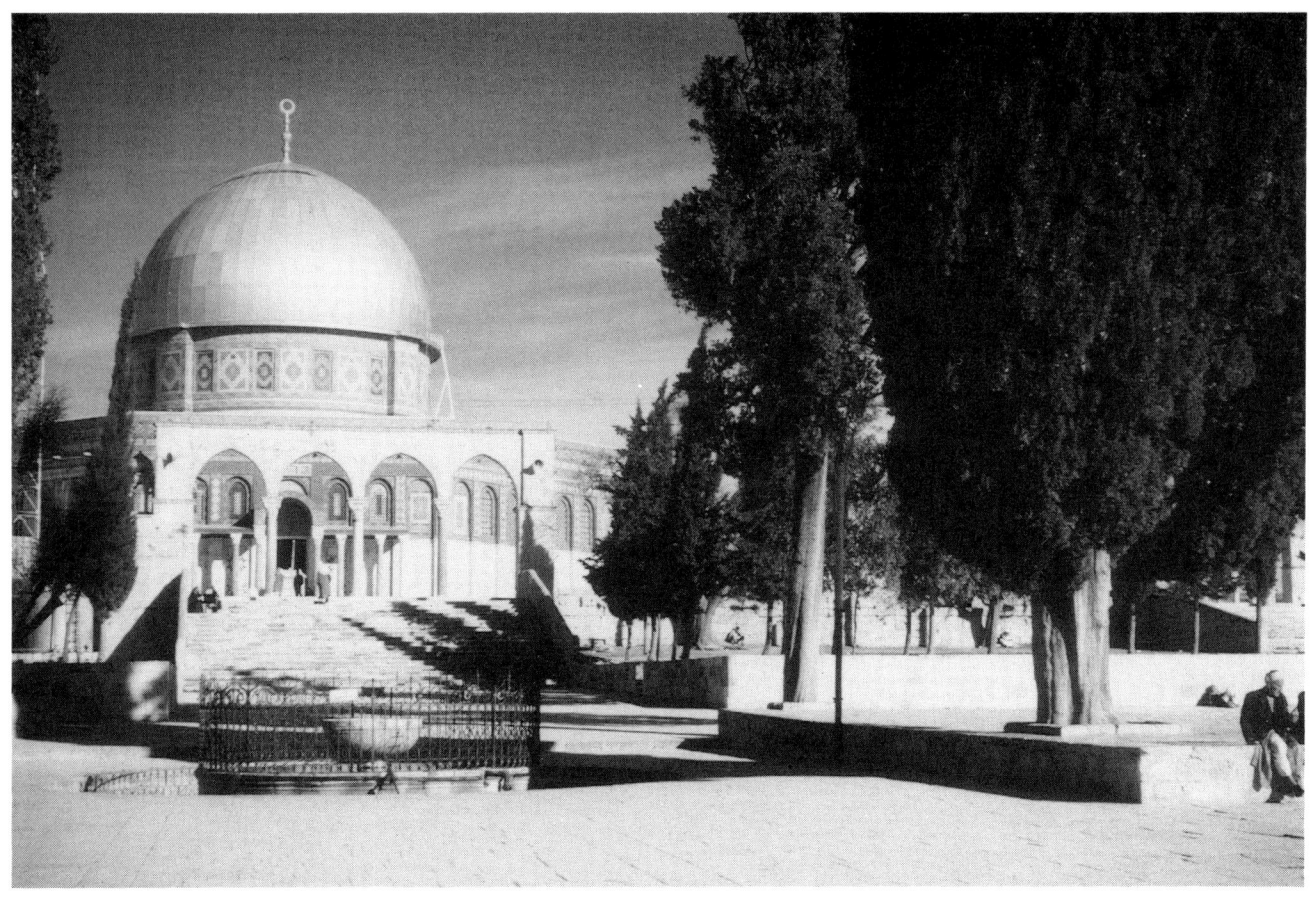

109. The Dome of the Rock, Jerusalem

The Dome

While the cosmic significance of the dome is universally recognized, the cosmic significance of the sky itself can be overlooked. But when Sinan built the Selimiye this ultimate dome over all domes[50] was deliberately made the visible, spiritual extension of the earthbound architecture.

Had it followed its aspiration to achieve the sublime in the form of the grand dome, Ottoman architecture would have been doomed to reach its own dead end early in the sixteenth century. The mosques of Bayazid at Edirne and of Selim I[51] in Istanbul are perfect hemispheres and their pendentives spring from almost the roots of the perfect cubes on which they rest. They achieve large, dignified and significant space: the reverse of the monolith.

But the internal perfection of the perfect hemisphere set on the perfect square was sterilized by this very perfection. Henceforth there was nowhere to go, for good workmanship meant that the domed cube had

The Dome

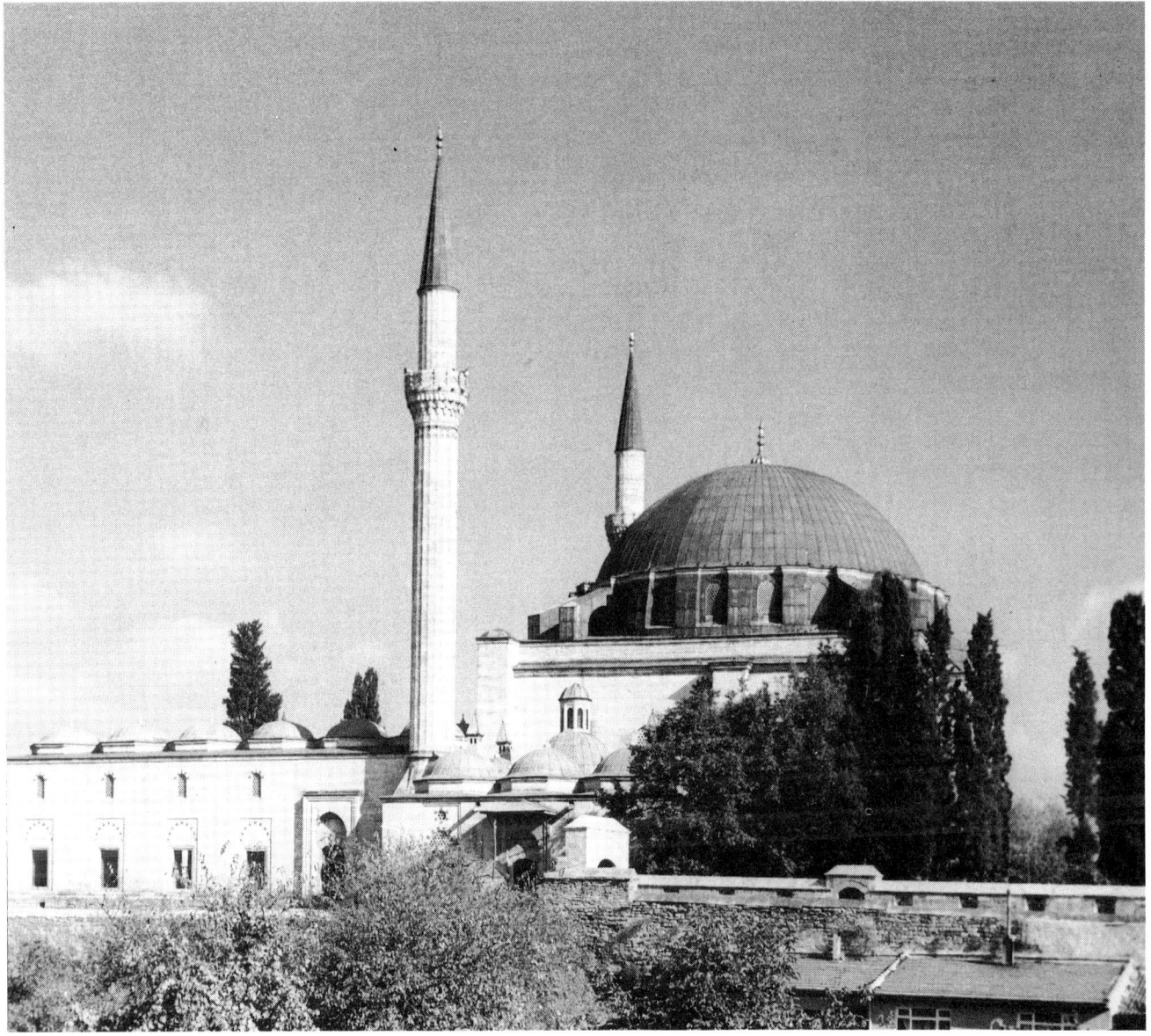

110. Sultan Selim mosque, Istanbul: exterior (Gurlitt)

reached its structural apogee. The need to combine a number of functional units—retiring rooms, areas for ritual eating and dancing, the prayer hall itself—meant that these were welded into a complex united whole. Because of this unification as one building with all the possibilities for variation, the fourteenth and fifteenth centuries had no reason to suppose that their work was approaching sterility. However perfect each domed section might be, the agglomeration had a life of its own. With the typical convent-mosque form, which spread all over Anatolia and the Balkans, the ability to divine the usage of each internal area from the outset gives them a certain dynamic: in a grander form, but much as a crossword addict is stimulated by finding the solution to a brilliantly devised clue.

This is not to disparage Ottoman architecture before 1540. There have been (and still are) plenty of architectural styles and periods where the ideal interior space cannot be enhanced any further and is unable to evolve because the problems of achieving a single aim have been resolved. It is the next event that matters, in architecture as in all other things: it was this ability to step through the mirror which was Sinan's unique achievement in the sixteenth-century period of Ottoman building. It faltered after his death for ultimately a brilliant achievement signals inevitable decline whether or not it can be postponed or disguised. Once every bone and ligament of the body had been analysed by Leonardo da Vinci all that remained to explore was malformity and the grotesque, as if the ultimate art were to be found among the specimens at the Wellcome Institute. A style of architecture also becomes distorted in the search for originality until the old forms give way to the new.

Haghia Sophia is among the greatest buildings in the world and even in its grand old age is in no way a freak. But any responsible engineer in the sixteenth century would have had cause for concern when he surveyed the distortions and patched wounds that abound in the great church. Sinan, as the overseer of Haghia Sophia, then the chief mosque of the sultanate, studied it from top to bottom and it is clear that as a trained engineer some of what he saw alarmed him.

The building had been in a poor state in 1453 when Constantinople was taken by the Ottomans and had only been patched up before Sinan was called in to save it from what was feared to be approaching collapse. Stallholders had burrowed into the walls at ground level, columns were askew, not one of the brick arches was a true hemispherical shape. The dome had a history which Sinan cannot have known although he may have been able to trace it by deduction from its distortions. It was misshapen due to earthquakes and to fourteenth-century repairs. The gallery of the dome slanted inwards at its base—and still slants—towards the floor and was strewn with stumbling blocks and bases. He was not to know that the huge building had shifted during its first century and crushed the Devonian rock on which it is built until it finally eased itself into stability like Dr Johnson into a favourite chair. To Sinan the building clearly appeared to be so unstable that he expended great sums and much time constructing massive buttresses to shore it up against its ruin.

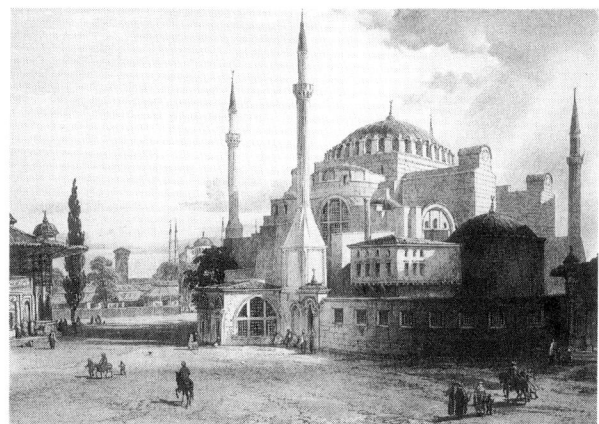

111. Haghia Sophia (Aya Sofya mosque), Istanbul: exterior by Fossati

Facing page:
112. Haghia Sophia (Aya Sofya mosque), Istanbul: exedra by Fossati

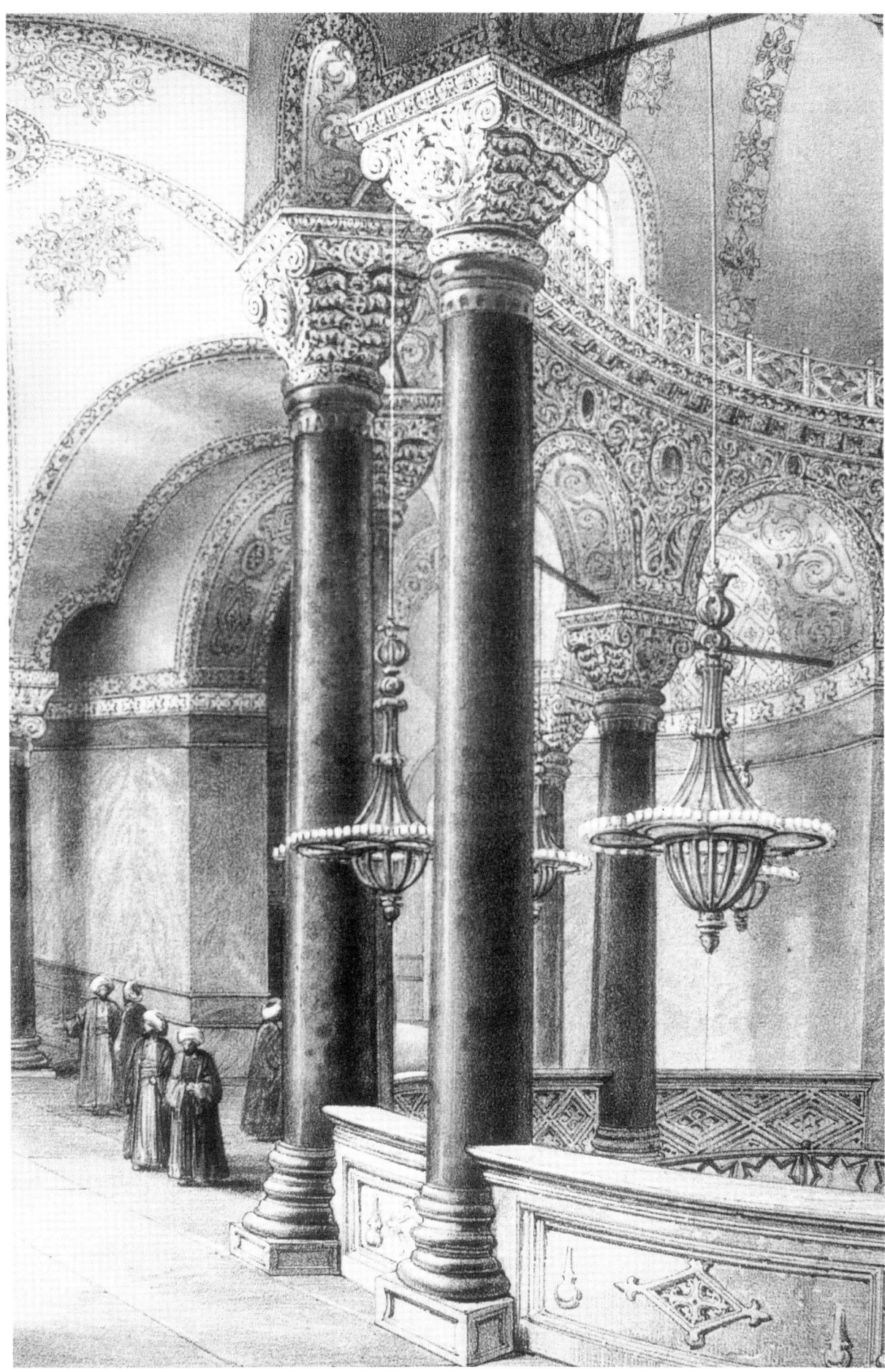

What Sinan did not learn from Haghia Sophia was how to build a dome. Nor was it Haghia Sophia's dome about which Sir Christopher Wren sought detailed information from Roger North,[52] the Turkey merchant, when Wren came to build St Paul's Cathedral in London—it was that of the Süleymaniye. Apart from the mosque of Murad Pasha above Üsküdar thirteen years after the conquest in 1466 and whose builder was undoubtedly Greek like the pasha, a Palaeologus, no Ottoman architect ever imitated the basically brick drum structure of the Byzantine canon. The two semi-domes of Bayazid II's mosque do indeed reflect Byzantine aesthetics but the structure was different—a fact made more difficult to analyse since the dome was rebuilt after it fell during the great earthquake of 22 May 1766, which decapitated mosques as fast as the revolution was to guillotine French aristocrats.

Sinan was to match the twin semi-domes of the Bayazidiye with those of the mosque of Süleyman and yet totally differently. Partly because it dominates the skyline of the old city of Istanbul, the Süleymaniye is often thought of as Sinan's masterpiece. But it is probably true that he himself said that the Şehzade mosque was his apprentice work and the Süleymaniye the achievement of his journeymanship, but that the Selimiye was his masterpiece. It has, apart from the mihrab recess, no semi-domes and nowhere for them to go. What Sinan did absorb from his study of Haghia Sophia was the use of exedras. These appear in his canon from the fourfoil plan of the Şehzade mosque onwards. They had not been understood by the builder of the Bayazidiye let alone incorporated into the mosque structure. He had responded to the idea of a dome between semi-domes although retaining old-fashioned small dome units down each side. He had been trained in the compartmentalized style of the old Ottoman technique: the very idea of an exedra would have been upsetting because it compromises space in a way that is hostile to the Ottoman style. Anxious above all not to lose that order which offers the best sense of security to a visitor in a building, the architect—Hayreddin, or whoever he was[53]—could not let the semi-domes and the main dome coalesce either. Seen from inside, each is kept to its own area. At the Süleymaniye the use of exedras lets space flow and intermingle.

The Süleymaniye, however, was the only mosque save Kılıç Ali Pasha that Sinan built with semi-domes fore and aft of the central dome nor did any of his students repeat the form. In chronological order, the influence of

Facing page:
113. Haghia Sophia (Aya Sofya mosque), Istanbul: interior (Gurlitt)

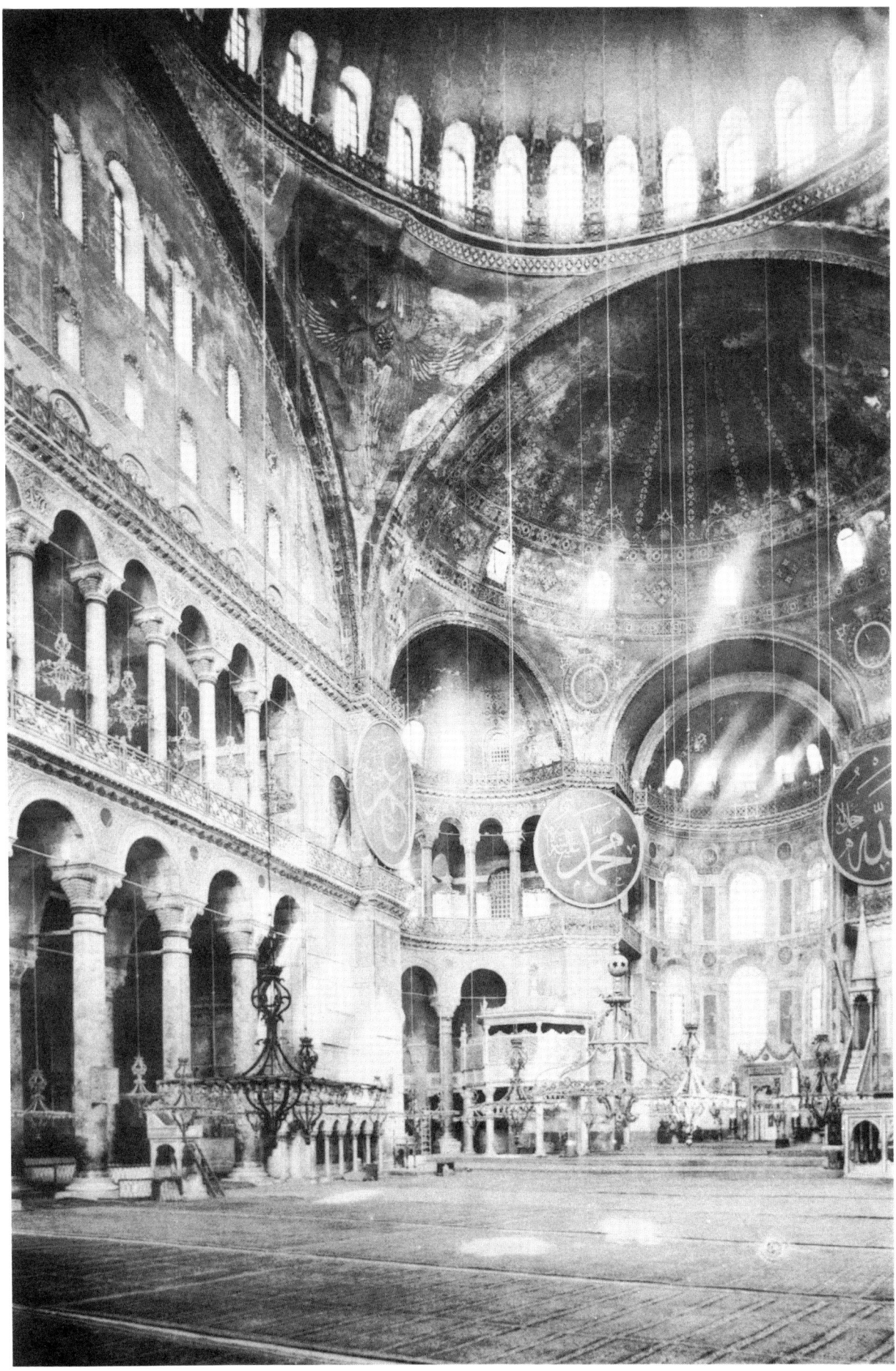

the basic plan of Haghia Sophia was confined to the mosques of Bayazid II in Istanbul (1506); of Fatih Pasha at Dıyarbekir (1517); of Süleyman in Istanbul (1551-8); and of Kılıç Ali Pasha in Istanbul (1580-1). This very late work of Sinan's was a failure if it is seen as a copy of Haghia Sophia and not as an Ottoman theme after the great church. So Kılıç Ali Pasha's mosque is filled with bright light and the variations in the spaces, the sequential glimpses across undefined areas and the sheer irregularity of the elements that make up the poetry of Haghia Sophia have here been rationalized. Sinan's precision, or that of his subordinates, destroyed the mystery as totally as electric light switches out the ghost.

After Sinan's death there were to be the Yeni Valide mosque and the rebuilt Fatih mosque after the earthquake of 1766. This last was a self-conscious attempt to resurrect the Grand Manner. Although structural necessity imposed good proportions, the detailing was coarse even before the nineteenth- and twentieth-century redecoration ravished the interior. There was the citadel mosque at Cairo, which in 1830 finally emerged as something of a caricature and which was built at vast expense. Hawksmoor's project to echo the Süleymaniye when commissioned to build the Radcliffe Camera was abandoned because of cost.[54] Oxford would never have been the same but it is to be noted that the work of Sinan was taken seriously in England at that time even if it has been neglected during this century.

Finally, the domescape itself in each and every mosque of any size is a remarkable achievement of interrelated spaces and lawns of lead. To walk among the turrets of the Süleymaniye, or only to look down on the roof from the gallery of a minaret, is to encounter an aesthetic no man's land at sky level which is also a tribute to the brilliance of the solution to the final engineering problems associated with a great mosque. And the even-handed treatment achieved by Sinan is the climax of his skills.

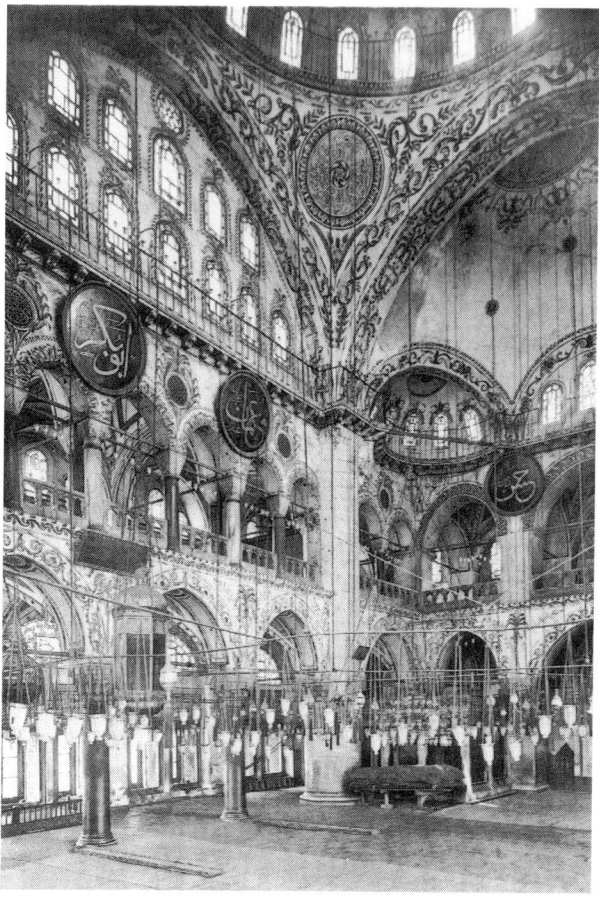

114. *Kılıç Ali Pasha mosque, Istanbul: interior* (Gurlitt)

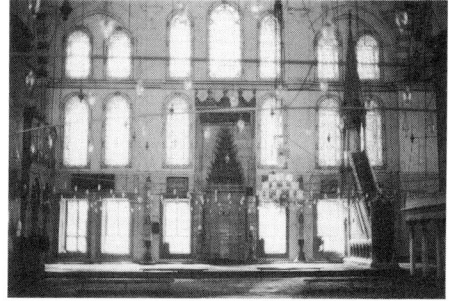

115. *Fatih, the mosque of Mehmed II the Conqueror, Istanbul* (Gurlitt)

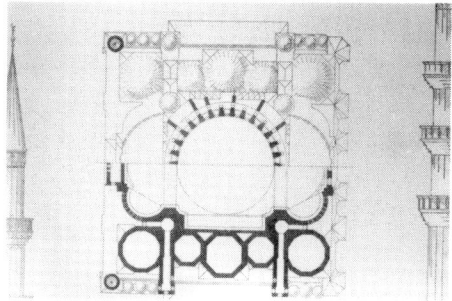

116. *Süleymaniye mosque, Istanbul: plan at dome level* (Gurlitt)

The Minaret

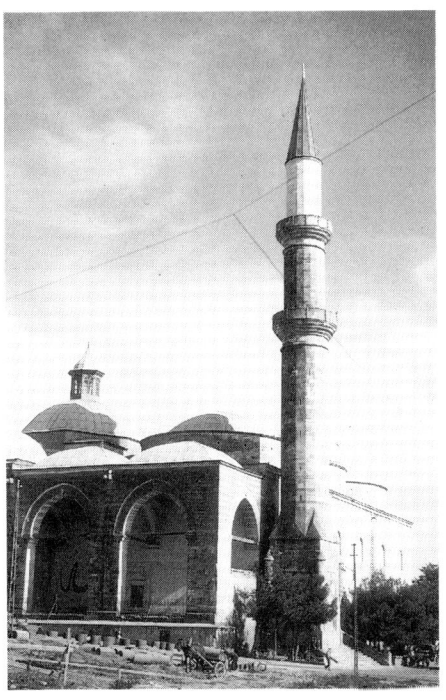

117. Yivli mosque, Antalya: minaret dating from first half of thirteenth century

118. Eski Cami (Old Mosque), Edirne

Ottoman minarets were always multifaceted or round and so easily distinguishable from the towers of most of Islam or the short pairs of turrets of Iran. They evolved from Seljuk ancestors for at first it was a refinement of ornament rather than of girth which developed from the twin guardians each side of a college gate such as that of the Gök *medrese* at Sivas. Early Ottoman minarets were no more lissom but much less ornamental as at the Ulu Cami (Great Mosque) at Bursa (*c*. 1400) or the Eski Cami (Old Mosque) at Edirne (1414). At the latter, the original minaret stood independently of the building and in the early days, indeed, there was no settled position for these towers. Moreover, the palace mosques at Bursa, whether of Bayazid I, Mehmed I or Murad II, originally had no minarets at all because they were chapels within the small palace enclosures. Early independent minarets may have been kept away from the footings of the mosque walls because their foundations had to be dug so much deeper that, in proximity, they could weaken the foundations of the building. The thick early minarets were decorated with glazed bricks or strips of marble but never in the three-dimensional and sensational Seljuk manner. Those of the Great Mosque at Bursa were faced with marble to some 5 metres of their height. The last important minarets in the old style were built at the extremities of the mosque of Bayazid II in Istanbul although his mosque in Amasya and his hospital at Edirne had limestone minarets, undecorated, in the new manner. If there was decoration other than the stalactite supports of the balconies, it was the blue tiles at topmost level inset as if fake windows. Occasionally the edge of the inner staircase was used to create a spiral pattern in the truthful manner traditional with Ottoman architecture.

By the beginning of Süleyman's reign any important mosque, including that of his father, had stone minarets. The work of building them was so skilled, as we know from the late Professor Barkan's monumental work on the accounts of the Süleymaniye complex, as to command high wages and master masons went from building to building as a team. The foundations were dug and at least part of the minaret erected before the main building, a sight which must have been fascinating.

Once the sultan's mosques had two minarets (not always the case in early times), their location at the end of the front portico was inevitable. The vezirial mosques anchored their single minaret in the north-west corner although there are such exceptions as the minaret of the Piyale Pasha mosque where it is in the middle of the entrance façade.⁵⁵ The Üç Şerefeli mosque of Murad II had introduced as many as four minarets which did not match but were logically placed at the four corners of the courtyard, offering a lesson in the development of Ottoman style from the most rotund with its three balconies to the final stone example. These four minarets set a precedent for those of the Süleymaniye mosque and later for those of the Selimiye at Edirne.⁵⁶ But in the latter, all four are equal in height and the drama lies in their symbolism as the four corners of the earth and as a message of exaltation round the heaven of the dome. The two concepts were to be compounded with the six minarets of the mosque of Sultan Ahmad to the weakening of the power of both statements. Yet this two-upmanship, which aroused so much hostility at the time, has an architectural force which compensates for the weakening of the symbolism of the abstract geometry.

With growing confidence, stone minarets grew taller and thinner still, in particular in the farther provinces of the empire. It is at the corner of the portico that the minaret has most aesthetic impact for there it is exposed from base to the lead cone that covers it and carries the horns of the crescent of its finial. It is the perfect foil to the dome, provided that it is slender and soars sufficiently high. But a minaret is totally functional because its gallery, or galleries with major mosques, is designed to project the call to prayer as far as possible.⁵⁷

With the work of Sinan the proportions of his minarets are always related to those of the mosque as a whole. Indeed, because the balance and interrelationships are delicate, the proportions relate to the dimensions of a complex as a whole. There is one striking exception to this rule with the pair which were begun for Selim II at Haghia Sophia and completed under Murad III. This building already had disparate minarets at each corner of the mihrab wall, which by the sixteenth century must have looked odd. They were there simply to direct the call to prayer, first and foremost towards the palace. For the citizens, a small turret had been converted above the west front immediately after the Conquest, 'defrocked' of its Christian appurtenances. The brick minaret of Mehmed II was followed by the stone minaret of his son Bayazid II and so did not match.

It was natural, therefore, for Sinan to build two grand minarets at each corner of the west front where they ought to have been. The turret then returned to its

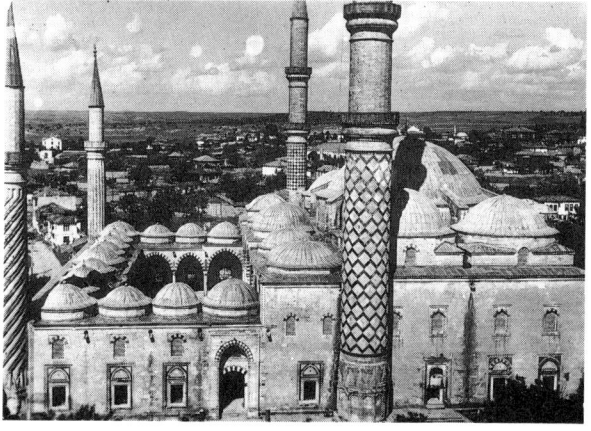

119. Üç Şerefeli (Three Balconies) mosque, Edirne. The domes show how it is composed of units.

The Minaret

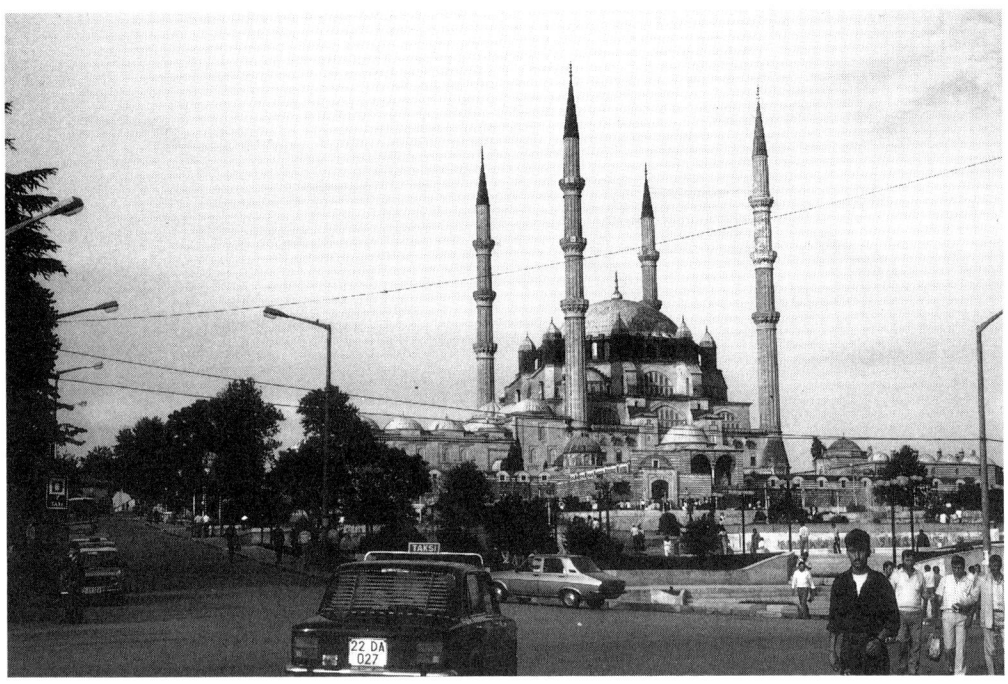

120. Selimiye mosque, Edirne

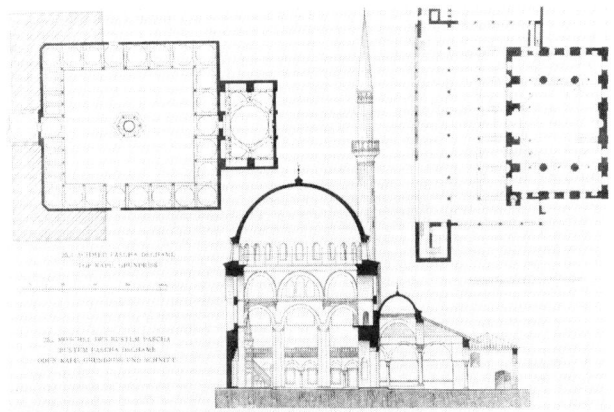

121. Rüstem Pasha mosque, Istanbul: elevation and plan. The cap of the minaret is the apex of a triangle. (Gurlitt)

original role. But the puzzle is that these new minarets were extraordinarily thick and in no way elegant although, in architectural terms, dogmatic. Haghia Sophia with its additional buttresses was bulky enough to require powerful counterfoils but these exaggerate such a duty. The north-west minaret suggests, however, that their intended heights were never achieved because its stairway continues after the one balcony to be blocked by the ceiling for no reason whatsoever. Had there been two balconies and many extra metres added to the height of the minarets, the older pair would have looked absurd: they would have to have been replaced to achieve the dramatic effect of the four at the Selim II mosque at Edirne. The expense would have been enormous and doubtless Murad III did not think it justified. The second balconies were then forgone so as not to throw the composition of the mosque into disarray at sky level. This is speculation, however, and new clues will doubtless be found together with new solutions to the conundrum.

It must be added that nothing contributes more to the decay of a minaret than the absence of the muezzins in their galleries in favour of loud and coarse tapes. Already stairs are difficult to climb. But, worse, minarets bereft of their function are as dead as drained teeth and belittle their architectural as well as their spiritual function.

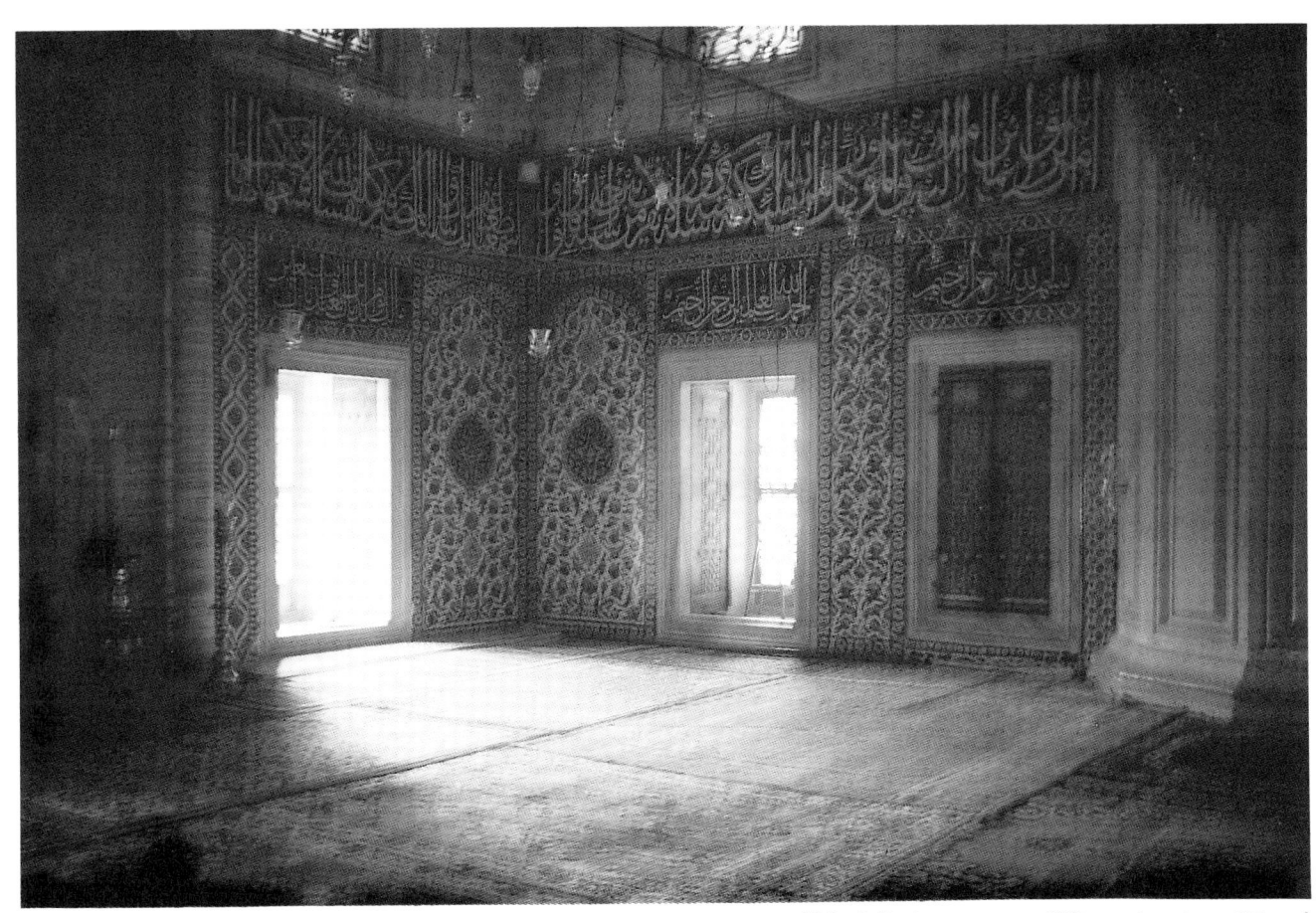

122. *Selimiye mosque, Edirne: interior of Royal Gallery (Hunkar Mahfile)*

Problems of Interior Space

Galleries

Building the Selimiye mosque, Sinan dealt with several problems of interior space quite apart from the use of light. There were the dead areas under the galleries and the conflict of dome and mihrab wall as opposing focal points, which may have been one reason why he made a feature of the apse; but the outward projection of the galleries requires investigation in order to be appreciated as the solution to a long-accepted weakness.

In the case of the Selimiye, the royal gallery is much more of a sanctuary set apart than in most others. From here it is quite difficult to look down on a small section of the worshippers. It is an intensely luxuriant garden because of the finest Iznik tile panels and a sense of withdrawal brings the chamber very close to the tranquillity of the paradise that it represents. Its mihrab at first glance is a typical richly framed niche, but with two

Problems of Interior Space

panels of inlaid woods and ivory (where tiles now usually occurred) in the centre. This break with normal practice in a sixteenth-century Ottoman mosque should not be overlooked or merely noted as something unique or idiosyncratic. These panels are probably the finest shutters ever made in Ottoman workshops and so they ought to be. For when they are flung open—particularly if viewed when kneeling—the sudden revelation of the sky, in whatever mood it may be cast, creates an emotion as near to the divine as any that architect has achieved before or since.

The history of the gallery in classical Ottoman mosques begins quite simply with the courtyard portico and the inescapable need to reinforce masonry walls with buttresses—buttressing by thickening the wall rather than in the Western sense. Because they cannot be exposed on the courtyard side of a mosque where they would block and deform the portico, the buttresses had to be erected inside where the space between them created useful and large alcoves which were disproportionate because of their lofty ceilings. Moreover they would have looked out of place, which indeed they were, had they not carried a gallery across the back of the mosque. This conveniently faced the mihrab and was usually reserved for women. Thus two levels were established for prayer and the north wall was made interesting but unobtrusive while masking the buttresses.

Lateral galleries were functional and were not simply to exploit lateral buttresses, for these were placed outside the mosque. Later Sinan was to make aesthetic use of them. Galleries appeared as early as such mosques as that of Bali Pasha in Istanbul (1504) where they were recessed into the thickness of the walls. Sinan inserted galleries down the sides of the prayer halls in most of his vezirial mosques, sometimes using them to fill in the wings and make a central square area out of a rectangle.

The overshadowed area beneath a gallery has no particular sanctity or symbolic importance. It tends to become a place apart. The supporting columns can obscure the view of the imam leading prayers and only when a mosque is crowded out will such a place be filled with worshippers. It was for this reason that Sinan's solution of setting galleries over external or semi-external porches, initiated at the mosque of Süleyman and finally achieved at that of Selim II, was important for he had got rid of the muted areas completely.

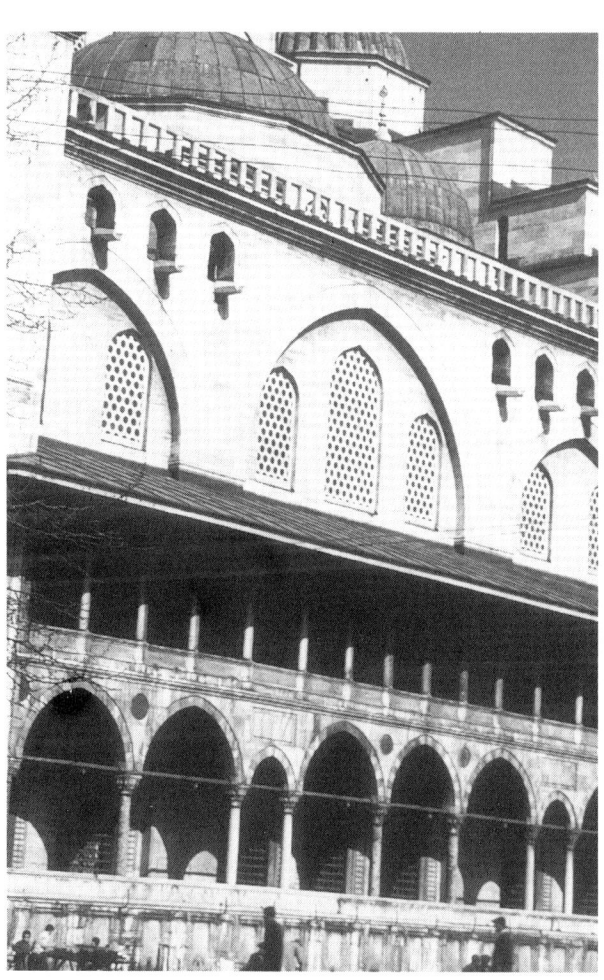

123. Süleymaniye mosque, Istanbul: elevation

Conflict of Dome and Mihrab

There remained a more important problem. To a Western visitor, the interiors of large mosques may feel dead—they are, of course, meant to be full and alive with the faithful and, at such times, are very moving. But they are also alive when deserted except for tourists, or at least they are in tension. This tension created a real problem for any Ottoman architect as opposed to a builder working to the excellent structural formulas evolved by experienced workmen. Although the architecture had wedded external and internal space into a near to divine balance, there was no seeming solution to the dichotomy in religious symbolism between the world when the worshipper stood with head bowed and the imperative need of the Mecca wall to draw everybody's attention in the direction to which prayers must be addressed. It is a problem which did not arise in mosques in the open or which were simple if spacious rooms. There, in a sense, the front rank of the faithful, the place of honour, was part of the architecture for the wider the mihrab wall the better. Islam, as we have seen, is not a processional religion and therefore needs no nave. The impact of that wall is just as immediate as are buffers to an engine. It was for this reason that the projecting apse, carrying the eye onwards beyond the severe rectilinear limits, was a liberation. It prolonged the view and relaxed it. It deepened the paradisaical garden. The door of the mihrab, metaphorically speaking, had been opened—if not with that magic with which the sultan's window was opened in his private retreat upstairs.

Space and Form

As long ago as 1914, Geoffrey Scott in *The Architecture of Humanism* wrote that criticism had singularly failed to recognize the supremacy of spatial values in architecture.[58] They were overlooked because they were read as the negative as opposed to the positive character of any solid.

Yet it is this delight, to echo Sir Henry Wootton who had learnt about it from Alberti, this three-dimensional magic, which Paul the Silentiary and others extolled when writing of the newly completed church of Haghia Sophia when it was lit by thousands of oil lamps at night. They saw its transubstantial quality, its dome seeming to float far above the earth, as the true achievement of the vastest dome in the Western world save the Pantheon.

They did not think to discuss its exact height or circumference. But we are temporal beings and need to know how the illusion works.

'Space', Scott recorded, 'is liberty of movement.' But here his view is only partial. The skies of the ancient Egyptians or the Greeks were not free because there dwelt the flycatcher gods breaking their own rules wantonly since they had been devised for an obedient humanity. Pleasure there may be in freedom of movement but space is not architectural at all unless it is limited by materials such as stone or brick: without them there is chaos, which humans cannot tolerate whether in politics, food or art. Confronted with an action painting, the eye looks for and finds form. Only certain paintings of the mad elude this levelling process of the brain and continue to disturb.

However, there is one substance, glass, that creates ambiguity through its reflections and counter-reflections. But glass is also a way of escape for eye and spirit and here space and solid are in tension. Nevertheless, no window can exist without a frame, a point which will be seen as important to an understanding of Sinan and the mind behind the creation of the Selimiye.

The architects of Haghia Sophia, Anthemius of Tralles and the equally illustrious mathematician Isidore of Miletus, took as positive a view of architecture as that which is ingrained in their heirs today. They supported the boundaries of space structurally before they achieved their miraculous dome.[59] Other mathematicians well versed in the dynamic of reversals—so often exploited in the art of Islam—have overlooked the dynamics of negatives: the rest of us may perhaps be excused for misunderstanding the creative force of the void. Yet it is much more common to feel at ease in uncapped space than when space is roofed. It is as if the casual visitor preferred the steam to escape. Photographers decapitate their interior shots but nobody reproves them or supposes that this distortion challenges their ability to assess the quality of the space pictured. Of necessity, we are all guilty and we are wrong—if less wrong than the great lie, the wide-angle lens. Life is, like it or not, a process of continual adjustment but one ought to know what it is that one is doing.

What is not relevant to Ottoman architecture, but has every right to its own crags and meadows, is romantic space. William Muschenheim, in *The Elements of the Art of Architecture* published in 1964, wrote that medieval courtyards are notable for dynamically balanced relationships achieved by the asymmetrical groupings of

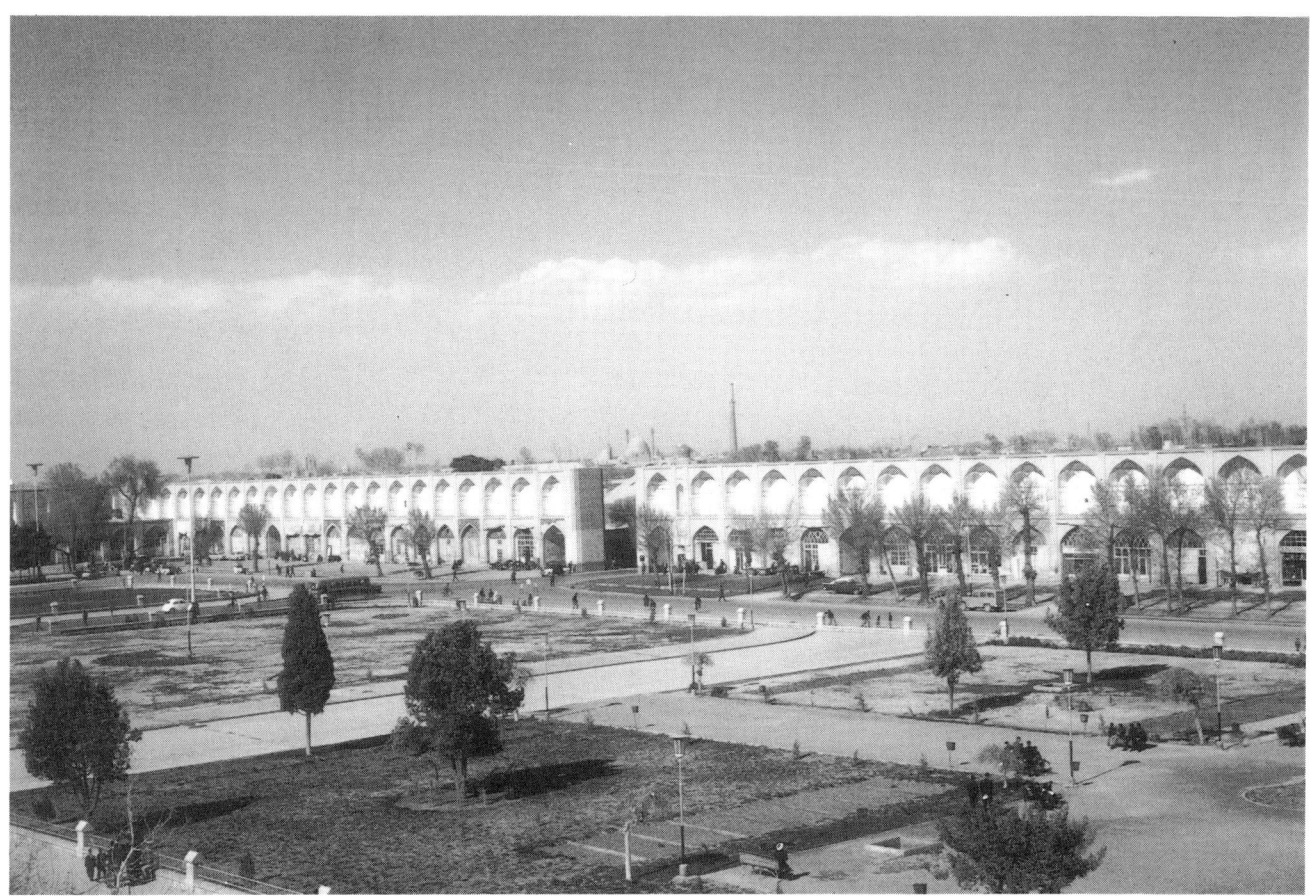

124. Isfahan: the meydan

such dissimilar elements as window bays, turrets, staircases and large building masses with steeply sloping roofs. This is a vision with which Sinan could have little sympathy. It might explain why he absorbed so little when he was on campaign in the Balkans. His courtyards were ordered squares and rectangles clearly defined by balanced limits. Even when he built in the suburbs or the country, where land was cheap, the boundaries were rigidly expressed and related to the scale of the complete complex. This is why when a site enforces distortion Sinan's frustration is apparent and troubling, as happened with the college of the mosque courtyard at the complex of Zal Mahmud Pasha, Istanbul. Stone and order were reserved for God and His shadow on earth.[60]

It is essential to recognize that architects by creating form create voids, which like mirrors in reverse are meaningful reflections of form. This does not preclude the deliberate creation of voids for their own sake: these can make the forms subordinate to their spaces, as with a walled garden where, crinklecranked or castellated as it

Space and Form

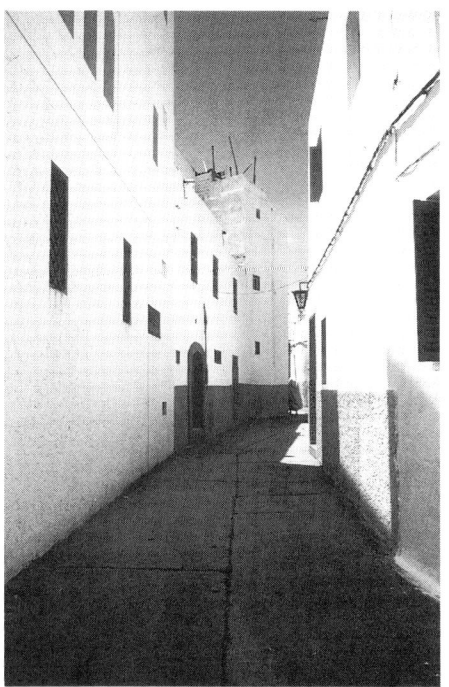

125. *Asilah, a street restored*

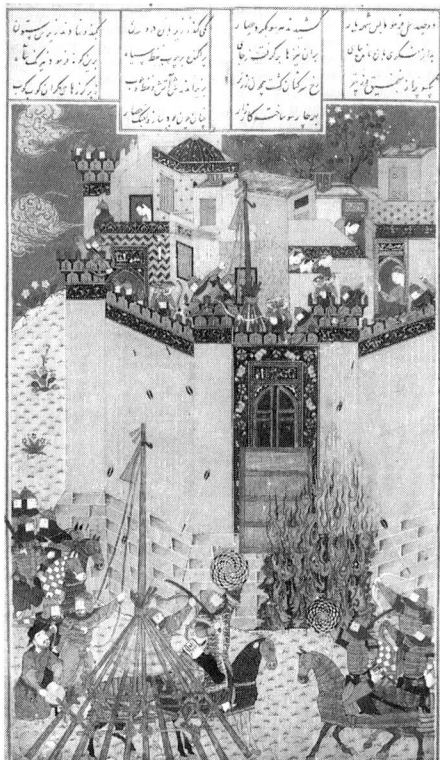

126. *Shahnama of Muhammad Juki: miniature* (by permission of the Royal Asiatic Society)

may be, and purposeful as the protector and supporter of plants, the wall is subordinate to the space. Again, space can be stretched too far even when confined so that a haphazard *meydan* (open square), such as that of Taksim in Istanbul or to some degree the Place de la Concorde in Paris, lose impact or conclusions for lack of defined form and function. The great meydan at Isfahan, however, takes the idea of space to its limits with Safavid aesthetics. It remains meaningful because the two-storey boundaries that enclose its vast rectangle keep the three-dimensional central space low and in check, leaving the domes of the mosques and the high gates to express the aspirations of the spirit.

Those living courtyards of former Chinese houses which evolved as the family evolved by keeping their roofs and eaves low similarly kept space low, enhancing the effect by offering glimpses of the courts beyond through open halls and loggias. Equally, those Near and Middle Eastern streets that use strong contrasts of light and shade on walls and alcoves create abstract art before its time, yet the blind meanderings of such lanes were not the work of architects but of property rights and the need for seclusion behind closed doors for the women and for the security of the whole family.

The depiction of architecture in Islamic miniatures helps the evaluation of Islamic concepts of space. The buildings, and especially walls and fortifications, are folded cut-outs which can be stuck where required. This is particularly true of tents and their awnings. In the Nakkaş Osman *Hünernama* or the *Shahnama* of Muhammad Juki—perhaps the noblest Timurid manuscript—the scene is watched as if by a bird from above. It is a theatre with no stalls but only a dress circle. Nature and architecture are manipulated to make this possible. And so they should be since the scenery should not obscure the players but enhance the action. With the fortress of Rhodes in the *Süleymannama* the walls and the hills are set aside accordingly or elsewhere a bluff can be used to screen posses of horsemen. Matrakçi Nasuh's *Beyan-i Menazil-i Sefer-i Trakyen* with his views of towns like Diyarbekir sticks the buildings on like stamps in an album. Similarly, with a miniature of the model of the Süleymaniye mosque it is not possible to be sure that it is only two-dimensional. With the scene of Sultan Süleyman sitting in state, interior and exterior, fountain court and upper storey rooms are each flattened like boxes yet to be opened. So with the view of the Divan court, which forms a wonderful stage upon which the illustrious sit or stand, the geometry at the corners of the arcades is shamelessly distorted.[61] Distorted, that is, for those who cannot decipher the codes.

It would seem that to miniaturists space mattered more than form, as it did with Byzantine mosaics at Hosias Lukas or Daphni, although Islamic miniatures do not draw the onlooker into the scene as do the mosaics. Architects must care about structure and their arcades to be able to turn the corner yet the miniaturists' vision of events within space offers a key to the fundamental dynamic underlying Sinan's perception of form. In the West, before Piero della Francesca performed miracles of perspective, composition was close to that of the miniature. Even in the fifteenth century, with Benedetto Bonfigli's view of Perugia, the architecture, although vertical, is still stacked behind disproportionate figures.

The Recognition of Apsidal Form

The apse of Selim II's mosque was an essential feature boldly stated. It was not completely new to Ottoman architecture but had made only rare appearances. No mosque belonging to the Bursa style had any need of it and this style prevailed with larger mosques of sultans and vezirs into the sixteenth century. Such mosques as that of Mahmud Pasha with its twin domes was a conservative development in 1467 and the architect took no notice of semi-domes belonging to an alien mode. It is true that Murad I's mosque above Bursa, the Hudavendigâr, built in the late fourteenth century, has a deeply recessed mihrab but this was not a true apse. The recess was there to support a curious cell built immediately over it, and perhaps associated with the college built at that first-floor level. Its purpose can only be guessed at but must have had importance since it called for much extra building work.

A true apse did occur in Istanbul in 1485 with the mosque of Davud Pasha but it is curiously deep and narrow and did not set a fashion. In domestic form, the projecting polygon at the Çinili Kiosk below Topkapısaray is more of a bay window or gazebo than an apse. Some recognition of the apisdal form had influenced the earliest Islamic architecture of the Umayyads in Spain but again this was not a question of a true apse but of a large and deep mihrab such as that of the great mosque at Cordoba.

The Recognition of Apsidal Form

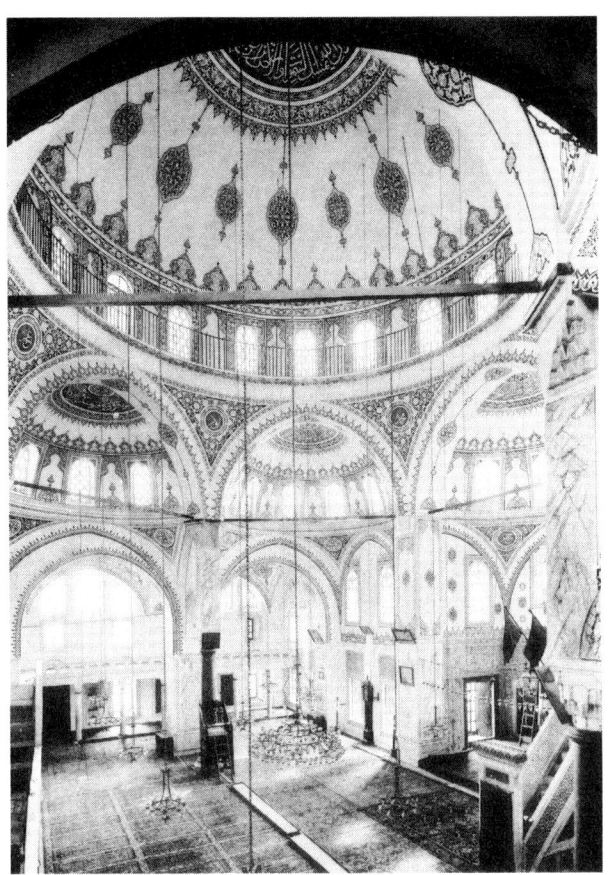

127. Atık Valide complex, Üsküdar (Gurlitt)

In Anatolia, no interest was taken in an apse and the outward expression of the mihrab niche was never made an important external architectural feature. One may list all the major mosques where no apse appears, including those of Bayazid II, Selim I and Şehzade in addition to that of Süleyman.

At the Atık Ali Pasha mosque the projection is vestigial, coming from the prayer area of the Bursa zaviye-mosque type. This is clear when its plan is compared with that of mosques like that of Rum Mehmed Pasha, where lateral rooms are still cut off from the body of the building unlike those of the mosques of Atık Ali Pasha or Bayazid II in Istanbul. It could be that working on the apse at Haghia Sophia awoke Sinan's interest in the form as a source of light: and of something else. The mihrab guides the prayers of the brotherhood of Islam towards their source in the man Muhammad, who was not divine. But Islamic mysticism is devoted to that light to which each human particle will return. In this lies a profound motive for illuminating the mihrab area in the Selim II mosque.

Sinan was to use the apse again in the mosques of Kılıç Ali Pasha and the Atık Valide. The latter was after all an imitation of Haghia Sophia, among other later mosques. His senior student and successor as Royal Architect, Mehmed Agha, rejected the concept when he built the mosque of Sultan Ahmad I but it reappears in the mosque of Hekimoğlu Ali Pasha in Istanbul and with the provincial and rebuilt mosque of Şerefeddin (1636) at Konya. With the coming of baroque in the 1730s it was a feature of many mosques including Laleli and the Nuruosmaniye, both in Istanbul.

The Yeni Cami (New Mosque), the main mosque of Tosya in Anatolia, dated 1574, achieved an apse by removing the south-east and south-west corners of the normal mosque grid plan exemplified by the Şehzade. This radical decision was taken further by the removal of all corner areas by the architect of the interesting Nişancı Mehmed Pasha mosque in Istanbul (1589). The mosque was possibly built by Sinan's gifted student Davud Agha, for it owes its eight piers, its exedras, its circular movement and its apse to the Selimiye, which has been discussed already.

The Courtyard

The courtyard and the piazza, which is the courtyard in its grandest form, offer the clearest definition of the void. The courtyard is also the largest chamber in a palace, with the loftiest ceiling of all. In Ottoman society, as in many others, the sovereign used the courtyard as his throne-room, as when the sultan sat in the gateway to the Third Court of the palace of Topkapı to receive the oath of allegiance upon his accession or just as the largest hall of the Vatican is the Piazza San Pietro, contained by Bernini's colonnades. The result was that Ottoman palaces had some large rooms but no great halls prior to the Europeanization of the nineteenth century. The internal court is essential to the architecture of grander buildings, as are walls and roofs and the vista of the enfilade of chambers in mansions or palaces such as the Villa Maser or Blenheim. It is to the Court and not the throne-room or the bedchamber of St James that ambassadors to Britain present their credentials.

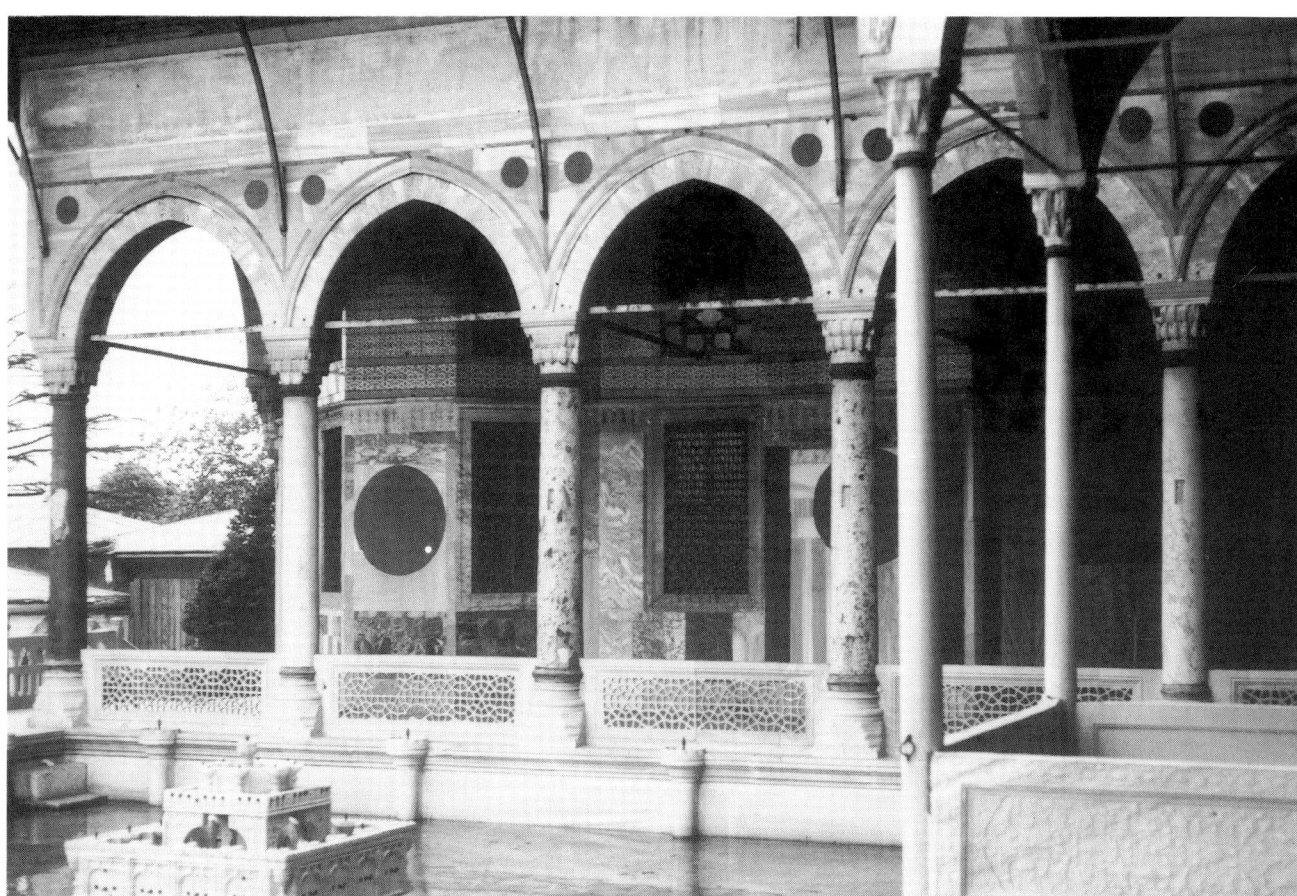

128. Fourth court, Topkapısaray, Istanbul: pool and Erevan Kiosk (Revan Köşkü)

The Courtyard

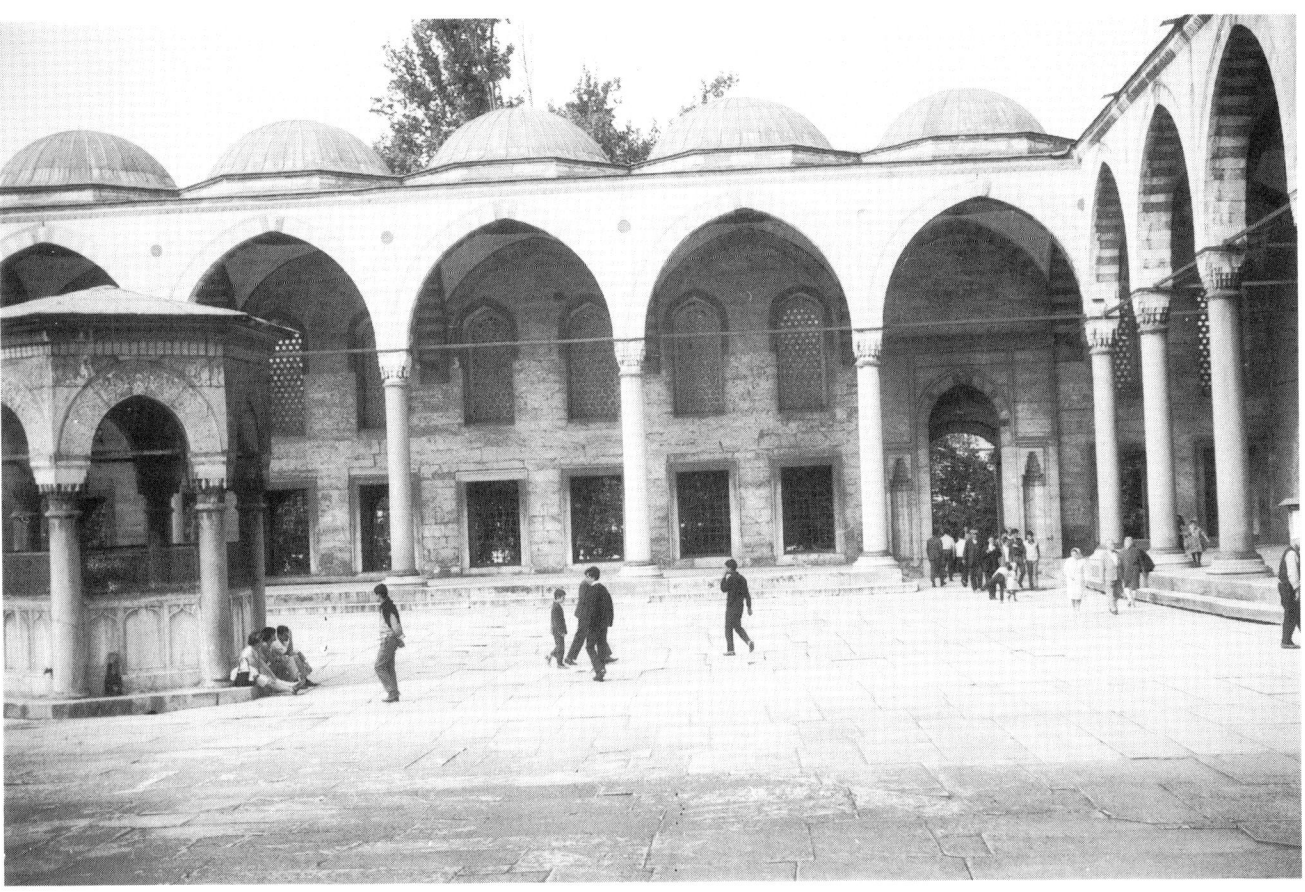

129. Sultan Ahmad mosque, Istanbul: court

During the fifteenth century Ottoman mosques developed a standard form of courtyard, either square or rectangular, with a tall portico of five or seven arches in front of the mosque itself. The arch before the central portal could have a wider span. Each of the two porticoes flanking the court usually had lower arcades and either a central entrance or a doorway that divided the mosque portico from that of the court, sometimes with a lodging over its arch. The entrance on the side opposite the mosque had the greatest door, which had to be centrally placed on the axis of the main mosque door and the mihrab.

With the fountain in the middle,[62] the success of the composition depended on the proportions of the arches in relation to the central space. They could be large as in the case of Sinan's Şehzade mosque or too mean as in the case of Mehmed Agha's mosque of Sultan Ahmad. But usually the proportions were good because structure dictates the width and height of free-standing columns in relation to the span of the arch that they have to carry. When, as was the case into the seventeenth century in Istanbul, there was a sufficiency of good Byzantine marble columns, the mathematics were precise and easy to calculate because the columns had already been cut to standard measurements evolved for convenience by Roman quarries. Later, defects appear but not during the sixteenth century.

Courtyards are refuges from the turmoil of the town[63] not just because they are havened off by stout walls but also because their proportions are simple and clear to read and so calm and ease the spirit. Even with the unexpectedly broad courtyard of the Üç Şerefeli mosque at Edirne, because it served former dervish areas at either end of the mosque, or with the square court of the mosque of the Bayazid hospital in the same city, or with the mosque of Selim I in Istanbul which mirrors it (to cite examples from before the work of Sinan), this sense of calm is achieved. The sense of confinement in the court of the mosque of Şehzade Mehmed, on the other hand, is not satisfactory. Sinan did not repeat this error, which arose from the ground plan of the court mirroring that of the interior of the mosque.

When designing the courts of his colleges, Sinan had to follow tradition. The open court, with its pool in the middle, was the centre of life for the students who slept two or three together in their cells but lived under the porticoes. The proportions could vary and, indeed, with the college of Rüstem Pasha in Istanbul the court is octagonal, a form always wasteful of space and masonry at the angles. But the central position of the teaching hall and the equal number of the cells each side of it were preordained. None the less, some courts have proportions more satisfying than others and the *tabhane* (dervish hospice) at the Süleymaniye complex is the finest of them all. As we have seen, it is enhanced by the dynamic effect of having columns which are all equal in height. Thus there is no interruption to the sequence of the arches at the corners of the porticoes but a continual movement so that the eye travels round a rectangle as if it were serpentine. That recesses or open chambers punctuate the sequence of the cells and that the central hall is lofty and light is additional to this delight.

The courtyard of the mosque of Selim II at Edirne also conforms to the accepted plan although it is on a grander scale which necessitates piers to stabilize the arches at the two north corners. It reflects Sinan's decision to abandon any attempt at a grand entry on the north side on the axis of the mihrab. The portico is handsome and defined but it does not rise above the cupolas on each side of it. This was because of the insuperable problem of joining a lower, lateral portico to a loftier. The last

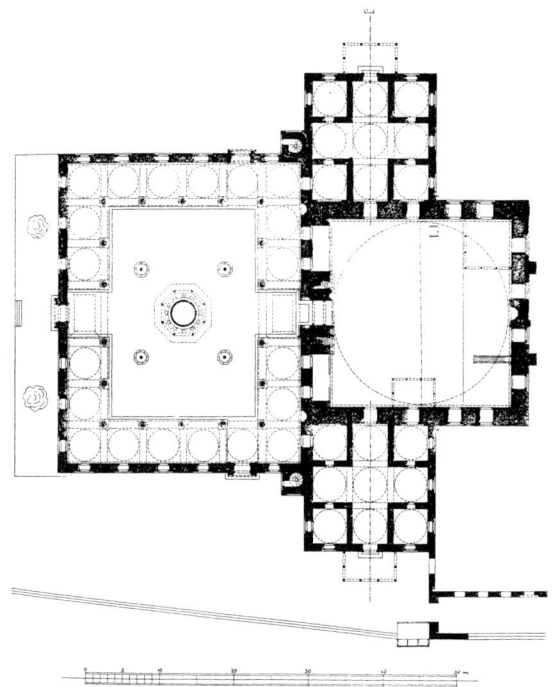

130. Selim I mosque, Istanbul: plan (Gurlitt)

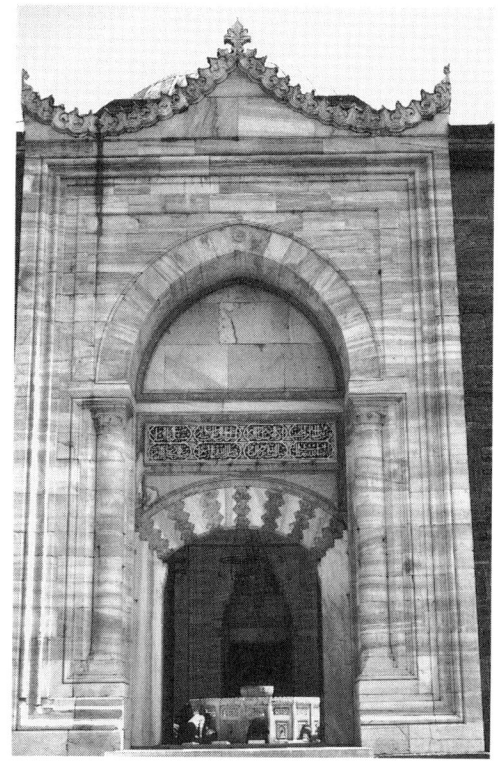

131. Selimiye mosque, Edirne

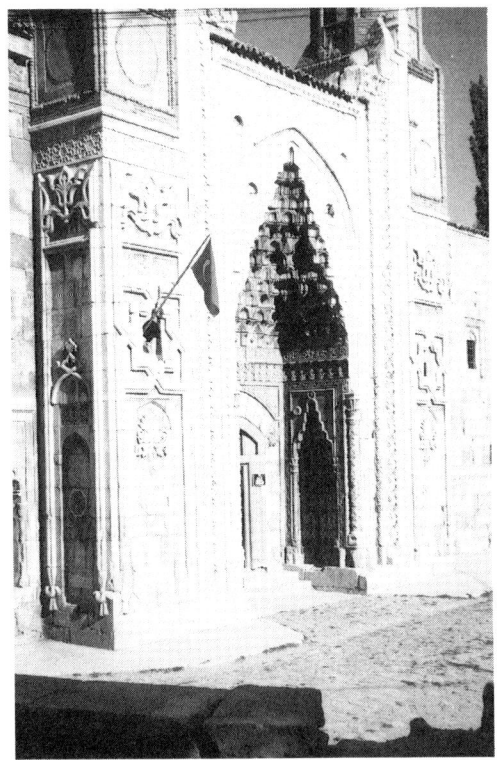

132. Gök Medrese (Heavenly College), Sivas: portal

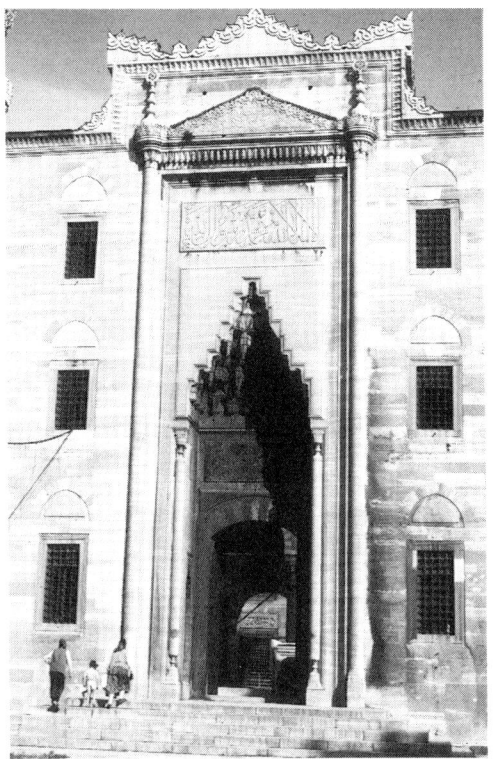

133. Süleymaniye mosque, Istanbul: external portal of court

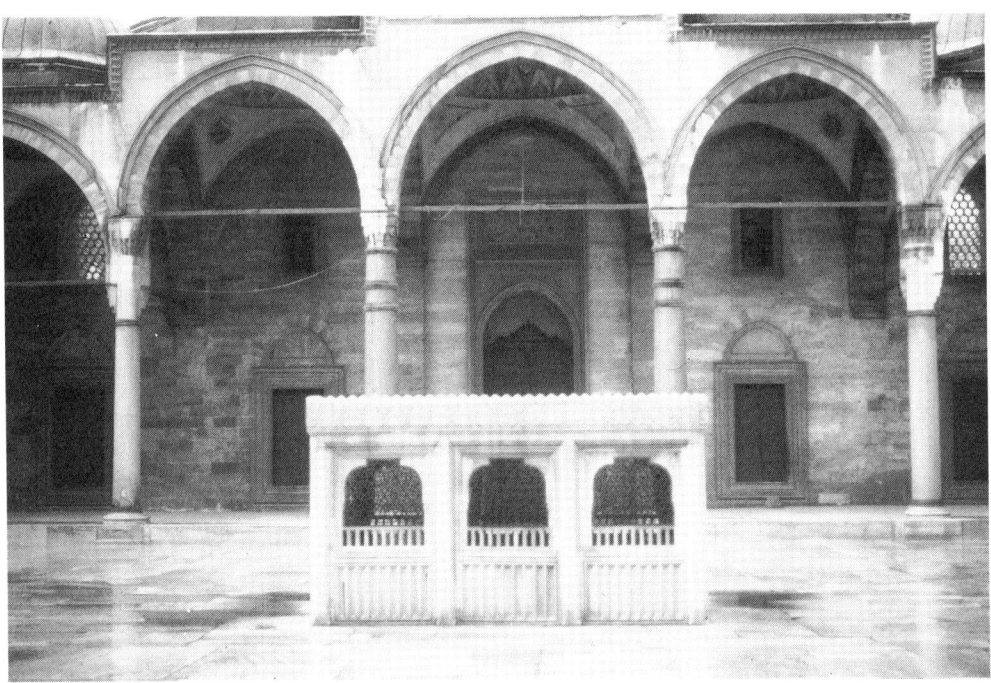

134. Süleymaniye mosque, Istanbul: court

Sinan

capital of the former has to be halved and springs from the large column of the mosque portico. Even when remarked on, this device is unobtrusive and does not offend. But at the Süleymaniye Sinan introduced a grand portal in the middle of the north side of the courtyard. From the outside this gives the entrance something of the appearance of a façade. Inside, there had to be three lofty arches in the centre of the north arcade in proportion to the great entry. These were flanked by the rest of the normally proportioned arches of the porticoes. The result was that where the arches joined at disparate heights, capitals were cut and bolstered to produce a hotchpotch of dissected stone. Proof that Sinan was displeased by this deformity is the fact that the loftier grand entrance to a court was not repeated: not even at Edirne where it might most have been expected.

The width of a courtyard was usually determined by the width of the mosque, or the mosque and any wing rooms that might be added to it. At the Selimiye this resulted in a spaciousness beyond previous imagining and because of the loftiness of the massive mosque it was essential to have a proportionally high main portico to front it. Exceptionally (for elsewhere Sinan used the traditional form of chevron or debased composite), the capital had to take on larger proportions to match these dimensions. To enlarge architectural forms is to set up continual eddies of the multiplication tables. At Edirne, the grander arches required a new rhythm in order to avoid a monotony that feeds on size—a feature of the Sultan Ahmad mosque. There all the courtyard arches are the same size. At the Selimiye, Sinan introduced a half-sized arch each side of the central arch before the great door. These created an interval which he filled with two monumental marble inscriptive discs to achieve movement and grandeur at the same time.

A second form of courtyard which Sinan developed was possible with country mosques or in the farther suburbs within the walls, where land was not as costly in the centre of a city. These courts were still rectangular or square but very large: they were effectively gardens with trees and cobbled paths rather than the marble pavements of the city mosques. Their size required careful planning. The success of Kara Ahmad Pasha's mosque and its garden court has already been studied. The synthesis of mosque and college had been achieved 100 years before in Anatolia as at the mosque of Işak Pasha, Inegöl (1482). Previously the two had stood aloof across an open space or had been placed side by side or, as at

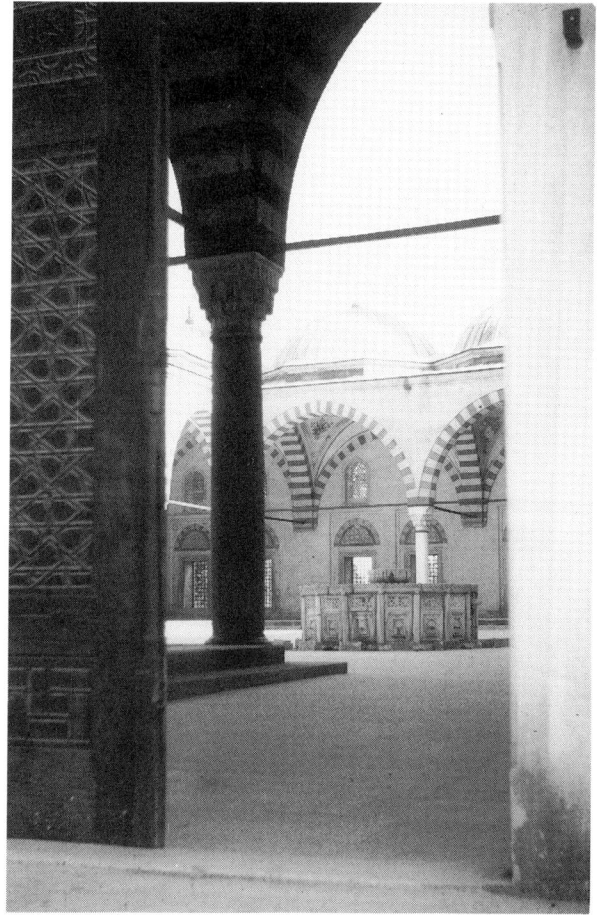

135. Selimiye mosque, Edirne: view into court

The Courtyard

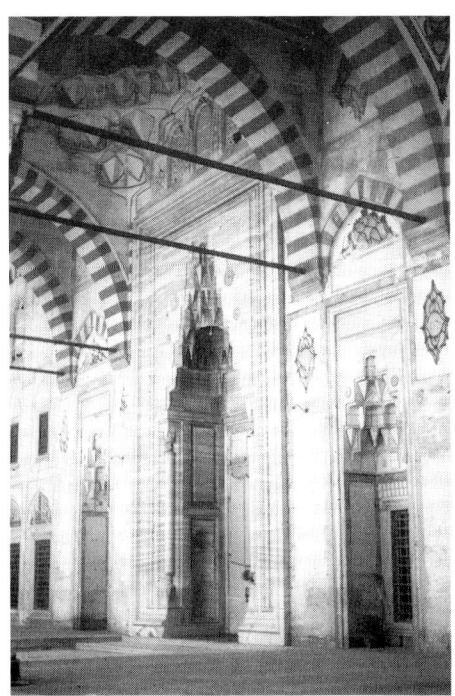

136. Selimiye mosque, Edirne: portico

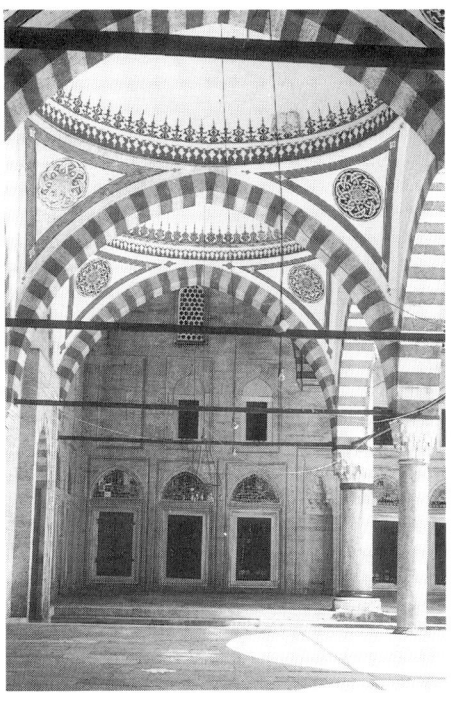

137. Selimiye mosque, Edirne: arches

the Yeşil Cami (Green Mosque) at Bursa, built in relation to the hillside but not to each other. There was an additional factor to the rule that only a royal mosque might have a courtyard as well as a portico: a vezirial mosque which combined a college in order to share a court had to be divided from it even in the sixteenth century. Hence, as at the Sokollu Mehmed Pasha mosque at Kadırga, gatehouses divided the portico from the arcades of the college while at Kara Ahmad Pasha's mosque there was a long stretch of wall beyond the arcading.

At the Sokollu Mehmed Pasha mosque at Lüleburgaz, half-way between Istanbul and Edirne, the court was too vast for there to be a simple solution. The space was reduced by the introduction of a second portico, which added a new dimension to the composition of mosque and courtyard apart from producing a handsome extravagance of columns. It served a function in sheltering worshippers who used courtyards for prayer when the mosque was shut or when it was full to overflowing. Aesthetically, with the Sokollu Mehmed mosque, the court increased the presence of the building in relation to the space, amplifying rather than aggrandizing which would have been out of sympathy with the cells and modest gatehouses of the garden court. Sinan was to use the portico in various ways. He created an impressive phalanx of arches across the façade of the Rüstem Pasha mosque at Tekirdağ because it was set on a ridge. He also used it to diminish and make intimate courtyards that could not expand because the site was too modest. Misshapen plots of land, sloping ground or sites along the seashore all presented problems which stimulated ideas. Indeed, many of Sinan's imaginative designs were responses to such difficulties.

Some were traditional and had traditional answers, as with mosques in markets which had to be built above the bustle of the streets and shops and hawkers. These were raised over storerooms, booths or even market courts of justice, thus making use of their street-level vaults as with the mosque of Rüstem Pasha in Istanbul. Here Sinan created a terrace and a double portico where no true courtyard could be, bringing the arcades down the flanks of the mosque. He removed the facilities for ritual washing to a large yard at ground level across a lane from the mosque.

The earlier of the two mosques which Sinan built for Mihrimah beside the water at Üsküdar had been too close to the shore for there to be a courtyard but, as we have seen, he elaborated a remarkable second portico

Sinan

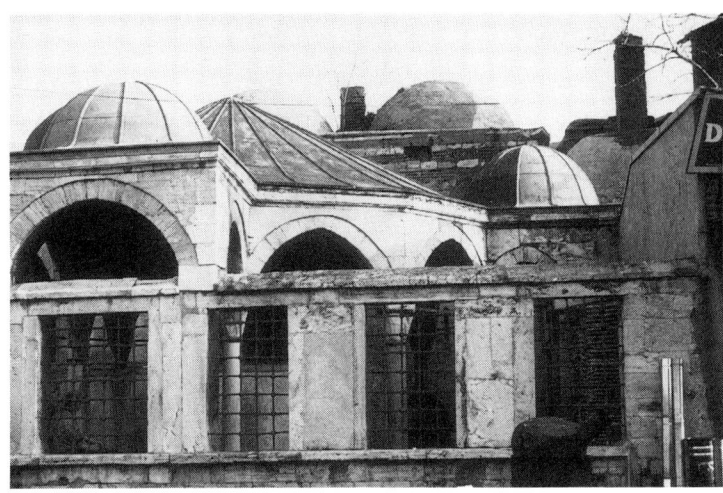

138. *Rüstem Pasha mosque, Istanbul: fountain house for ritual washing*

with belvedere which houses the fountain. With the grander and later Mihrimah complex at Edirnekapı, the problem was ruder since the land came right up under the city wall. He placed the mosque on a terrace as far back as he could but the garden court was narrow for its width and overshadowed by the ramparts. His response to this was to employ vistas into other open areas down the flanks of the mosque and extend the long portico of the façade by a second, even though it reached the fountain, as if to emphasize the restrictions of the lopsided terrain. Worse, the college cells were forced to merge with the wall and come to a stop. This second portico has disappeared, probably when the mosque was repaired after the earthquake of 1894, but the position of the columns and the marks of the roof joints on the flanking wall are easy to trace.

It is not without interest that Sinan used two forms of arch to form the arcades of courtyards, as indeed he did with those supporting the galleries inside his mosques. The most important monuments all had the slightly pointed arch which had become the traditional Ottoman form. But with more lyrical settings such as the court of the Sokollu Mehmed Pasha college at Kadırga he used an ogee arch, the shape of an Ottoman bow.

If the mood varies according to the purpose and dignity of a courtyard, it remains passive and reflective under the dominance of dome and minaret. In order to be their foil, the courtyard must accentuate detachment and tranquillity either by a wholly satisfying balance of the movement of the arcades and the regular, contained central space open to the sky or by a romantic rustic disorder due to trees: but always within a harmonious boundary.

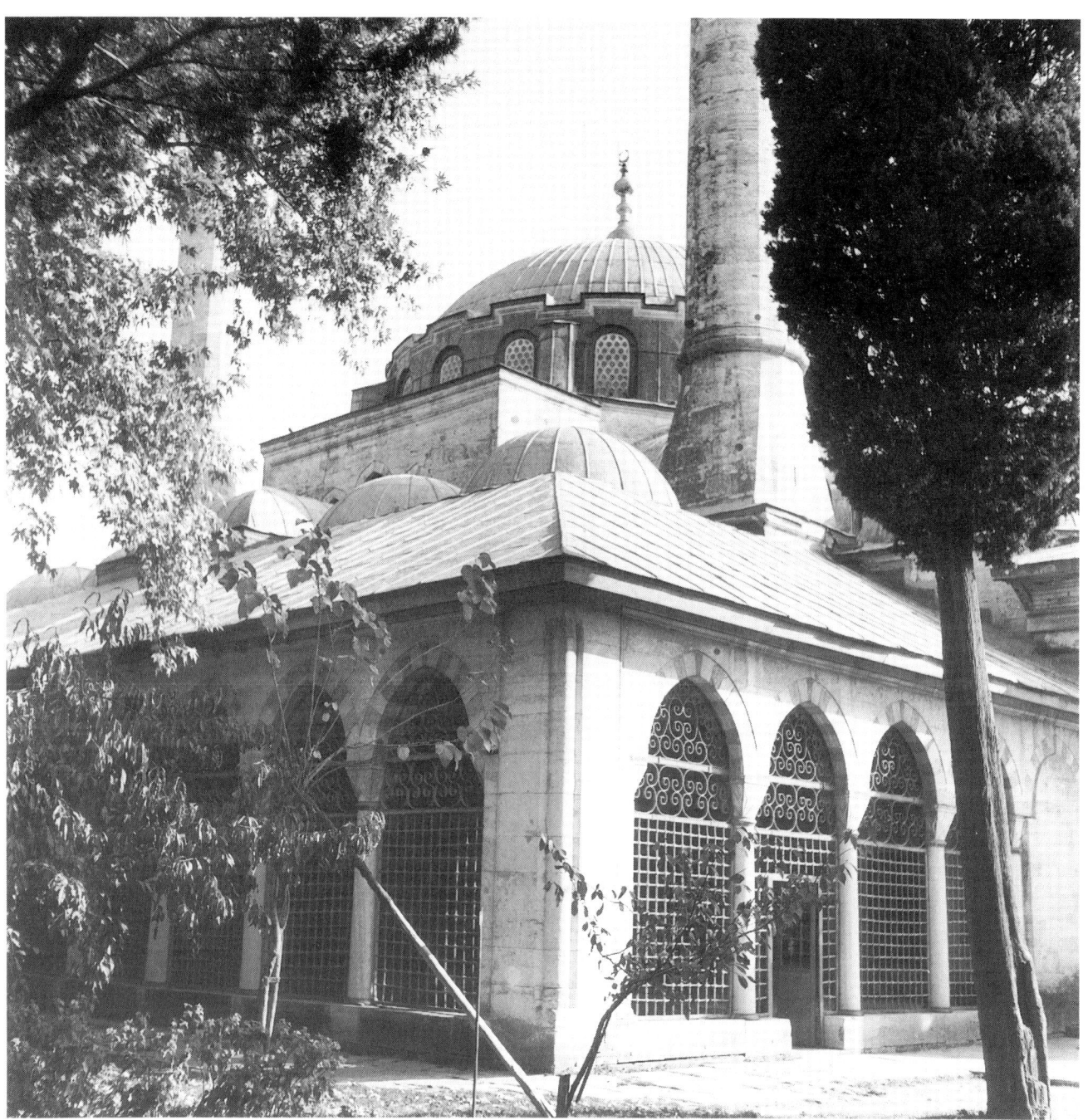

139. Atık Valide mosque, Üsküdar

Sinan

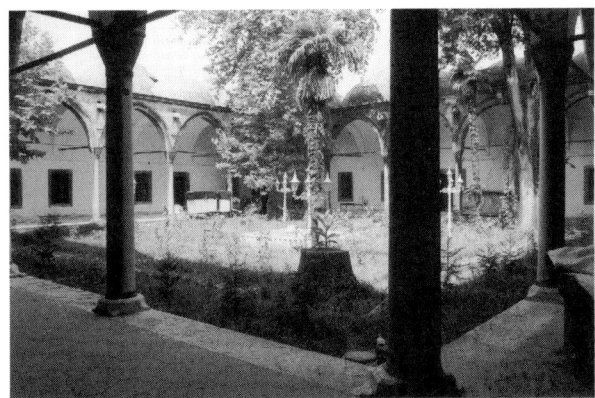

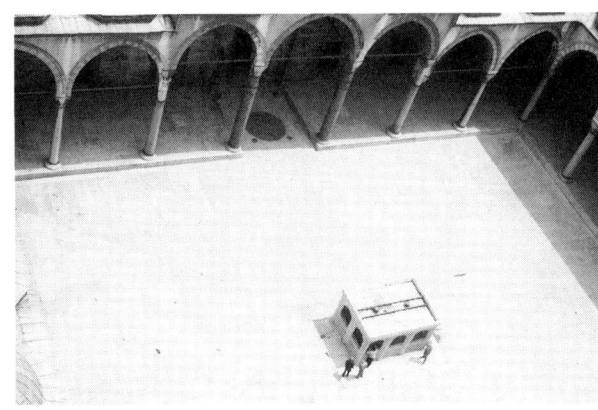

141. Süleymaniye mosque, Istanbul: court

Left:
140. Süleymaniye complex, Istanbul: kitchen (imaret) court

Measuring the Void

To have a value, space must be defined by either visible or implied boundaries. In Ottoman architecture, a courtyard is bound on all four sides by porticoes and the volume is measured by the eye from the entrance or, when standing in it, by the width and height of the small cupolas of the arcades punctuated by their horned finials. The higher portico fronting the mosque will rise above this level and a continuum of domes and semi-domes build up to the emotional climax of the main dome. This does not relate directly to the volume of the courtyard, the more so because in the centre will be found an ablution or ornamental fountain which acts, as it were, as the anchor of the enclosure. But seen from outside, at a suitable distance, experience informs the onlooker where the courtyard lies behind flanking walls and their inward porticoes. The void may be glimpsed through a grilled window but, even if it is not, the spectator is well aware that it exists and that it responds to the crown of the great dome.

Turkish architectural historians have long seized on this point. The minarets, if there is a pair, create an imaginary volume related to the enclosed space under the dome; this can be experienced by sensing the height of the minarets and the width between them. At the Süleymaniye mosque where there is a further pair of minarets at the farthest corners of the courtyard, besides the taller two where court and mosque unite, there is a sense of incline from the main dome which has a dynamic of its own. The loftiness of the minaret is a measure of its aspiration.

To consider the unique geometric function of the courtyard in relation to the pyramidal silhouette of a royal mosque is to recognize that it becomes, effectively, the reversal of the dome like a majestic letter S upon its side thus: ∽ . The hollow of the court enhances the upward sweep of the domes and the caps of the minarets become the apex of a triangle with all the structural security implied by a silhouette in pyramidal form.

In a complex as extensive as the Süleymaniye there have to be related spaces between buildings which must be expressed and demarcated. On the west side there is a long rectangular piazza bounded by colleges and the wall of the mosque garden. This piazza is closed by walls and domes of the hospital and the kitchens with their pronounced chimney hoods. Only when one reaches these buildings can another dimension be appreciated for between them, as we have seen, wide steps descend to a street far below revealing the secret: the complex is raised on a vast man-made terrace. On the east and seaward side, on the contrary, the garden of the mosque is bounded by a terrace with views over the Golden Horn and the Bosphorus. Here the dimension is outgoing, to be bound only by the buildings of Galata and the high hills beyond the Anatolian shore.

In reverse, when seen from Galata across the water, the mosque looms above the city together with the mausoleum of the sultan and that of his wife, Haseki Hürrem. Before the twentieth century the mosque was a focal point from all over the city. The drama of the view from Galata is as good an example of Sinan's mind in action as can be found.

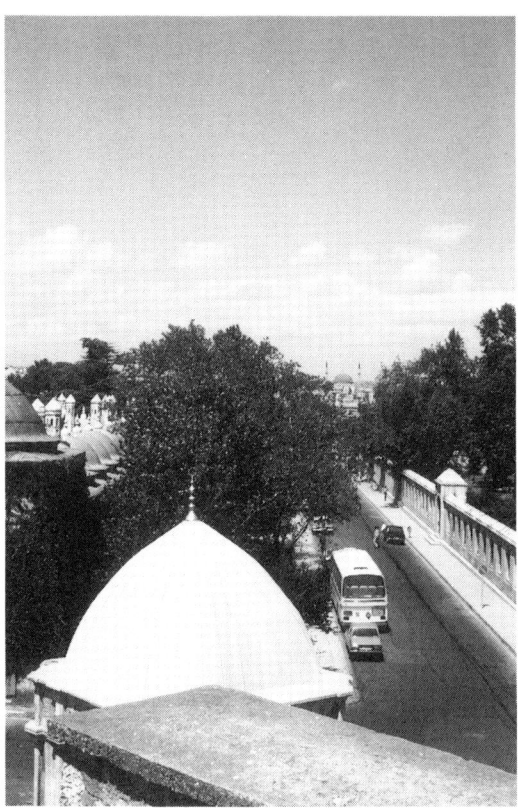
142. *Süleymaniye complex, Istanbul: the Addicts' Parade (Tiryaki Meydani)*

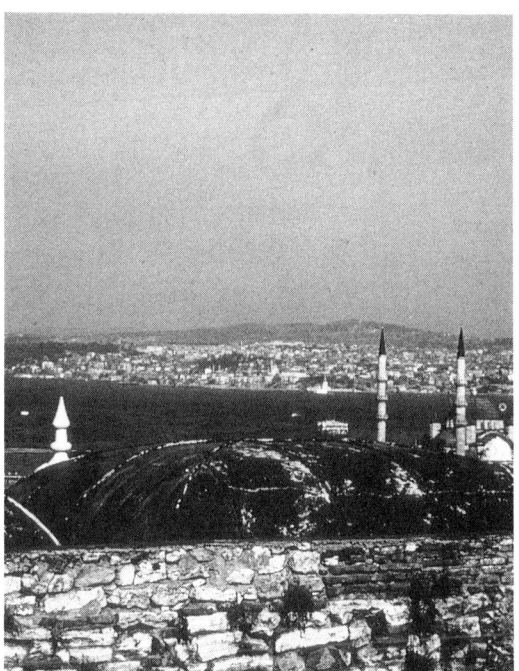
143. *Üsküdar from Süleymaniye terrace*

Decoration

The loss of their original painted decoration has damaged the interiors of Sinan's buildings although, fortunately, most of the tiles survive. Decoration is an aspect of architecture where the builder is frequently governed by the availability of craftsmen, the dictates of custom and the taste of the patron. For a Muslim the most important decoration is inscriptive but calligraphy dating from as early as the sixteenth century has been restored in almost every one of Sinan's mosques or else entirely rewritten. Even those nineteenth-century inscriptions which were applied directly to the plaster have suffered, whereas framed examples happily survive, as do the great targets which are so merciless to the architecture of Haghia Sophia.

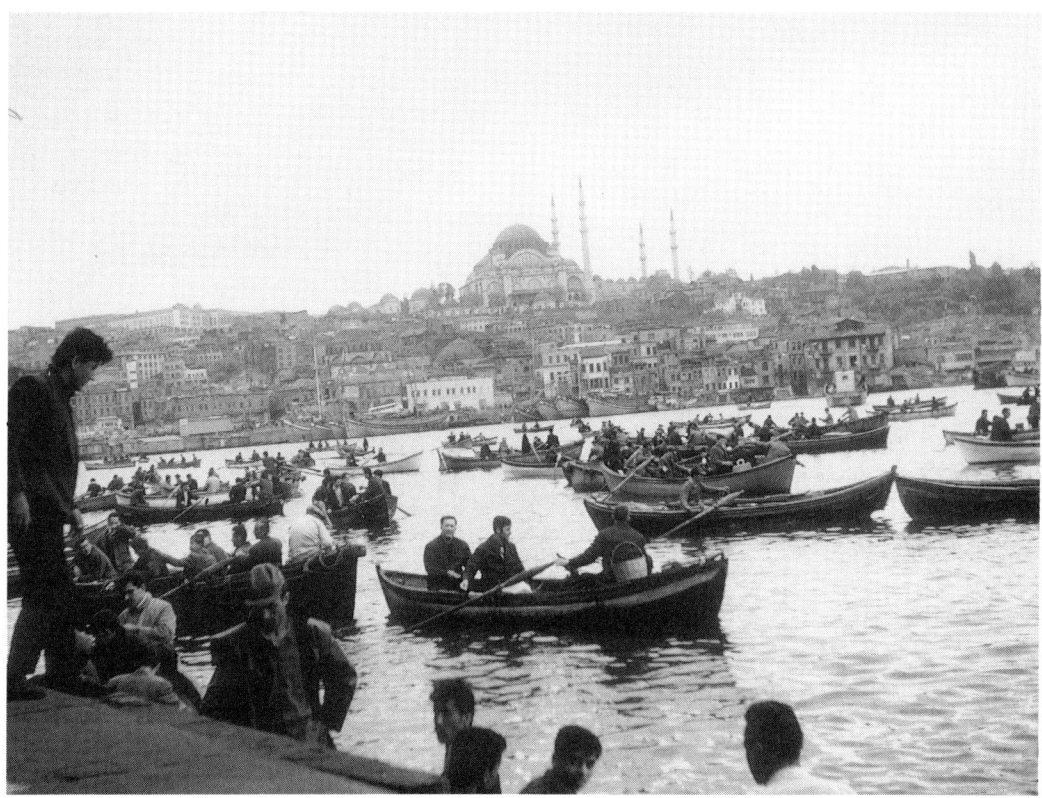

144. Süleymaniye mosque, Istanbul, viewed from Galata

It is possible to surmise something of the original character of these mosques from studying the painted decoration on the ceilings under the galleries in the Sokollu Mehmed Pasha mosque at Kadırga, or the Muradiye at Manisa. At the Selim I mosque the decor under the sultan's loge was restored in the eighteenth century complete with little ribboned posies but retains the quantity of colours and gilding that must once have adorned it. Such work is intricate and close to fabric design in its proportions because it covers relatively intimate areas. What wallscapes can have been like, it is impossible to judge when so little remains of such frescoes as those of the Muradiye tekke, Edirne, or the royal tombs at Bursa. There are indications of whole woods and pastures above the dado at the Muradiye in particular and of inscriptions on richly painted backgrounds at Bursa. The restored dome of the mausoleum of Süleyman the Magnificent, repainted in terracotta and black with white ribbon and with rosettes set with crystal roses, suggests a colour scheme for great mosque domes although there is no reason to suppose that all were painted a dusty red rather than that blue which its heavenly symbolism might be expected to command. What they were never adorned with was the shoddy

Decoration

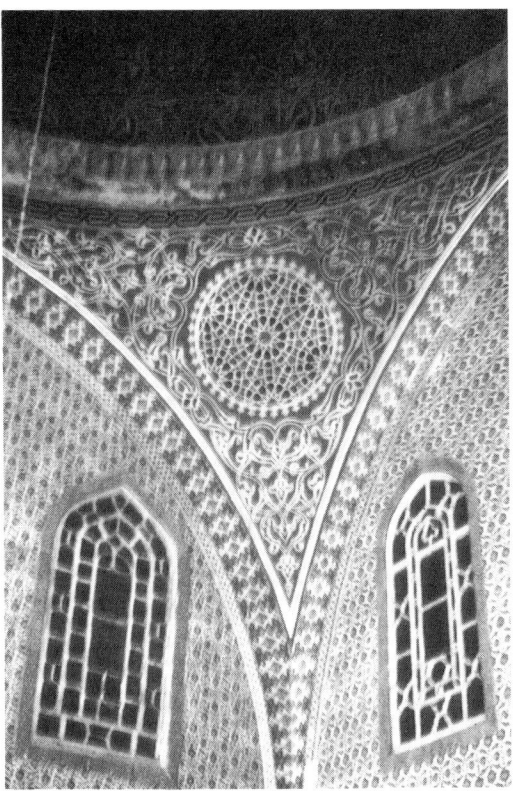

145. Murad III chamber, Topkapısaray: painted pendentive

Right:
146. Süleymaniye mosque, Istanbul: window and wheel of inscriptive tiles

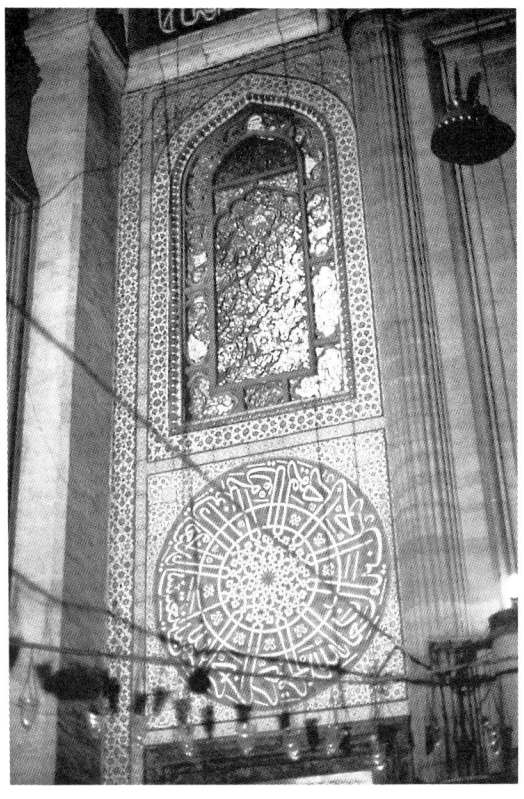

stencil work of restored or rebuilt mosques such as that of Fatih's great complex or that of Mihrimah at Edirnekapı. Affronted by such decoration as this, one must lament that there is no hadith, an edict of the Prophet evoked over the years by a continuing oral transmission, which states that religious foundations are to be restored to their original state exactly. Holy Writ anywhere is wine in a clouded glass.

It is said that a newly fledged architect, but not one supposes Sinan, graduated by presenting a Koran box as his masterpiece. These finely inlaid boxes which stood on small tables offer an important clue as to the nature of the decoration of mosque domes, for the inside surfaces of their own domical lids are handsomely painted in just such designs as a mosque dome would require. They and the reading desks were also inlaid with precious woods, mother-of-pearl and ivory or bone, and the preacher's chairs, which survive in several mosques, indicate the richness of the furniture although Koran boxes and their contents have rightly escaped to the protection of museums.

The Koranic texts had their exact position in the mosque just as the Virgin was lodged in the eastern semi-dome under Byzantine ordinances. The original handiwork is the greatest loss but at least the magic of that calligraphy has been preserved in the Iznik panels over the windows of many mosques or in those vast ceramic roundels which Ahmad Karahisarı[64] is said to have invented. They are celestial chariot wheels, with sweeping alifs (the first letter) and lams for their spokes, in circles which are surrounded by clouds of afterthoughts. Sometimes blue on white and at other times white on blue, the letters occasionally have colour-filled loops or flowers scattered amongst them for letters and flowers are so closely associated that they are likened to each other by the poets; hence the floral borders of many inscriptive panels. Such calligraphic designs on paintwork are to be found heavily restored at the Süleymaniye mosque but, elsewhere, are lost. The tall and narrow mimbers with balusters of stone interlace, which replaced the venerable wooden tradition in the fifteenth century,[65] sweep up to a hooded belvedere with that same elegance that Sinan pursued when transforming stone walls into honeycombs of glass.

Altar and mihrab are equally bound by doctrinal rules. The mihrab had grown to be a gateway with a deep recess. Its stalactic arch and vault expressed the limits of grandeur within a prayer hall for its dimensions determined the success or failure of that interior space—that and the carving of the frame, its precious marble colonnades and all the etiquette of tile or marble decoration where no real door could be. It must be remembered that to a believer mihrabs were indeed doors to which no one might have the key until their death, when they would find no use for keys at all. This is as important for the understanding of any mosque as is the knowledge that the altar is the table where the apostles took communion with God if one is to understand the architectural language of a church.

Mosque floors were tiled and covered with elegant Egyptian matting or cheaper local reeds, for the congregation brought their own rugs with them. The present array of knotted rugs and, worse, wall-to-wall Manchester woven carpets is out of place. Something spiritual is lost for when a passer-by went in and unrolled his modest mat or rug on which to perform his devotions, he was with his soul on his own island on the sea-bed of a mosque such as the Sülemaniye; however humble he may have been, he was a signal to all comers of all men's devotion.

The sumptuously painted mosque lamps are now a grievous loss doomed never to shine, whether in museums or private collections, like dumb nightingales. In winter and on dark days when their floating wicks

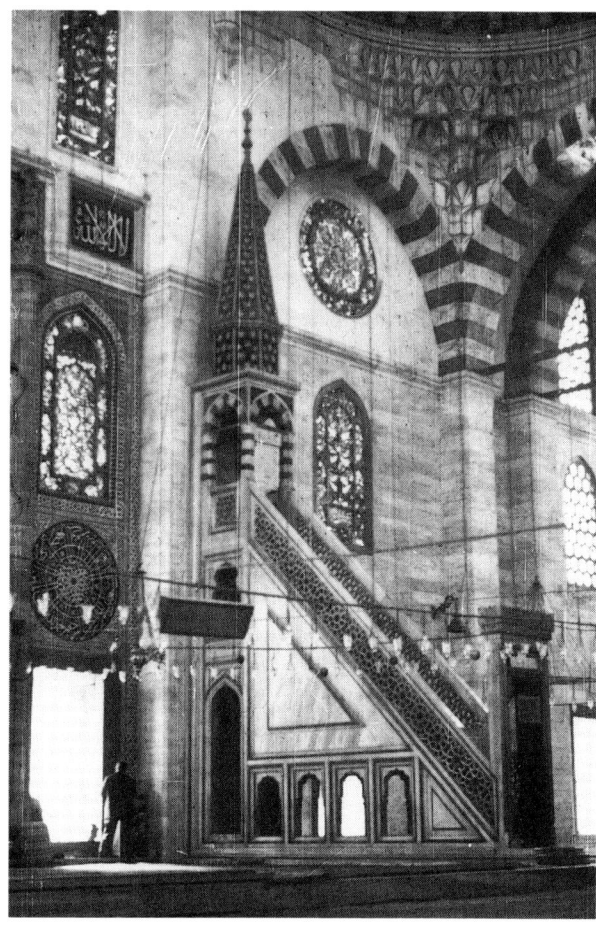

147. Süleymaniye mosque, Istanbul: mimber

Facing page:
148. Süleymaniye mosque, Istanbul: mihrab wall

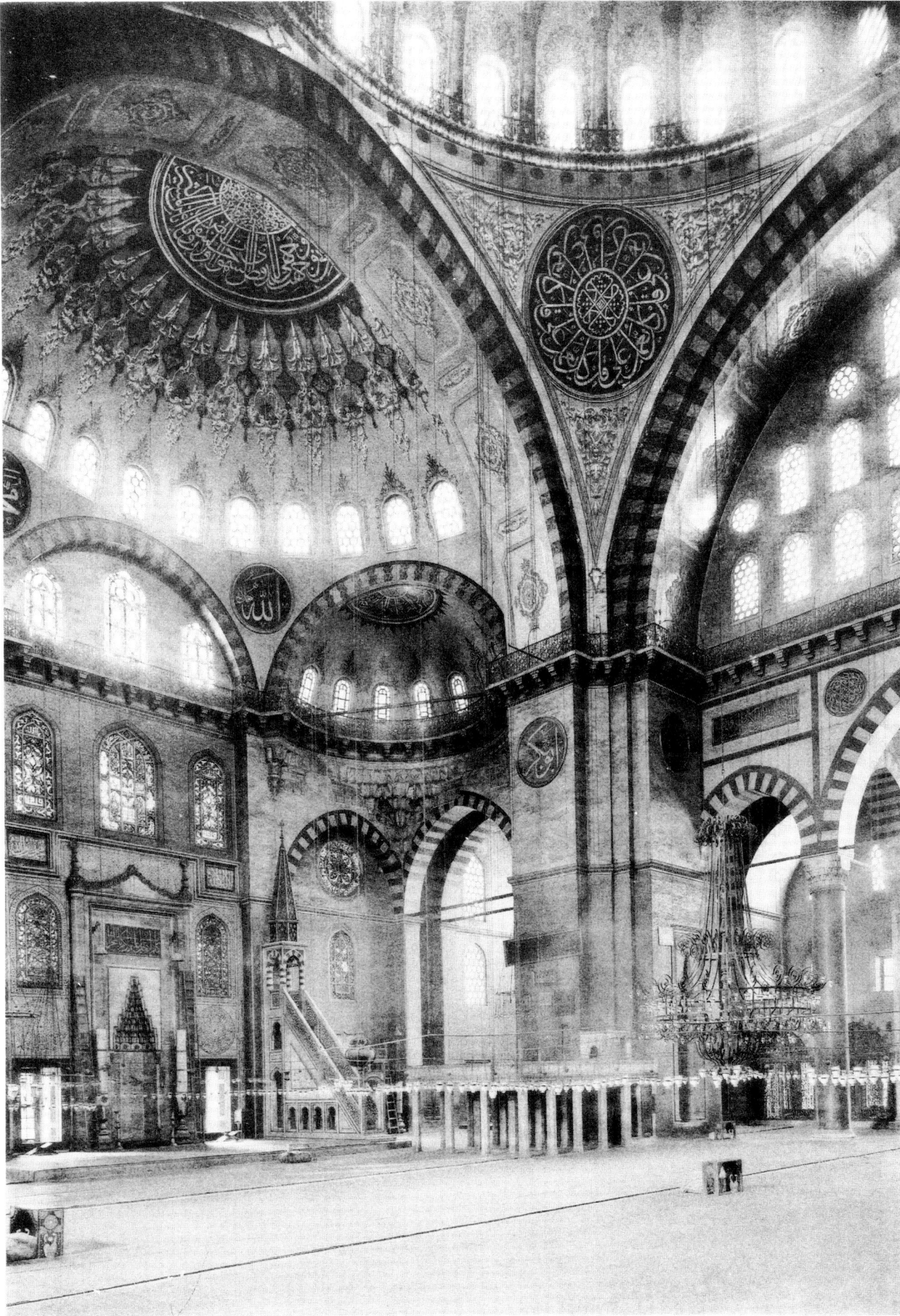

Sinan

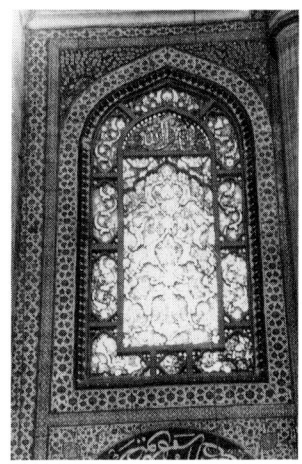

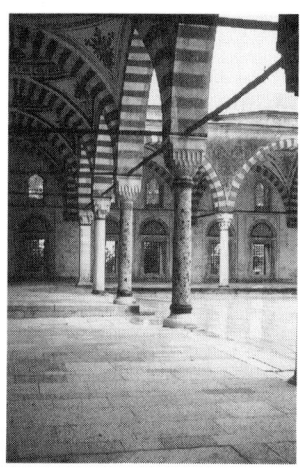

150. Selimiye mosque, Edirne: court (Graeme Gardiner)

Top left:
149. Süleymaniye mosque, Istanbul: mihrab wall

were fed on oil, their light was diffused. In place of their warmth, nineteenth-century glass cups hanging from iron rings create an artificial ceiling a few metres above the heads of the congregation and now contain a bare bulb here and there which casts a merciless spasm of light. Between these lights, the ostrich eggs from Mecca (few now brightly painted) and fertility emblems made of straw, as they are the world over, still hang dustily. Of chandeliers and modern strip-lighting nothing can be said.

Much of the original coloured glass came from Venice and was set in plaster to create flower patterns. The windows can be viewed best at an angle of 45 degrees. They are to be admired as moments of blazing light within the grey limestone of the walls.

Outside, the courtyards and their marble pavements and columns are no longer polished any more than are the dirt-engrained columns of Venice's San Marco above shoulder level. Nor do the window grilles shine; still less are they regilded. Yet after rain something of the lost gleam returns and the courtyard is momentarily alive again.

Tiles

Sinan could not ignore, nor would he have wished to ignore, the fashion for Iznik tiles. His own time was the great period of their manufacture and they brought delight to Ottoman architecture. They were used over the soffits of arches at the college of the Haseki Hürrem foundation where Sinan began his career as a Royal Architect, but his first important use of them was in the

Tiles

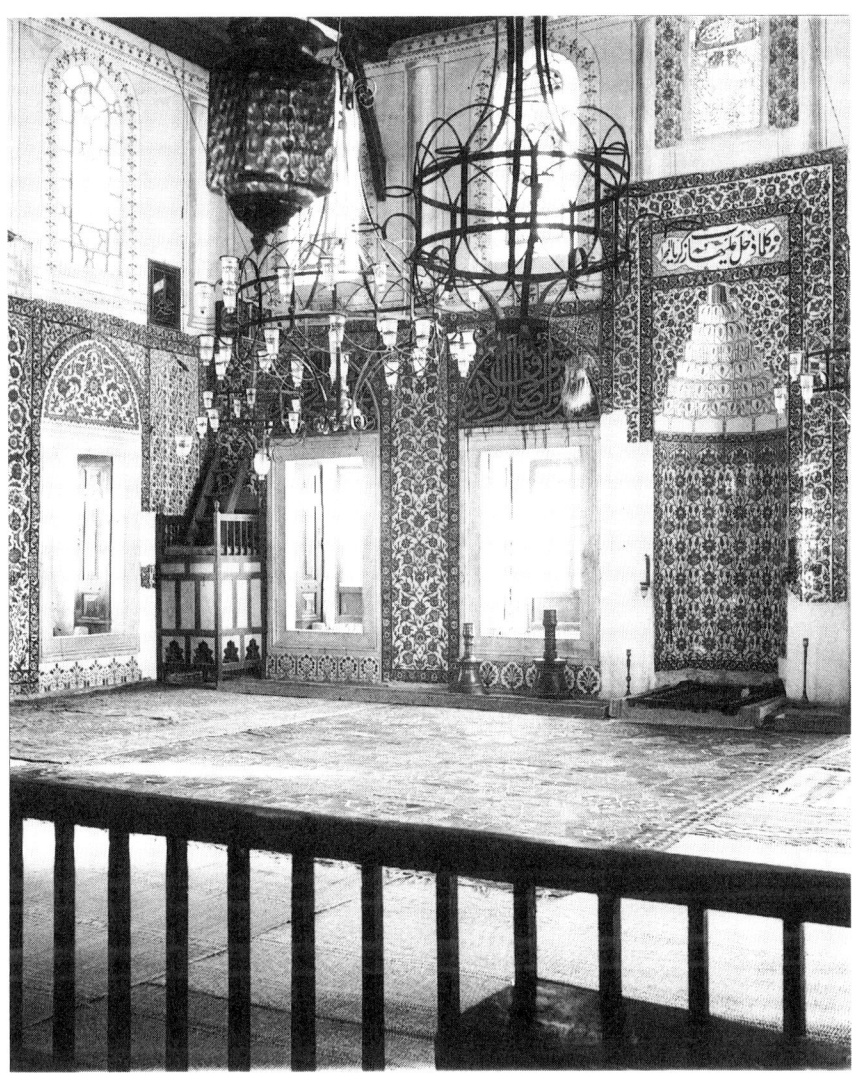

151. *Takkeci Ibrahim Çavuş mosque, Istanbul: Iznik tiles*

mosque of Süleyman where the mihrab wall is clad in them. They include large circular inscriptive tiles based on the calligraphy of Ahmad Karahisarı, who was the foremost penman of his age in the Islamic world. Since heaven is a garden, tile designs were made up of flowers and blossom and sometimes cypress trees. Their heads dipped in the wind, they were the earthly echo of the celestial palace, to quote from Finster.[66] The echo became a clamour when the mosque of Rüstem Pasha[67] was completed in 1562 after the Grand Vezir's death. Every wall, including that of the portico and the circles in the soffits of the arches of the outer portico, is clad in tiles in two styles. That of the mihrab includes stylized lamps defined with hard black lines and an entangled garden. Those of the galleries and piers form large panels of strictly repeated patterns that, mischievously speaking, recall dress lengths. They avoid axial symmetry in most cases but are rational and closely woven decoration. In the galleries the repeat panels are widely spaced so that unity is not lost although dispersed. None the less, no mosque ever had such a display again, with two exceptions (see below), and one may conclude that Sinan saw that the building had been weakened by excess. The overwhelming quantity of ceramic can only have been due to the patronage of the sultan's daughter, Mihrimah, Rüstem Pasha's widow.

It is important to assess the power that a patron as strong-willed as Mihrimah could exert over her architect, even one as illustrious as Sinan. When her brother, Selim II, succeeded to the sultanate she was to rule the palace. Clearly at the Rüstem Pasha mosque, the deceased parvenu and his royal widow required an excess of splendour. This excess was exceedingly costly and was certainly ordered specifically for this building because some tiles clad the piers which support the dome and were made to measure. Money or no money, no mosque under Ottoman patronage was coated in such abundance again, in contrast to the mosques of Safavid Iran. There were to be two exceptions, one of which, that of Ramazan Efendi, was built by Sinan in 1585-6; the other was that of Takkeci Ibrahim Çavuş,[68] built after his death in 1592, beyond the city walls. Both these mosques are small and modestly built with painted wooden roofs. Their walls are completely covered in composite panels of tiles of multiple floral and foliate patterns creating a high hedge of beauty beyond which lay actual paradise, sleeping. All the panels are related by their subject matter and their borders. They include vines as well as court flowers; the colours are intense while the whites have that purity which only pertains to the finest creations of Iznik. Because the prayer rooms are not large the effect is not to overwhelm or weary with profusion but to give pleasure. At the mosque of Rüstem Pasha the space is too great for the patterns not to merge and lose form, as does the architecture, even when discounting the lamentable paintwork. Intense as the blues and reds of individual panels are, the effect is of a green haze.

At the most beautiful of Sinan's vezirial mosques, that for Sokollu Mehmed Pasha at Kadırga below the Hippodrome of Istanbul, the mihrab wall from the pendentives to the floor is a single tiled cascade of flowers and fine calligraphy. The tiles are of a particular purity of colour, especially the white ground, and even include fake marble skirtings. The whole wall was designed as one and no other Iznik composition as grand was ever achieved again. Inscriptive tiles over windows and the original paintwork of ceilings under galleries and tribunes, along with the fine quality of the masonry, create a tall prayer hall able to sustain the energy of the tile wall with all the variations and richness of its colourscape.[69] The whole mosque is not draped in tile, however, and the monumental panel is contained within the central third of the mihrab wall area but echoed by the elegance of the ceramic hood to the member. For a mosque of its dimensions, it would seem that the perfect balance between ashlar and tile had been achieved.

In later mosques, such as that of the thuggish Zal Mahmud Pasha, tiled panels were modestly restrained to the mihrab surrounds. This was probably due to a shortage of tiles on the market—since the palace was voracious and had first call—or to cost. Vezirs might well regard the immediate surrounds of the mihrab as representing the minimum area that must be tiled. Probably it was as much as they chose to afford.

At no point did Selim II economize over the building of his mosque or, for that matter, his tomb, which was tapestried with tiles and of soaring loftiness. It is reasonable to suppose that Sinan concentrated the tile panels between the windows of the Selimiye apse for aesthetic harmony as well as metaphysical symbolic reasons. Elsewhere he placed fine inscriptive tiles above the windows and in addition there are grand circular discs which dominate the portico onto the courtyard. Inside, unique designs appear in the triangular shoulders of the arches and the galleries but great areas of stone are undecorated, notably the vast north wall opposite the mihrab. Sinan was to repeat this powerful but restrained use of tile at the very late (1579–83) mosque of the Atık Valide Sultan above Üsküdar and to some extent with Murad III's mosque at Manisa. Fortunately for Sinan, the rapid decline in the quality of colour of Iznik tiles did not begin until the seventeenth century.

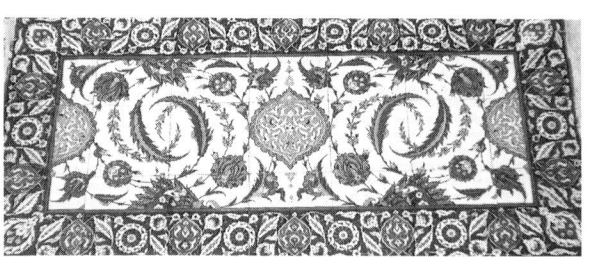

152. Sokollu Mehmed Pasha mosque, Kadırga (Istanbul): tile above window

Mathematics and Architecture

Each year at least 200,000 theorems are recorded representing the narrower and narrower borings of research.[70] Like lost souls, most of them talk only to themselves. It is not only mathematicians but art and architectural historians who are afflicted with that disease of the insect kingdom: inflexibility of limited purpose. In the sixteenth century there were few theorems and those few could all be read. They could accommodate an ants' nest of nuances such as awake interest when considering Pythagoras but they remained thought-producing rather than sprouting further analyses and further records. The obvious sterility of self-absorbed research is that the time free to look around is too limited to allow a glimpse of similar work and progress, even if the dimensions and the time, the function and the purpose, are different in scale.

Ideas form the apex of the pyramid of tradition and this is visibly demonstrated in the development of the buildings of Sinan, who, by bringing Ottoman tradition to its terminus with the Süleymaniye complex, could forget its origins. Tradition is nothing if it is not the forgetting of origins.[71] This is to return to the theory that the next development must be to postulate new forms supported by the evolution of existing structural concepts. Just as in mathematics the aim is to explain a situation by using abstract models. In architecture this perception of conjectural space is expressed in very tangible plans and models. If this be so, it is pardonable to be confounded by the metaphysical problem of relating spirit and matter. To ask an architect whether a precise map of a road to paradise is superior to faith is to forget that he, by his very nature, must match the former to the latter in order to avoid the chaos of Beauvais[72] and the world before God, remembering that it is in his image as an architect that God has been perceived; and not only by William Blake. Ottoman building methods were profoundly concerned with stability. There is, therefore, no history of collapse during construction, as was the case with the cathedral at Beauvais, but only damage due to subsequent earthquakes.

No Building is an Island

There are buildings which are expressive of a period: although their structural elements may reappear in new achievements, they have no true offspring. The Eiffel Tower, for example, was a single gesture; engineering elements were repeated from the warehouses of the Bronx to electricity pylons but these are not monumental gestures, they merely show a common vocabulary of open steel trusses. Indeed it is difficult to find a

Western monument, one that was built and not just a fantasy of Leonardo da Vinci or Piranesi, that did not go on influencing future design. The mosque of Selim II had almost no influence at all. It was the earlier Süleymaniye complex in Istanbul which was the apotheosis of the Ottoman styles—the plural is intended. The Selimiye mosque developed ideas beyond the imagination and grasp of the successors to Sinan's architectural supremacy. It was unique and unrepeatable because it could only have had descendants if the character and intellectual development of Islam had not been petrified. Moreover, Sinan himself went no further as the cold records show. This is not simply because he did not receive a comparable commission but because he had achieved all that he, as an architect of his time and society, could achieve. What followed in his own work was a series of experiments with smaller mosques, of varying interest and success, that exercised his wits but when he died his subordinates had waited too long for the throne. They retreated to past forms. Their works might be grand but they are of secondary interest because they were entrenched in the fourfoil plan which Sinan had already taken to its limit and then discarded. This nostalgic and conservative tradition was fertilized by French baroque elements but no architect succeeded in assimilating the odalisque curves into the basic square form required of a mosque; religion emasculated the builders and Ottoman baroque escaped to adorn minor works and its fountains frolic cheerfully.

So it was that no architect attempted to copy, let alone emulate, the genius of Sinan's concepts. It is brutal but honest to say that no successor came who could divine the thought which grew to be the Selimiye except for Davud Agha. Because Sinan left no texts behind him for students to study and digest, the task was impossible. A builder may copy a building with the old materials or with new because he is an artisan, an artisan who has been trained in the tradition. But an architect needs to recreate and to dispute the past. Thus the classical tradition which continued through Palladio and Lord Burlington or Jefferson produced a Chiswick House in London; but it is not a villa on the Brenta. There was a new movement of columns as expressed at St Paul's in London or in the totally different mood of the Pantheon in Paris or the serried ranks of the Capitol. And so with domes, where the understanding of the forces at large in them was revolutionized by the commission that studied the cracks in St Peter's dome and reported their findings in 1742.

The Dimensions of Genius

The no man's land between good workmanship and ordered development and the somewhat braggartly concept of genius has to be forayed; braggartly because with buildings art is much more the creation of a team than in any other save for music. Moreover all periods have suffered from idiosyncracy masquerading as genius. Sometimes it is just bad manners, as when a classical portico in London's Strand has no supporting columns, like a child on a bicycle waving and crying, 'Look! No hands!' With Sinan there was nothing braggartly or idiosyncratic in relation to classical—that is, Ottoman classical—architecture. Still less did Sinan seek a quasi-hieroglyphic or mystical disposition of marble symbolism as occurs on the brick flanks of Michelangelo's Porta Pia in Rome.

It is important to understand the problems which were posed. The problem was how a mosque of a certain size, with all its appendages from its courtyard to the latrines, could be placed and correctly oriented on a site within the limitations of the endowment. Luckily, enough of Sinan's monuments exist for comparisons to be made within a chronological framework. One may divine how his solutions changed, what innovations he made and what forms he discarded. Examples mark Sinan's rejection of certain elements and the re-use and amplification of others. It is possible to recognize a feature that is not repeated although the circumstances in which it had been used before recur. If the circumstances recur often enough it is reasonable to discount such extraneous influences as the whims of individual patrons or patronesses, a glut of lead or the legend that Rüstem Pasha had a large collection of Iznik tile panels, hence the quantity used in his mosque. To omit a feature time and again is to reject it: such rejections give a critical insight into Sinan's thinking and if such negative clues are easier to notice than positive, the latter certainly exist. The development of the façade has already been studied. Here it is only pertinent to remark that it is an indication of Sinan's commitment to the Renaissance, if only by instinct or osmosis, that he attacked the problem of the façade in relation to his greater mosques until with the Selimiye he constructed a building lofty enough for, in a sense, all four sides to be façades.

In this lay the difference between solving a problem (as with the slypes through the college at the Kara Ahmad Pasha complex), which is commendable, and

The Common Denominator...

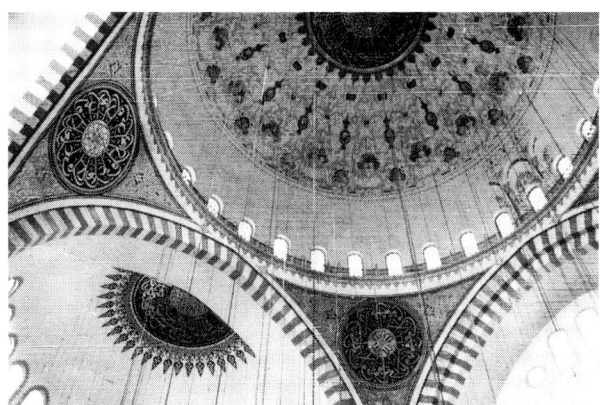

153. Süleymaniye mosque, Istanbul: interior domes. The paintwork is not original.

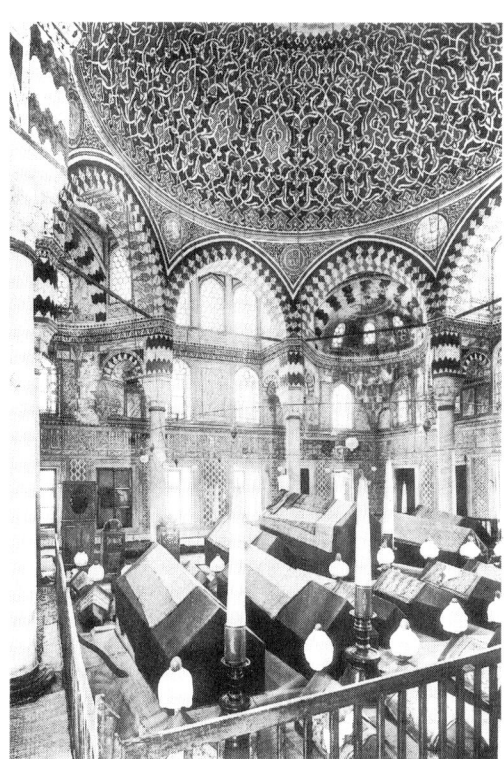

154. Selim II mausoleum (türbe), Istanbul: interior (Gurlitt)

creating a new form (such as the teaching hall raised above the entry to the Sokollu Mehmed Pasha complex at Kadırga), which is much more commendable. To add a new dimension altogether, as with the minarets of the Selimiye, may be called genius. It is genius when the relationship of the structure that is essential to all architecture—if it is to function—is as much part of the invented form as the skeleton is of the individual.

All architects work under restraints imposed by established methods of construction so that any radical change or development requires new construction techniques. Apart from metal clamps, tie-beams and such, structure until the nineteenth century was dependent upon the behaviour of timber, brick or stone under stress or compression. The span of an arch set limits to its proportions, even if the limit was disguised or augmented by additional structure devised to distract attention from worldly problems of walls and piers. All this was subordinate to the ultimate purpose of architecture: for example, to make a heavenly dome float. This is the secret of the masked piers of Haghia Sophia; and subterfuge plays the same role at St Paul's in London, where the spiritual dome of the interior is enhanced externally by a second vaster dome which overrides the city. In both Western and Ottoman architecture it is structure that is felt to generate form. In any tradition, any architect who evolves a new form has to know what is possible within the limitations of the materials he is able to employ. He also needs that visual imagination which cannot be taught but must be nurtured. Knowledge of the stresses and tensions, or their lack, accounts for many disappointments. Sinan's buildings always contained a structural margin of safety which could withstand all but the most vicious earthquake. His engineering discipline prevented his imagination from being a flight of fancy like a stage set or, for that matter, spires of Gothic churches.

The Common Denominator of Ottoman Architecture

Architecture is an elemental art because it simply relates the qualities of span and materials or, to put the point in a psychological form, it relates pre-spatial time and post-material consciousness. We have, then, space and material as the passive and active components, the spatial body and the material spirit. In this lies a paradox: it is common to consider materials as the body and space as the spirit, but in architecture the spiritual quality of a space is due to its containment or definition by the material.

Architecture is about the relationship of space and material and with these combined as exterior and interior. Within the dimension of achieved form, space differs from material as the general from the particular. Space is existential in an interior and functional in an exterior juxtaposed, indeed, as is the hollow to the solid. Even when, for example, a courtyard is measured by its void, buildings are space-positive. Space-positive, that is, according to the predominance of verticality or horizontality in terms of content.

Ottoman architecture kept interior and exterior completely balanced whereas the Western basilica stressed the interior and the Eastern temple stressed the exterior. This is one reason why Sinan rejected the dimensions of Haghia Sophia. Being nodally pure in its conjunction and absorption of elements, Ottoman architecture was the culmination of formal relationships. It avoided the imbalance of architectures that stress either interior or exterior so that, quasi-sculpturally, space survived the material and the material space: their harmony was complete.

Ottoman architecture also achieved harmony between horizontal and vertical, exterior and interior; its apotheosis was that perfect balance achieved in the unique relationship of the objective general potentiality and the suggestive particular realizations. The difference lies between passive space and active material. But space is positive in relation to the content and material also is positive in relation to enclosed form.

In Sinan's mature buildings the beauty of all the details cohere, are part of a whole and cannot be considered individually on their own account. Hence the rejection of non-functional structural ornament by Sinan after his first major building, the mosque of Şehzade Mehmed in Istanbul. The result in this building was wonderful and unique in more than just permutations of the square and circle. It follows that the summation of classical Ottoman architecture was to result from the cumulative experience of the past in the mind and eye of a single man. For Lethaby's axiom that no great art is only one man deep has yet to be refuted. And this concept of Ottoman architecture was to be

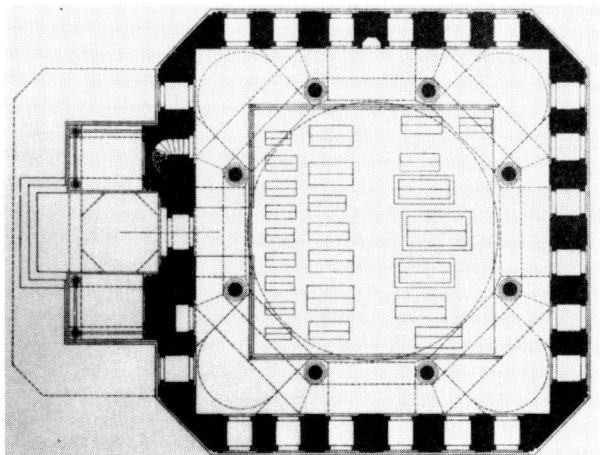

155. Selim II mausoleum (türbe), Istanbul: plan (Gurlitt)

Facing page:
156. Selimiye mosque, Edirne

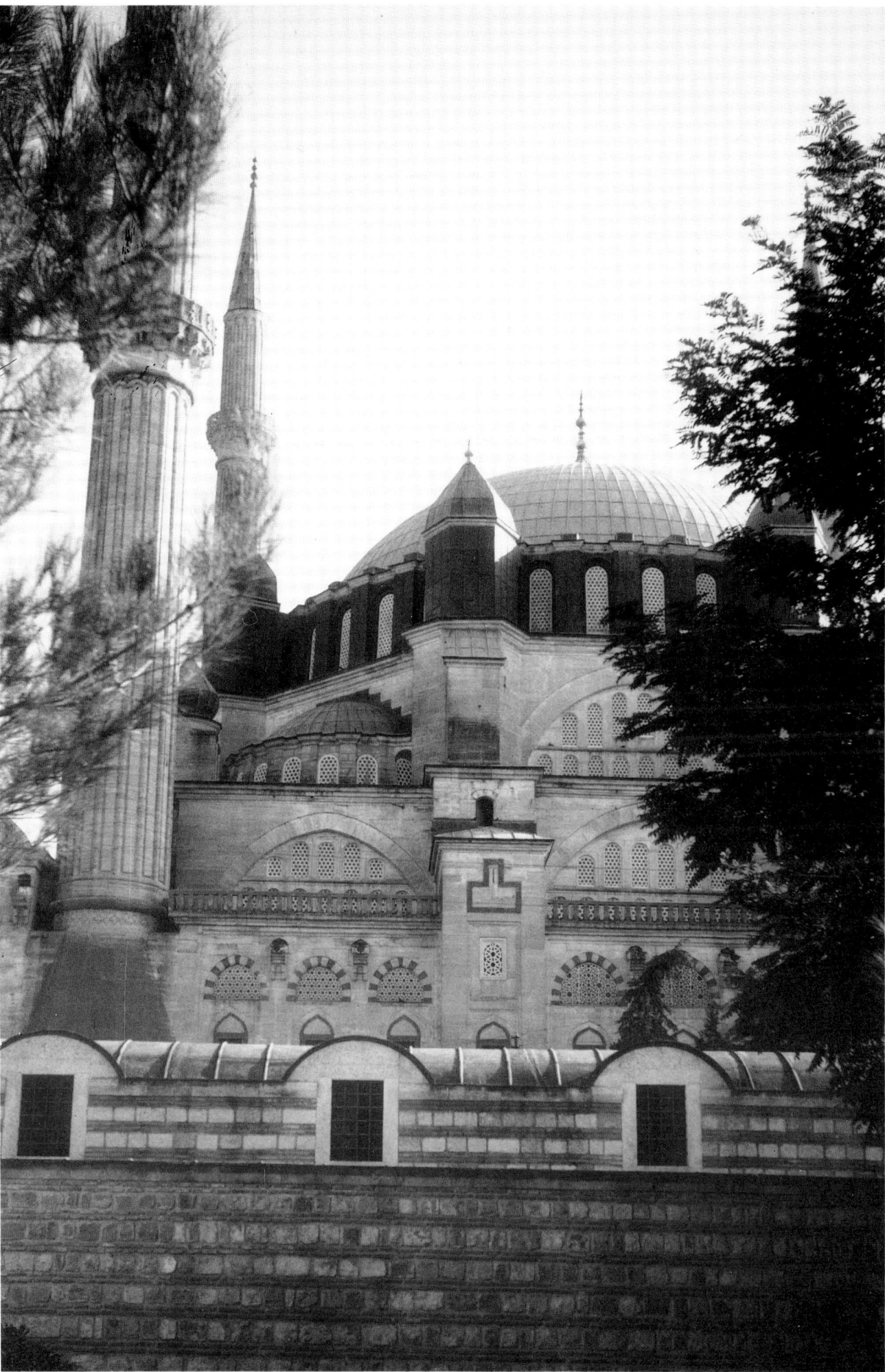

absorbed by the twentieth-century modern movement at its inception and at its best.

The perfection of the Ottoman achievement in classical terms was the Süleymaniye complex in Istanbul. It was built when the great river was in full spate, fed by tributaries of ceramics, craftsmanship and wealth deeper than any that previous sultans could employ or were ever to employ again. Sinan probably did say that this remarkable concourse of monuments and ordered open spaces was the work of a journeyman whereas the Şehzade complex had been the work of an apprentice. But he went on to say (just as all who have made the pilgrimage to Edirne are aware) that the mosque of Selim II was for him, as it is for us, his masterpiece. It was a unique achievement and intellectually as much a work of genius as any one of the monuments achieved elsewhere in its time. This was because it was beyond the wit or inventive experience of those who followed after. The monotony of late twentieth-century commercial blocks is due to the inability of all but a few architects to orchestrate such complex scores as the Selimiye or Chartres, even if there are patrons with the vision to employ them.[73]

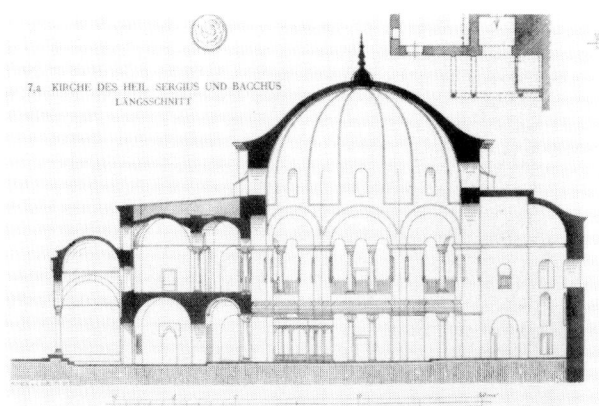

157. *SS Sergius and Bacchus church (Küçük Aya Sofya mosque), Istanbul: cross-section* (Gurlitt)

Counting the Dead

This monograph has been concerned with the work of one man. Unlike other Islamic builders about whom we know little or nothing as individuals, it is possible to discover the development of his mind. All mathematical solutions have been approximate since the first tides turned. Pythagoras discovered that the most illustrious number was 6. Let us put aside Edison's 137 or whatever peculiar figure this or that computer may find compatible, positive or negative or neither. For Sinan, the ideal number is likely to have been 8 and this is because it has its own significance. It was 8 that liberated him from the traditional Ottoman mould where 6 had failed the anonymous builder of the mosque of Üç Şerefeli. Nothing less than 8 could approximate closely enough to the circle to be easily read as such, just as Anthemius of Tralles had discovered with the precursor of Haghia Sophia, the church of SS Sergius and Bacchus. Eight has the curious property of being the number of times that a human hand can fold a sheet of paper. It is the omega of manipulative power and as such has its own symbolism.

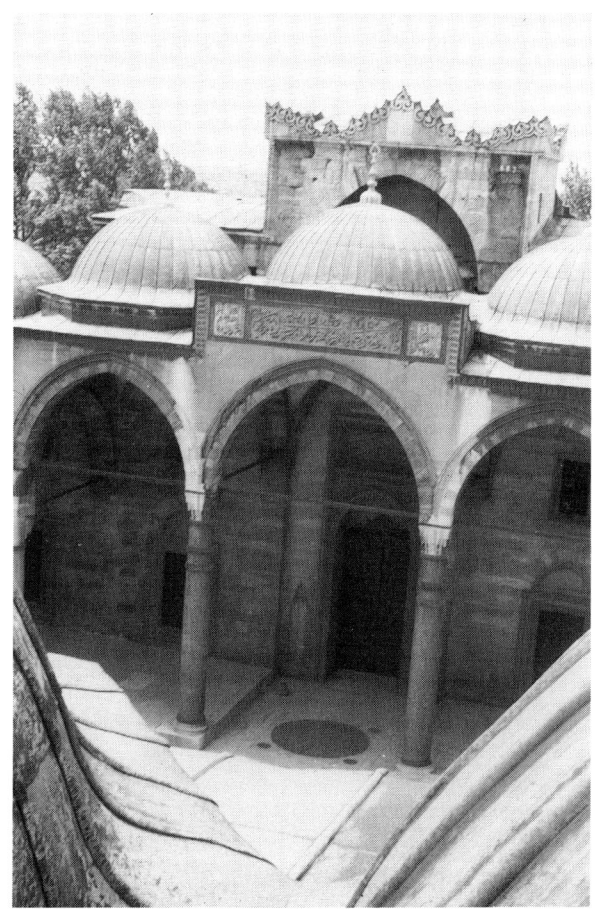

158. *Süleymaniye mosque, Istanbul: court*

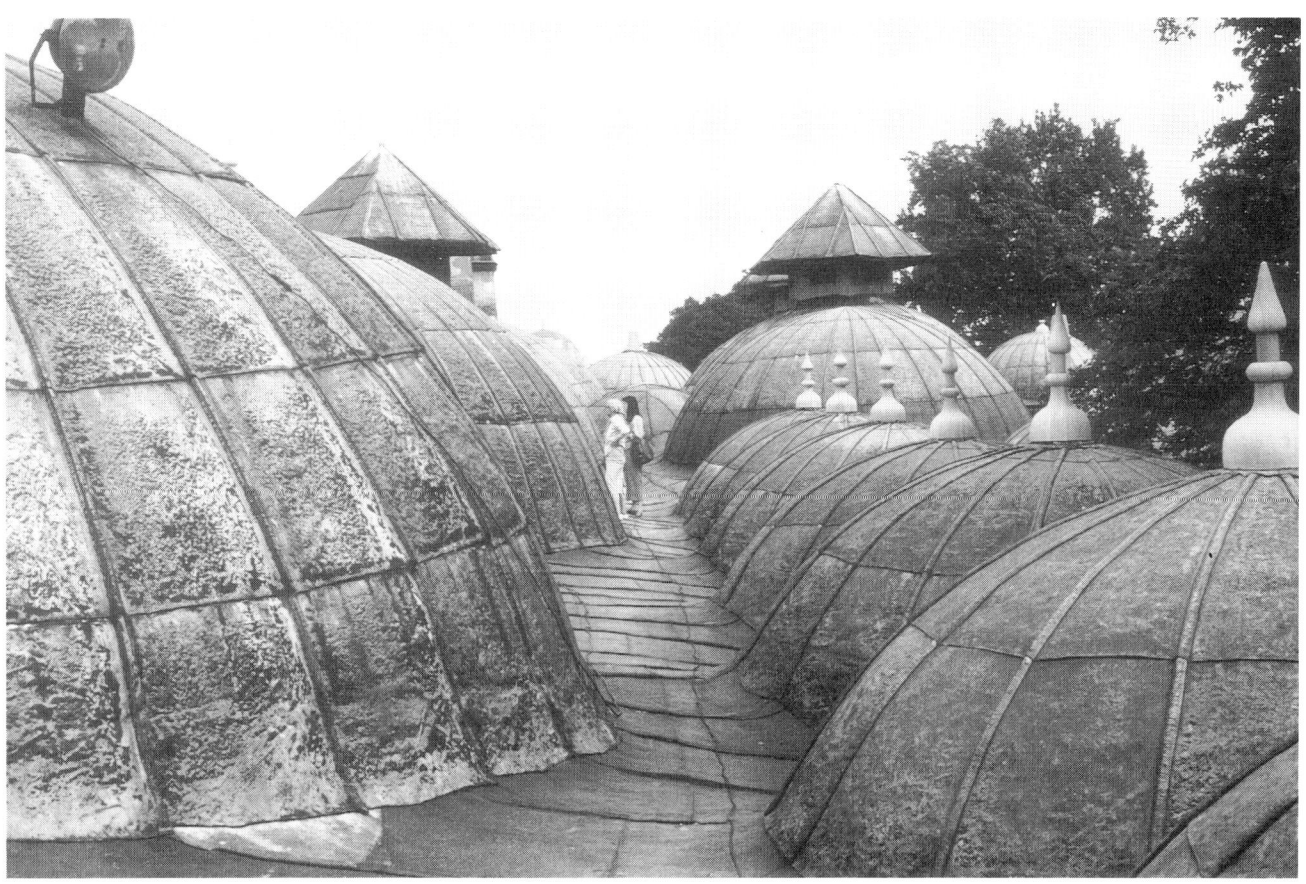

159. Süleymaniye complex, Istanbul: domes of refectory (imaret) and kitchen ventilators in the distance

To consider the work of Sinan is not to consider a style of architecture which is only one man deep. But it is, indeed, a question of profundity. What has been postulated here is that he has until now been seen in the narrow concept of only one style as if he were a silhouette or a stage set of a single culture. This is to exile the mind to the level of popular guidebooks. To be understood, Sinan must be seen standing along with other great men of the sixteenth century. He had the rare ability to change the forms, and therefore the proportions of the elements, of his architecture. For this reason alone he is remarkable in much more universal terms than those of national pride. He brought new enlightenment when he was alive yet he would only be a memory were that all. It is not. He is one of those who went before and left an example with which to stimulate the living eye.

Notes

For a complete bibliography, the reader is referred to Godfrey Goodwin, *A History of Ottoman Architecture* (London/Baltimore, Md, 1971).

1. 'In this manner do those individuals who possess the quality of uniqueness refute the theories of determinism... If the history of the world is due to the operation of identifiable forces other than, and little affected by, free human wills and free choices (whether these occur or not), then the proper explanation of what happens must be given in terms of the evolution of such forces... This unlimited extension of necessity... becomes intrinsic to the explanation of everything.' I. Berlin, *Historical Inevitability* (London, 1954), pp. 25-6.

2. The greatest proportion of art and architecture develops inevitably. If there had been no Borromini or Guarini there would have been someone else. The great architects or artists were those who evolved elements of complete monuments which were not inevitable. The Porta Pia is one such example. There was no reason whatsoever why the mosque of Selim II should have evolved or been predetermined. Had Sinan never lived, nothing like it would have been achieved. Sinan dead, moreover, nothing like it was to recur.

3. Ömer L. Barkan, *Süleymaniye Camii re Imareti Ins'atti: 1550-7*, vols. I and II (Ankara, 1972-9). This prodigious work on the detailed accounts of the building of the Süleymaniye complex is of signal importance.

4. Dalgıç (The Diver) Ahmad Agha, killed in battle against Kalender rebels, 1608. Specialist in inlay. Chief Architect, 1598-1606, when appointed *beylerbey* (governor) of Silistre and promoted Pasha. Worked on tombs of Murad III and Mehmed III; continued Yeni Valide complex.

Davud Agha *floruit* 1575-98. Chief Architect, 1588-98. Built: mosque and mausoleum of Mehmed Agha, Çarşamba, Istanbul, 1585; Incili Kiosk, 1589; Sepetciler Kiosk, 1591; Sinan Pasha complex, 1593; Cerrah Mehmed Pasha complex, 1594; tomb of Murad III, 1595+; Gazanfer Agha complex, 1598(?); left Yeni Valide complex incomplete on death or execution, September 1598.

5. Ibrahim Pasha was created the first *Sadrazam* (Grand Vezir as opposed to Chief Vezir). This dashing boon companion shared the government of the empire with his sultan until, growing all too grand, he was strangled in 1536. Kara Ahmad Pasha was Grand Vezir from 1553 to 1555 while Rüstem Pasha was temporarily out of office because of his unpopularity with the army. Rüstem was restored to office as soon as was possible and Kara Ahmad executed.

6. Rowland J. Mainstone, *Hagia Sophia* (London, 1988), pp. 177-8, quoting Evagrius on the measurements of the Basilica.

7. Aptullah Kuran, *Sinan, the Grand Old Master of Ottoman Architecture* (Washington & Istanbul, 1987). I think that Sinan's structural concepts were closer to Alberti (and therefore closer to Vitruvius than to the later Palladio) than does Kuran, who states, 'Palladio's architecture goes beyond the High Renaissance style' (p. 246). Palladio himself learnt from Alberti but it is when his genius develops that he also diverges from the Roman past which relied, as did Ottoman architecture, on the mathematics of engineering. Byzantine builders translated this superior prose into verse—the exedra, for instance, which Sinan learnt from Haghia Sophia, was a key to imagination cast in space. The centripetal Tempio della Consolazione at Todi, built to the plan of Bramante and not completed until 1606, is several times cited in architectural history books as a parallel to the Şehzade mosque in Istanbul. It is not, even when viewed from the outside, because the semi-domes have less to do with the support of the dome than with the expression of a central cube. Inside, with its windows high above ground level and its total concern with the former shrine under the crown of the central dome, it is as unlike the mosque in its use of space as it is structurally different.

8. Summarized by Rudolph Wittkower, *Architectural Principles in the Age of Humanism* (London, 1962), p. 7: 'According to Alberti's well known mathematical definition, based on Vitruvius, beauty consists in a rational integration of the proportions of all the parts of a building in such a way that every part has its absolutely fixed size and shape and nothing could be added or taken away without destroying the harmony of the whole.' Of no architecture is this more true than of Ottoman architecture and its respect, like Brunelleschi's, for the proportional system that lay behind classical structure —see Richard A. Goldthwaite, *The Buildings of Renaissance Florence* (Baltimore, Md, 1980), p. 361.

9. Dr Aptullah Kuran prefers to treat the reference to 100 years on Sinan's epitaph as hyperbole and so make him as much as 5 years younger when conscripted. It was the gifted painter Abidin Dino who realized the significance of these caves.

10. Mohacs (1526) was the major battle of Süleyman's campaign against the Hungarians during which their army was decimated and the king was killed. The Ottoman forces went on to take Buda and rule most of the country for a period.

Sinan was promoted to the rank of captain on this campaign and began his ascent of the military ladder while gaining experience in a variety of corps.

11. Because of this event, Vicenza contributed two galleys to the fleet of Don Juan of Austria. The consequent lack of funds prevented the completion of the Loggia del Capitano. J.S. Ackerman, *Palladio* (Harmondsworth, 1966), p. 122.

12. See Le Corbusier (C.E. Jeaneret-Gris), *My Work*, trans. Palmes (London, 1960).

13. Mathematical principles, said Galileo, are the language in which God wrote the world. M. Kline, *Mathematics in Western Culture* (Harmondsworth, 1973), p. 128.

14. Note the restrained use of tiles in most vezirial mosques like those of Hadım Ibrahim Pasha or Zal Mahmud Pasha. Cost and the palace monopoly of production were responsible. But by the end of the sixteenth century the demand for tiles for royal buildings diminished. It has been suggested that the tiles of the mosque-tekke of Ramazan Efendi were surplus to palace needs and sold off.

15. Mihrimah, daughter of Süleyman, wife and later widow of the Grand Vezir Rüstem Pasha, was reputedly the richest woman in the world. Her father broke with precedent when he permitted the building of two minarets at her mosque at Üsküdar. Her brother Selim II only permitted her to build one at her mosque at Edirnekapı.

16. Ahmad I loved hunting, women and God in that order. He himself worked on the foundations and building of his mosque.

17. See Ahmet Refik, *Istanbul hayatı, on altına asırda*, 4 vols (Istanbul, 1930–5).

18. Kuran, *Sinan* . . .

19. Şehzade Mehmed, Süleyman's eldest son, died on 6 November 1543 at the age of 22. The magnitude of the complex (built 1543–9) is a measure of the sultan's grief. Although it was more highly decorated externally than any other Sinan mosque, one assumes that Sinan rejected those Iranian influences that detracted from purity of form.

20. The repetition of a basic architectural concept ensures safety even when the traditional form requires daring domes: 'and even the barbarous Turks are in this glorious, who cover stupendous fabricks with hemisphere volts and open the 4 sides; as well as abutt the whole with 4 quarter spheres, which is a figure of so great perfection, I wonder it is not introduc't with us, who so much love room and lofty coverings'. H. Colvin and J. Newman (eds), *Of Building: Roger North's writings of architecture* (Oxford, 1981), p. 114.

21. In the seventh book of Alberti's *De re Aedificatoria*, the author eulogizes the circle as preferred by Nature—Wittkower, *Architectural Principles* . . ., p.3. It may also relate as a form to the importance of astrology for, like Ottoman builders, work could not begin without determining the auspicious day (Alberti II, p. xiii).

22. Depending on the area of the mosque, the ratio of window to wall at its greatest extent is approximately 1:3.

23. The Süleyman I complex, Istanbul, built 1551–8. The dome was completed on 16 August 1556. The ceremonial opening was held in October 1557. The tomb of Haseki Hürrem, Süleyman's wife, was built in 1558 and his own after 1566. 'Süleymaniye beyond all description beautiful', Evliya (Çelebi) Efendi, trans. J. von Hammer, *Narrative of Travels in Europe, Asia and Africa* (London, 1834), Book 1, p. 74.

24. But it was *architecture* surely and it expressed that freedom with vision and splendour—and a uniformity—worthy of the vigour and durability of the empire. Marshall G.S. Hodgson, *The Venture of Islam*, vol. III (Chicago, 1974), p. 124.

25. The *tabhane* is now difficult of access because it has become a public record office. The metal shelving, left out in the rain, has badly stained the marble pavement.

26. Mehmed Agha *floruit c*. 1570–1617; died 1622. Chief Architect, 1606–22. Known as Sedefkar (Worker in Mother-of-Pearl). Worked on the Selimiye complex; completed the Muradiye mosque, Manisa; deputy governor of Dıyarbekir, 1593; military command in Syria, 1595; repaired the Ka'ba and rebuilt the Great Mosques at Mecca and Medina; built the Sultan Ahmad complex, Istanbul, 1609–16.

27. *Cuerda seca* tiles have their glazes divided by a thread. This perishes in the firing leaving distinctive clear-cut designs.

28. The second of Süleyman's Grand Vezirs. At one point he was married to a daughter of Selim I. A Grand Vezir was expected to marry into the royal family whatever his social shortcomings.

29. See note 5 above.

30. In other words, the church was used for ceremonial, which was antipathetic to Islamic prayer, but the octagonal support for the dome was influential in the development of the Ottoman mosque in the sixteenth century.

31. This dome is a cautious innovation and massively supported. Builders needed to learn both from inherited and from new experience. History is littered with fallen buildings: see, for example, L.F. Salzman, *Building in England* (Oxford, 1952), pp. 25–6. The list includes the fall of Abingdon Tower because of the way in which the newly enlarged chancel joined it, the fall of the West Tower, Gloucester, because of the inadequate foundations and the fall of the West Front of St Albans.

32. There appears to be no doubt that Mihrimah Sultan took a personal interest in all her remarkable foundations.

33. It was felled in the 1894 earthquake.

34. These massive towers are unique.

35. Gothic architecture is another matter.

Notes

36. Endowed in the year of his death, 1561. The plan is related to that of the Selimiye at Edirne but without an apse.
37. Zal Mahmud Pasha was said to be brutal. He and his royal wife were to die in bed together on the same night.
38. Sokollu Mehmed Pasha was the third of the great vezirs of the sixteenth century along with Ibrahim Pasha and Rüstem Pasha. He became unpopular because he filled too many appointments with his Bosnian relatives. Sinan built some of his finest works for this patron. 'For an architect, the site is usually the fundamental spatial constraint,' Kanan Makiya, *Post-Islamic Classicism: A Visual Essay on the Architecture of Mohamed Makiya* (London, 1990), p. 43.
39. Mosques in the courts of kervansarays and in the middle of open markets were raised on terraces in order to achieve peace above the clamour of commerce.
40. The mosque was built in two stages: begun in 1549, it was enlarged in 1569 with an extensive kervansaray and markets.
41. For an authoritative account of the office of the Şehir Emini see H.A.R. Gibb and H. Bowen, *Islamic Society and the West*, vol. I, part I (OUP, 1950), pp. 356–7.
42. An important contribution in this field was made by Dr Aptullah Kuran in a paper delivered at the 7th Congress on Turkish Art, 1974, when he analysed the proportional system employed on the mosque of Selim II at Karapınar: *Mimar Sinan yapısı Karapınar II Selim cami'inin proporsyon sistemi üzerinde bir deneme*.
43. See the important article by Gülru Necipoğlu-Kafadar, 'Plans and Models in 15th and 16th century Ottoman architectural practice' in *Journal of the Society of Architectural Historians*, vol. XLV, no. 3 (Sept. 1986). Goldthwaite, *Buildings of Renaissance Florence*, p. 372, states that Florentine models were made in wood or plaster as entries for architectural competitions. Not all models were completed down to the decorative details, p. 375. They were costly and might take six months to complete, pp. 378–9. Filarete and Alberti were explicit on the need, pp. 374–5. Ground plans were the least important but models or drawings approximated to modern elevations in medieval building practice in England—see Salzman, *Building in England*, pp. 16–17.
44. One regrets the death of Mustafa since the originality of the plans for Murad's mosque implies adaption to a difficult site and therefore considerable freedom for him to develop his own initiative. Not all the innovations, which include windows that slope inwards, were successful.
45. Commissioned by Safiye Valide on her son Mehmed III's succession while engaged in ousting the redoubtable Venetian Nurbanu, widow of Selim II and mother of the cultured Murad III.
46. The six minarets also created hostility among members of the religio-legal establishment or ulema.
47. 'Mathematical style aimed at brevity and formal proportions. It sometimes succeeds too well and sacrifices the clarity its precision seeks to guarantee,' Kline, *Mathematics in Western Culture*, p. 25.
48. But lights were needed in winter, for special festivals and at dawn and dusk, creating a false ceiling some 2 metres above the worshippers and making a mystery of the dusky void between them and the dome. At holiday time, the royal mosques hung lanterns between their minarets calling on Allah to bless the occasion.
49. Geoffrey Scott, *The Architecture of Humanism* (London, 1961), p. 226.
50. Width 31.28m; height 43.40m. By comparison, the dome of Haghia Sophia is 30.90–31.80m in width and 55.60m high.
51. 'Selim I has no fine columns in it like other mosques. It is only an elevated dome supported by four walls', Evliya, *Narrative of Travels . . .*, Book 1, p. 73.
52. Roger North was asked by Wren to investigate the principles of the construction of the dome of the Süleymaniye but he did not apply them, not even the long-established rule that lead should rest on the bed from which it came—clay—and not on wood which hastens warping and decay.
53. R.M. Meriç, 'L'Architecte de la Mosquée de Beyazid d'Istanbul'. The *First International Congress of Turkish Art* (ICTA, Ankara, 1961) pp. 164–5 states that it was not Hayreddin Usta who built the Bayazidiye, although he was trained in the Ottoman tradition, but the mysterious Yakupşah bin Sultanşah who with all his preposterous royal affixes could only have been a Persian. He was succeeded by Ali bin Aptullah or Yakut bin Papas, or both, and both presumably Greek in origin.
54. T. Downes, *Hawksmoor* (London, 1979), p. 29.
55. The mosque of Piyale Pasha at Kasımpasha is only listed on one of the *tezkirets* and not the more reliable records. It is a splendid if clumsy building externally due to the six domes and the hoisting of the minaret among the external galleries (which abound) of the entrance wall. It was once a romantic country mosque in meadows but is now the prisoner of a mob of singularly ugly and ill-built twentieth-century apartment blocks. One would like to claim it as the work of Sinan because of the galleries, where the dervishes and others could sit and deliberate. Before the earthquake of 1894, they hemmed in three sides of the mosque with grace. On the other hand, the buttresses of the mihrab wall are merely tough.
56. The height of the Selimiye minarets is 70.89m.
57. The contrast of dome and minaret, female and male symbols, is not an aesthetic Freudian slip. Both features have their function.
58. Scott, *Architecture of Humanism*, p. 227.
59. 'If voids are a necessary medium of movement, solids are the essential instrument of support,' ibid., p. 201.

Notes

60. Brick and wood built the homes of the people, often in a disorderly fashion.
61. All these miniatures are in the Topkapısaray library except for the Muhammad Juki example, which is on loan to the British Library in London.
62. The şadırvan was originally for the ritual wash before prayers but would have been too small for a large congregation. It is permissible to wash at home.
63. After a fire or an earthquake, possessions could be stored in a mosque and its courtyard.
64. For the importance of Ahmad Karahisarı, see Annemarie Schimmel, *Calligraphy and Islamic Culture* (New York, 1984), pp. 72-3.
65. '. . . such effects were especially sought by the Islamic designers, who knew how to keep the mind busy without allowing variety to turn into confusion.' E.H. Gombrich, *The Sense of Order* (Oxford, 1979).
66. See also N. Menemencioğlu (ed.), *The Penguin Book of Turkish Verse* (Harmondsworth, 1978), pp. 72, 98, 111, etc.
67. It is strange that the Grand Vezir who was anathematized for taxing flowers should be immortalized by a mosque which suffers from a surfeit of them.
68. The felt hat-maker's mosque.
69. The original paintwork survives at this mosque, those of Atık Valide, Takkeci Ibrahim Çavuş and a handful of others. Some, like Selim I's mosque, have pretty seventeenth- and eighteenth-century floral work and calligraphy.
70. P.J. Davis and R. Hersch, *The Mathematical Experiences* (Harmondsworth, 1983), p. 24.
71. Particularly now that we know that Plato's *True Knowledge* is a myth sustained until the last century by Euclid. What the mind conceives is intellectual and not God-given and so is inevitably found wanting.
72. After the collapse.
73. William Pitt, 1st Earl of Chatham, 18 February 1783: 'Necessity is the plea for every infringement of human freedom. It is the argument of tyrants; it is the creed of slaves.' This is true of patronage and the demands of businessmen can be worse, as much of London and most other cities show. Meaningless blocks are the unlimited extension of necessity.

Ottoman Sultans and their Mothers, 1444–1595

Mehmed II Fatih (The Conqueror)
born 1432, acceded 1444–6; 2nd reign 1451, died 1481
=Gülbahar, valide sultan (Queen Mother), Slav

Bayazid II
born 1448, acceded 1481, deposed and died 1512
=Ayşe (Dulkadir princess)

Selim I Yavuz (The Grim)
born 1470, acceded 1512, died 1520
=Hafise, valide sultan, Circassian

Süleyman Kanuni (The Codifier), known in the West as Süleyman the Magnificent
born 1494, acceded 1520, died 1566
=(exceptionally, married) Haseki Hürrem (Roxelane), Slav

Selim II Sarhoş (The Drunkard)
His sister Mihrimah Sultan acted as valide sultan because his mother Roxelane predeceased his father.
born 1524, acceded 1566, died 1574
=Nurbanu (Venier-Baffo), valide sultan, Venetian

Murad III
born 1546, acceded 1574, died 1595
=Safiye, valide sultan

An Abbreviated List of Sinan's Buildings

Dr Aptullah Kuran has published a definitive register of works attributed to Sinan in the three lists issued in his period. These differ in their attributions. They are the *Tezkiret ül-Bünyan, Tezkiret ül-Ebniye* and, the least reliable, *Tuhfet ül-Mi'marin*. Of the 477 buildings recorded 173 no longer exist, 52 have been virtually rebuilt, 32 cannot be traced and 25 are in ruins. It is difficult if not impossible to assess the depth of Sinan's contribution to such works beyond, in effect, adding his stamp of approval to plans that in the main reflect the disciplines of his office.

Sinan cannot have supervised work on buildings far from Istanbul or Edirne and I would suggest that work on site was that of well-trained subordinates using the simplest plans and models, if models there were. Structural traditions governed building methods. In distant areas the employment of local masons led to many variations of the Ottoman theme, both structural (as at Lala Mustafa Pasha's mosque at Erzerum) and material (as at the Ahmad Pasha or Kurşunlu mosque at Kayseri). This leaves out of account the decoration of the Süleyman complex at Damascus and Sokollu Mehmed Pasha's vast kervansaray at Payas.

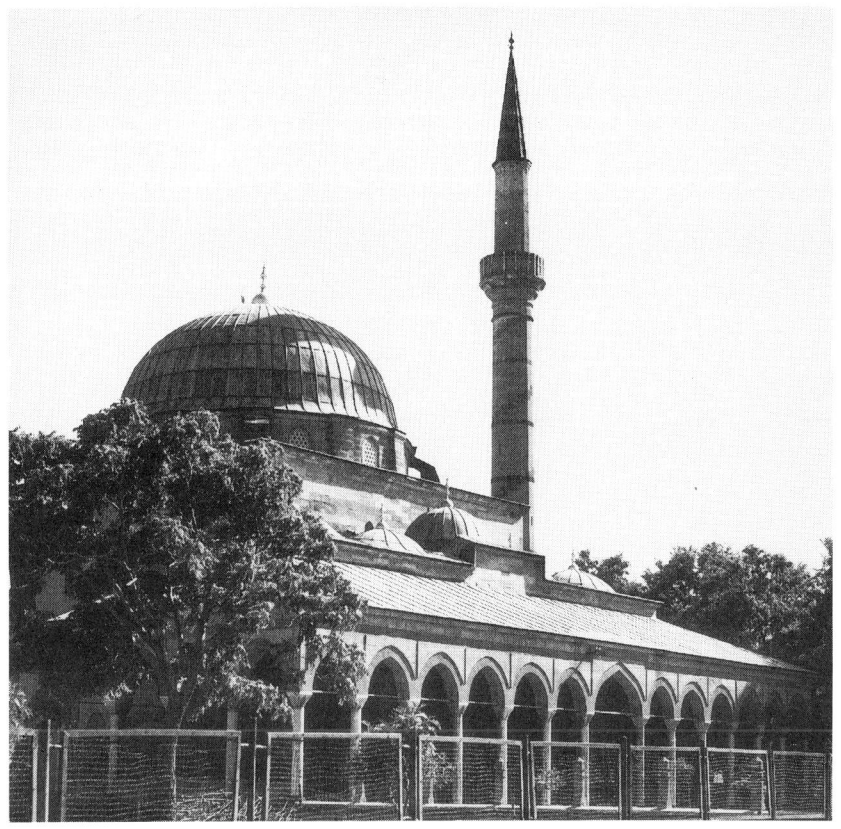

160. *Ahmad Pasha (Kurşunlu or lead-roofed) mosque, Kayseri*

List of Sinan's Buildings

Leaving aside Sinan's mosques in Istanbul or elsewhere while he was still a serving soldier, and which are only of esoteric interest to the specialist, my short list, A, covers those monuments where Sinan exercised supervision of the building and those foundations executed for his sultan where one may be certain that he kept constant watch on the work in progress. List B covers the principal buildings on Kuran's list of extant monuments where Sinan's connection seems to me to have been exercised at a remove. List C covers work which is of interest but I do not believe that Sinan can ever have seen: the journey to Edirne might take ten days while that across Anatolia involved several weeks. List D includes a few minor works. No building appears which is not listed in at least two out of three *Tezkirets*.

A. Monuments Built by Sinan
(Istanbul and Area unless Stated Otherwise)

Haseki Hürrem complex (part of)	1538–40
Barbaros Hayreddin Pasha tomb	1541–2
Şehzade Mehmed complex, tomb	1543–9
Hüsrev Pasha tomb	1545–6
Mihrimah Sultan complex, Üsküdar	1547–8
Selim I medrese	1548–9
Rüstem Pasha kervansaray, Galata	1550
Rüstem Pasha medrese	1550
Hadım Ibrahim Pasha complex	1551
Süleymaniye complex, including Haseki Hürrem tomb	1551–8
Sinan Pasha mosque	1555–6
Haseki Hürrem hamam	1556–7
Rüstem Pasha kervansaray, Edirne	1560–1
Molla Çelebi mosque	1561
Rüstem Pasha tomb	1561
Kara Ahmad Pasha complex	1561–2
Rüstem Pasha mosque	1561–2
Hadım Ibrahim Pasha tomb	1562–3
The dams and aqueduct system	1563–4
Mihrimah Sultan complex, Edirnekapı	c. 1565–70
Süleyman I bridge and Sokollu Mehmed Pasha complex, Büyükçekmece	1566–8
Sokollu Mehmed Pasha hamam, Edirne	1568–9
Various works at Topkapısaray	c. 1569 onwards
Sokollu Mehmed Pasha complex, Lüleburgaz	1569–70
Gazi Iskender Pasha tomb	1571–2
Sokollu Mehmed Pasha complex, Kadırga	1571–2
Selim II complex, Edirne	1572–5
Selim II tomb, Haghia Sophia	1576–7
Sokollu Mehmed Pasha mosque, Azapkapı	1577–8
Murad III pavilion, Topkapısaray (only in *Tuhfet ül-Mi'marin*)	1578–9
Atık (Nurbanu) Valide Sultan complex, Toptaşı	1579–83
Zal Mahmud Pasha complex	c.1580
Güzel Ahmad Pasha tomb	1580–1
Şemsi Ahmad Pasha complex	1580–1
Kılıç Ali Pasha complex	1580–1

Siyavuş Pasha family tomb	1583
Ramazan Efendi mosque	1585–6

B. Monuments Built to Plans by Sinan

Svilengrad Çoban Mustafa Pasha bridge	1528–9
Bosnalı Mehmed Pasha mosque, Sofia	1547–8
Rüstem Pasha complex, Tekirdağ	1552–3
Süleyman complex, Damascus	1554–5
Cafer Agha medrese, Istanbul	1559–60
Selim II complex, Karapınar	1563–4
Cenabi Ahmad Pasha mosque, Ankara	1565–6
Semiz Ali Pasha bazaar, Edirne	1568–9
and mosque, Babaeski	c. 1569
Defterdar Mustafa Pasha mosque, Edirne	c. 1576
Sokollu Kasım Pasha mosque, Havsa	1576–7
Hacı Pasha tomb, Istanbul	1576–7
Sokollu Mehmed Pasha bridge, Visegrád	1577–8
Pertev Pasha complex, Izmit	1579–80
Mehmed Agha complex, Istanbul	1585
Hacı Evhad mosque, Istanbul	1585
Murad III mosque, Manisa	1586–7

C. Monuments Planned (but never Seen) by Sinan

Sultan Süleyman kervansaray, Belen	1550
Iskender Pasha mosque, Dıyarbekir	1551
Karagöz Mehmed Pasha mosque, Mostar	1557–8
Gazi Iskender Pasha mosque, Istanbul	1559–60
Damad Ferhad Pasha mosque, Kastamonu	1559–60
Lala Mustafa Pasha mosque, Erzerum	1562–3
Adliye mosque, Aleppo	1565–6
Sokollu Mehmed Pasha hamam, Medina	1565–6
Sultan Selim medrese, Damascus	1566–7
Lala Hüseyn Pasha mosque, Kütahya	1570
Sokollu Mehmed Pasha complex, Payas	1574–5
Lala Mustafa Pasha mosque, Ilgın	1576–7
Hacı Ahmad Pasha mosque, Kayseri	1585–6

D. Minor Works

Sultan Süleyman mosque, Van	1533–4
Çavuş medrese, Istanbul	1560–1
Firdevs Bey mosque, Isparta	1561
Ferrah Kethüda mosque, Istanbul	1562–3
Hacı Hamza mescid, Istanbul	1577

Illustrations

1. Selimiye mosque, Edirne (*Ara Güler*)	[*jacket illustration*]
2. Süleymaniye mosque, Istanbul	14
3. Hudavendigâr mosque-zaviye, Bursa: loggia	18
4. Bridge at Büyükçekmece	19
5. Thirteenth-century Seljuk bridge at Çeşnıgar	19
6. Loggia del Capitano, Vicenza	20
7. Muradiye mosque, Bursa: support for subsidiary dome	21
8. Firuz Agha mosque, Istanbul: a single-domed unit	21
9. Bayazid Pasha mosque-zaviye, Amasya	22
10. Bayazid Pasha mosque-zaviye, Amasya: portico	22
11. Green Mosque (Yeşil Cami), Bursa: plan	22
12. Firuz Agha mosque-zaviye, Milas	23
13. Orhaniye minaret, Bilecik	23
14. Üç Şerefeli (Three Balconies) mosque, Edirne: elevation	23
15. Üç Şerefeli (Three Balconies) mosque, Edirne: interior (*Graeme Gardiner*)	24
16. Bayazidiye mosque, Istanbul: elevation (*Gurlitt*)	25
17. Bayazidiye mosque, Istanbul: exterior (*Gurlitt*)	25
18. Bayazidiye mosque, Istanbul: plan (*Gurlitt*)	26
19. Bayazidiye mosque, Istanbul: interior (*Gurlitt*)	26
20. Mihrimah mosque, Istanbul: portico	27
21. Haseki Hürrem complex, Istanbul: court of medical college	27
22. Bayazidiye hospital, Edirne	27
23. Mihrimah mosque, Istanbul: below Theodosian walls (*Graeme Gardiner*)	28
24. Rüstem Pasha mosque, Tekirdağ: portico	29
25. Atık Valide mosque, Üsküdar: panel of Iznik tiles	30
26. Rüstem Pasha mosque, Istanbul: interior (*Graeme Gardiner*)	31
27. Haseki Hürrem complex, Istanbul: plan	31
28. Şehzade mosque, Istanbul: exterior	32
29. Şehzade mosque, Istanbul: plan (*Gurlitt*)	32
30. Şehzade mosque, Istanbul: elevation (*Gurlitt*)	32
31. Şehzade mosque, Istanbul: interior (*Gurlitt*)	34
32. Süleymaniye complex, Istanbul: vaults	35
33. Süleymaniye complex, Istanbul: seen from Zeyrek mosque (Pantocrator)	36
34. Şehzade mosque, Istanbul: plan (*Gurlitt*)	36
35. Süleymaniye mosque, Istanbul: plan	36
36. Şehzade mosque, Istanbul: lateral arcades	37
37. Süleymaniye mosque, Istanbul: lateral arcades	37
38. Süleymaniye mosque, Istanbul: roof level	38
39. Süleymaniye mosque, Istanbul: roof level	38
40. Süleymaniye complex, Istanbul: plan	39
41. Süleymaniye complex, Istanbul: first and second colleges	40
42. Süleymaniye complex, Istanbul: lane of steps to vaults	40
43. Süleymaniye complex, Istanbul: kitchen court	41
44. Süleymaniye complex, Istanbul: kitchen court (*Graeme Gardiner*)	41
45. Süleymaniye complex, Istanbul: gate of dervish hospice	41

46. Süleymaniye complex, Istanbul: court of dervish hospice	41
47. Süleymaniye complex, Istanbul: Sinan's tomb	42
48. Süleymaniye complex, Istanbul: Sinan's fountain	42
49. Süleymaniye complex, Istanbul: court of fourth college	43
50. Süleymaniye complex, Istanbul: court of fourth college	43
51. Süleymaniye complex, Istanbul: apprentice college	43
52. Tomb of Süleyman the Magnificent and cemetery	44
53. Tomb of Süleyman the Magnificent: elevation (*Gurlitt*)	44
54. Tomb of Süleyman the Magnificent: interior (*Gurlitt*)	45
55. Hadım Ibrahim Pasha mosque, Istanbul: plan	45
56. Kara Ahmad Pasha complex, Istanbul: plan (*Gurlitt*)	46
57. Kara Ahmad Pasha complex, Istanbul	46
58. Kara Ahmad Pasha complex, Istanbul: court and portico	46
59. SS Sergius and Bacchus church (Küçük Aya Sofya mosque), Istanbul: plan (*Gurlitt*)	47
60. Üç Şerefeli mosque, Edirne: plan	47
61. Üç Şerefeli mosque, Edirne: court	47
62. Mihrimah mosque, Üsküdar: elevation and plan (*Gurlitt*)	48
63. Mihrimah mosque, Üsküdar: view from south	48
64. Mihrimah mosque, Üsküdar: ritual fountain (*Gurlitt*)	49
65. Mihrimah mosque, Istanbul: exterior	49
66. Mihrimah mosque, Istanbul: interior after 1894 earthquake (*Gurlitt*)	49
67. Mihrimah mosque, Istanbul: elevation	50
68. Rüstem Pasha mosque, Istanbul: interior	50
69. Zal Mahmud Pasha complex, Istanbul	50
70. Zal Mahmud Pasha complex, Istanbul: mosque court	51
71. Sokollu Mehmed Pasha complex, Kadırga (Istanbul): elevation (*Gurlitt*)	52
72. Sokollu Mehmed Pasha mosque, Kadırga (Istanbul): interior	52
73. Sokollu Mehmed Pasha mosque, Azapkapı (Istanbul): elevation (*Gurlitt*)	53
74. Sokollu Mehmed Pasha mosque, Azapkapı (Istanbul): plan (*Gurlitt*)	53
75. Sokollu Mehmed Pasha complex, Lüleburgaz: plan	54
76. Sokollu Mehmed Pasha complex, Lüleburgaz: portico	54
77. Haseki Hürrem hamam, Istanbul (*Graeme Gardiner*)	55
78. Bridge at Büyükçekmece	55
79. Yeni Valide mosque, Istanbul (*Gurlitt*)	56
80. Muradiye mosque, Manisa	56
81. Nişancı Mehmed Pasha mosque, Istanbul	57
82. Selim II mosque, Karapınar	57
83. Süleyman complex, Damascus: mosque	58
84. Süleyman complex, Damascus: court	59
85. Osmaniye dervish convent, Aleppo: minaret	59
86. Piyale Pasha mosque, Istanbul (*Gurlitt*)	60
87. Hacı Ivaz Efendi mosque, Istanbul (*Graeme Gardiner*)	61
88. Muradiye mosque, Manisa: interior	61
89. Semiz Ali Pasha mosque, Babaeski: interior	62
90. Kılıç Ali Pasha mosque, Istanbul: exterior	62
91. Kılıç Ali Pasha mosque, Istanbul: plan and elevation (*Gurlitt*)	62
92. Kılıç Ali Pasha mosque, Istanbul: interior at gallery level (*Gurlitt*)	63
93. Nişancı Mehmed Pasha mosque, Istanbul: exterior	63
94. Nişancı Mehmed Pasha mosque, Istanbul: plan	64
95. Sultan Ahmad mosque, Istanbul (*Gurlitt*)	65
96. Sultan Ahmad mosque, Istanbul: build-up to dome	65
97. Selimiye mosque, Edirne: towards the dome (*Graeme Gardiner*)	66

Illustrations

98. Selimiye mosque, Edirne: the centre (*Graeme Gardiner*)	66
99. House by Richard Neutra, Santa Barbara	67
100. Mihrimah mosque, Istanbul: exterior showing damage after 1894 earthquake (*Gurlitt*)	67
101. Haghia Sophia (Aya Sofya mosque), Istanbul: interior by Fossati	68
102. Selimiye mosque, Edirne: interior	68
103. Selimiye mosque, Edirne: cross-section (*Gurlitt*)	69
104. Selimiye complex, Edirne: plan	70
105. Selimiye mosque, Edirne: north wall	70
106. Selimiye mosque, Edirne: side galleries	71
107. Selimiye mosque, Edirne: south wall	71
108. Selimiye mosque, Edirne: shadow areas (*Graeme Gardiner*)	71
109. The Dome of the Rock, Jerusalem	72
110. Sultan Selim mosque, Istanbul: exterior (*Gurlitt*)	73
111. Haghia Sofya (Aya Sofya mosque), Istanbul: exterior by Fossati	74
112. Haghia Sofya (Aya Sofya mosque), Istanbul: exedra by Fossati	75
113. Haghia Sofya (Aya Sofya mosque), Istanbul: interior (*Gurlitt*)	77
114. Kılıç Ali Pasha mosque, Istanbul: interior (*Gurlitt*)	78
115. Fatih, the mosque of Mehmed II the Conqueror, Istanbul (*Gurlitt*)	78
116. Süleymaniye mosque, Istanbul: plan at dome level (*Gurlitt*)	78
117. Yivli mosque, Antalya: minaret dating from first half of thirteenth century	79
118. Eski Cami (Old Mosque), Edirne	79
119. Üç Şerefeli (Three Balconies) mosque, Edirne	80
120. Selimiye mosque, Edirne	81
121. Rüstem Pasha mosque, Istanbul: elevation and plan (*Gurlitt*)	81
122. Selimiye mosque, Edirne: interior of Royal Gallery (Hunkar Mahfile)	82
123. Süleymaniye mosque, Istanbul: elevation	83
124. Isfahan: the meydan	86
125. Asilah, a street restored	87
126. Shahnama of Muhammad Juki: miniature	87
127. Atık Valide complex, Üsküdar (*Gurlitt*)	89
128. Fourth court, Topkapısaray, Istanbul: pool and Erevan Kiosk	90
129. Sultan Ahmad mosque, Istanbul: court	91
130. Selim I mosque, Istanbul: plan (*Gurlitt*)	92
131. Selimiye mosque, Edirne	92
132. Gök Medrese (Heavenly College), Sivas: portal	93
133. Süleymaniye mosque, Istanbul: external portal of court	93
134. Süleymaniye mosque, Istanbul: court	93
135. Selimiye mosque, Edirne: view into court	94
136. Selimiye mosque, Edirne: portico	95
137. Selimiye mosque, Edirne: arches	95
138. Rüstem Pasha mosque, Istanbul: fountain house	96
139. Atık Valide mosque, Üsküdar	97
140. Süleymaniye complex, Istanbul: kitchen court	98
141. Süleymaniye mosque, Istanbul: court	98
142. Süleymaniye complex, Istanbul: the Addicts' Parade (Tiryaki Meydani)	99
143. Üsküdar from Süleymaniye terrace	99
144. Süleymaniye mosque, Istanbul, viewed from Galata	100
145. Murad III chamber, Topkapısaray: painted pendentive	101
146. Süleymaniye mosque, Istanbul: window and wheel of inscriptive tiles	101
147. Süleymaniye mosque, Istanbul: mimber	102
148. Süleymaniye mosque, Istanbul: mihrab wall	103
149. Süleymaniye mosque, Istanbul: mihrab wall	104

Illustrations

150. Selimiye mosque, Edirne: court (*Graeme Gardiner*)	104
151. Takkeci Ibrahim Çavuş mosque, Istanbul: Iznik tiles	105
152. Sokollu Mehmed Pasha mosque, Kadırga (Istanbul): tile above window	107
153. Süleymaniye mosque, Istanbul: interior domes	111
154. Selim II mausoleum, Istanbul: interior (*Gurlitt*)	111
155. Selim II mausoleum, Istanbul: plan (*Gurlitt*)	112
156. Selimiye mosque, Edirne	113
157. SS Sergius and Bacchus church (Küçük Aya Sofya mosque), Istanbul: cross-section (*Gurlitt*)	114
158. Süleymaniye mosque, Istanbul: court	114
159. Süleymaniye complex, Istanbul	115
160. Ahmad Pasha (Kurşunlu) mosque, Kayseri	121

Index

Acemi Agha 33
acemioğlan 17
Adam, Robert and James 38
Adrianople *see* Edirne
Agyrnas (Mimarsinanköy) 16
Ahis 21, 23
Ahmad I 31, *n*.16; mosque, Istanbul (Sultan Ahmad mosque) 56, 63, 64, 80, 89, 91, 94, *n*.26
Ahmad Karahisarı 102, 105, *n*.64
Ahmad Pasha mosque (Kurşunlu), Kayseri 60
Alberti, L.B. 15, 35, 84, *n*.7, *n*.8, *n*.21, *n*.43
alem 18
Aleppo 16, 58
Ali bin Aptullah *n*.53
Amasya 23, 24
ambiguity *see* glass
Anatolia 16, 17, 18, 20, 21, 26, 57, 64, 73, 89, 94, 99
Ani 33
Anthemius of Tralles 68, 85, 114
apse 52, 61, 63, 70, 82, 84, 88-9, 107
Apulia 18
arch 19, 20, 35, 40, 64, 91, 94, 95, 96; ogee 31, 53, 96; span 58, 111
architecture: Armenian 33; Byzantine 19, 21, 33, 66, 68, 88, 101, *n*.7 (*see also* Haghia Sophia, SS Sergius and Bacchus); Greek classical 15; Ottoman *passim*; Seljuk 19, 20, 79; Syrian 58; *see also* balance, centripetality, exedra, façade, galleries, pendentive, piers, portico, prefabrication, space, squinch, supplies, triangles, units, vaults and foundations
army and architects 64
Atık Ali Pasha mosque, Istanbul 89
Atık Sinan 49
Atık Valide mosque, Üsküdar 66, 89, *n*.69; tiles 107

Babaeski 62
balance 33, 35
Bali Pasha mosque, Istanbul 83
Balkans 16, 18, 20, 21, 26, 58, 73, 86
Barkan, Prof. Ömer L. 14, 79, *n*.3
baroque 89, 109
Bayazid I mosque, Bursa 79
Bayazid II 80; mosque, Amasya 23, 24, 79; mosque, Istanbul 26, 29, 76, 78, 79, 89, *n*.53; hospital, Edirne 26, 72, 79, 92
Bayazid Pasha *zaviye*, Amasya 23

Beauvais, cathedral 108
Berlin, I *n*.1
Bernini, G.L. 69, 90
Beyan-i Menazil-i Sefer-i Trakyen 87
Bilecik 23
Blake, W. 108
Blenheim Palace 90
Bonfigli, B. 88
Bor 57
Borromini, C. *n*.2
Bosphorus 99
Bramante, D. 15, *n*.7
Brenta, river 109
British Library, London *n*.61
Brunelleschi, F. *n*.8
Buda 19, *n*.10; bridge 19
Burlington, Earl of 109
Bursa 19, 20, 23, 26, 79, 88, 89, 95; royal tombs 100
Büyükçekmece, bridge 19, 20, 56
Byzantine 26, 56, 58, 70, 76, 91

Cairo 16, 60, 78
calligraphy 99, 102, 105, 106, *n*.69
Capitol, Washington 109
ceilings 45, 101, 104, 107
Çekirce (Bursa) 19
centripetality 21, 23, 33, 64, 109, *n*.7
Cervantes, M. de 63
Chartres, cathedral 114
Chinese houses 87
Chiswick House, London 109
Christian levy (*devşirme*) 16, 17
Çinili Kiosk, Istanbul 88
circle 69, *n*.21
columns 26, 40, 54, 57, 58, 83, 90, 91, 92, 96, 104, 109, *n*.51; register of 58; quantity 60, 95; ill-matched 62
Concorde, Place de la, Paris 87
Consolazione, Tempio della, Todi 24, 26, *n*.7
Constantinople *see* Istanbul
Cordoba 88
Corfu 18
court(yard) 23, 31, 33, 37, 38, 40, 46, 49, 52, 54, 58, 60, 64, 80, 85, 86, 87, 90-6, 98, 99, 104, 112
Cyprus 63

Index

Dalgıç Ahmad Pasha (Ahmad Agha) 14, 18, 56, 64, *n*.4
Damascus 16, 58
Dante 68, 70
Danube, river 21
Daphni, monastery 88
Davud Agha 14, 56, 63, 89, 109, *n*.4
Davud Pasha mosque, Istanbul 88
dervish 21, 23, 40, 47, 52, 92, *n*.55
devşirme see Christian levy
Dino, A. *n*.9
Diyarbekir 33, 78, 87
dome 18, 23, 24, 26, 33, 35, 36, 37, 45, 47, 49, 53, 55, 63, 64, 69, 70, 72-8, 80, 84, 85, 88, 96, 98, 109, 111, *n*.31, *n*.50; decoration 100ff; and mihrab 84; unit 21, 33; floating 84, 111
Dome of the Rock, Jerusalem 45
Dvina, river 19

earthquake 35, 59, 74, 108, 111, *n*.63; (1766) 76, 78; (1894) 96, *n*.33, *n*.55
Edirne (Adrianople) 13, 17, 20, 23, 24, 26, 29, 31, 47, 54, 56, 57, 62, 63, 65, 68, 72, 79ff, 92, 94, 95, 100, 114
Edison, T. 114
Eiffel Tower, Paris 108
Ertuğrul Bey 20
Erzerum 59
Eski Cami (Old Mosque), Edirne 79
Euclid *n*.71
Evliya Çelebi *n*.23, *n*.51
exedra 19, 26, 35, 36, 76, 89, *n*.7

façade 35, 37, 110
Fatih Pasha mosque, Diyarbekir 33, 78
Firuz Agha mosque, Milas 23
Florence 15
flowers 102, 104, 105, 106, *n*.67, *n*.69
follies 20
foundations *see* vaults and foundations
fountains 16, 21, 31, 33, 43, 49, 69, 91, 96, 98, *n*.62

Galata, Istanbul 43, 53, 99
Galileo *n*.13
galleries 47, 53, 61, 70, 80, 82ff, *n*.55; lateral 36, 37, 60
galley slaves 15, 18
glass 66; Venetian 46, 64, 104; ambiguity 85; extravagance 50, 68
Gök *medrese*, Sivas 79
Golden Horn, Istanbul 15, 40, 63, 99
Gombrich, E.H. *n*.65
Guarini, G. *n*.2

Hacı Ivaz Efendi mosque, Istanbul 60, 63
Haghia Sophia, basilica, Istanbul 26, 35, 45, 49, 55, 63, 68, 69, 70, 74, 76, 78, 80, 81, 84, 85, 89, 99, 111, 112, 114, *n*.6, *n*.7, *n*.50; and Kılıç Ali Pasha mosque 63
Haseki Hürrem (Roxelane): *hamam*, Istanbul 55; complex, Istanbul 29, 31, 51, 104; tomb, Istanbul 45, 99, *n*.23
Hawksmoor, N. 78, *n*.54
Hayreddin 24, 26, 76, *n*.53
Hekimoğlu Ali Pasha mosque, Istanbul 89
hexagon 47
Hippodrome, Istanbul 16, 29, 55, 56, 106
Holy Apostles, church of, Ani 33
Hosias Lucas, monastery 88
houses, Chinese 87
Hudavendigâr mosque, Bursa 19, 88
Hünernama 87
Hüsrev Pasha mosque, Aleppo 58

Ibrahim Pasha, Grand Vezir 14, *n*.5, *n*.38
Ibrahim Pasha (Hadım) *n*.28; mosque, Istanbul 29, 45, *n*.14
Inegöl 94
inflation 63
Işak Pasha mosque, Inegöl 94
Isfahan 87
Isidore of Miletus 85
Istanbul (Constantinople) *passim*
Izmit 62
Iznik (Nicaea) 20; *see also* tiles

janissaries (*yeniçeri*) 16, 17
Jefferson, T. 109
Jerusalem 45
Juki, Muhammad 87, *n*.61

Kara Ahmad Pasha, Grand Vezir 14, *n*.5; mosque, Istanbul 29, 46, 66, 94, 95, 110
kalfas 45, 56
Karapınar 57
Kayseri 16, 60, 63
Kılıç Ali Pasha mosque, Istanbul 29, 63, 76, 78, 89
Kilim Museum, Istanbul 56
Kline, M. *n*.13, *n*.47
Konya 57, 89
Koran boxes, lids 101
Küçük Aya Sofya mosque *see* SS Sergius and Bacchus church
Kuran, A. 31, *n*.7, *n*.9, *n*.42
Kurşunlu (Ahmad Pasha) mosque, Kayseri 60

Index

Lala Mustafa Pasha mosque, Erzerum 59; archaic squinches 59
Laleli mosque, Istanbul 89
lamps 102, 104, *n*.48
Le Corbusier (Jeanneret) 26, *n*.12
lead 26, 78, 110, *n*.52; use of by Sinan 63
Leonardo da Vinci 74, 109
Lethaby, W.R. 112
levy, Christian *see* Christian levy
light 20, 45, 50, 61, 65, 66ff, 78, 89
loggias 37
London, Strand 110
Lüleburgaz 54, 62, 95
Lutfi Pasha, Grand Vezir 17

Mahmud Pasha mosque, Istanbul 23, 88; *hamam* 56
Mainstone, R.J. *n*.6
Mamluks 16, 20, 60
Manisa 17, 56, 57, 61, 100, 107
Marmara, Sea of 20, 49, 55
Maser, Villa 90
Matrakçi Nasuh 87
matting 102
Mecca (and Medina) 45, 57, 58, 84, 104, *n*.26
Mehmed I 21; mosque, Bursa 79
Mehmed II, Fatih 21, 26, 49, 56; and Old Rome 21; complex, Istanbul 40, 49, 78, 80, 101; decoration 78
Mehmed III 49, 64, *n*.4, *n*.45
Mehmed Agha 43, 56, 57, 63, 64, 89, 91, *n*.26
Mehmed Şehzade *see* Şehzade Mehmed
Michelangelo 110
Mies van der Rohe, L. 66
mihrab 24, 61, 70, 82ff, 84, 88, 89, 102, 105, 107
Mihrimah 29, 30, 31, 49, 106, *n*.15, *n*.32; mosque, Edirnekapı 29, 31, 49, 52, 66, 68, 96, 101, *n*.15; mosque, Üsküdar 38, 49, 95, *n*.15
Milas 23
mimber: hood 53; decoration 102
minaret 33, 58, 79ff, 98, 99, 111, *n*.56, *n*.57; position of 23, 26, 38, 52, 53, 60, 79ff, *n*.55; number of 38, 45, 49, 57, 64, 69, 79, 80, *n*.15, *n*.46; slender 23, 31, 49, 58, 68, 80; stumpy 59
miniatures and architecture 87, 88
models 57, 108, *n*.43
Mohacs 17, 19, *n*.10
Mongols 20
Murad I 19; *see also* Hudavendigâr
Murad II 47, 80; *tekke*, Edirne, decoration 100; mosque, Bursa 79

Murad III 15, 55, 61, 80, 81, *n*.45; tomb 56, *n*.4; mosque, Manisa (Muradiye) 17, 56, 57, 60, 61, *n*.26, *n*.44; decoration 100, 107
Murad IV 33
Muschenheim, W. 85
Mustafa 56, 57, 61, *n*.44
mysticism, mystery 50, 68, 78, 89, 110

Nakkaş Osman 87
Necipoğlu-Kafadar, G. *n*.43
Neumann, B. 18
Neutra, R. 66
Nicaea *see* Iznik
Nısançı Mehmed Pasha mosque, Istanbul 63, 89
North, R. 76, *n*.20, *n*.52
number, discussed 114
Nurbanu, Valide Sultan *n*.45
Nuruosmaniye mosque, Istanbul 89

octagon 33, 47, 63, 92
Ohrid 19
Orhan Gazi 20; mosque, Bilecik (Orhaniye) 23
Osman I 20
Osmaniye *medrese*, Aleppo 58
Oxford 78

paintwork 61, 100ff, 106
Palladio, A. 15, 109, *n*.7
Pantheon: Rome 21, 84; Paris 109
Pantocrator 70
pendentive 21, 56, 59, 72
Pertev Pasha mosque, Izmit 62
Perugia, view of 88
Piero della Francesca 88
piers 24, 26, 47, 64, 69, 70, 89, 92, 106, 111
Piranesi, G. 109
Pitt, William, Earl of Chatham *n*.73
Piyale Pasha mosque, Istanbul 60, 80, *n*.55
plans 36, 38, 57, 58, 61, 64, 78, 108, *n*.43, *n*.44
Plato *n*.71
Porta Pia, Rome 110, *n*.2
portal, grand 94
portico 19, 21, 23, 33, 49, 52, 53, 54, 57, 59, 60, 70, 79, 80, 83, 91, 92, 94, 95, 98, 110; second 49, 51, 54, 59, 95, 96, 98
prefabrication 18
proportions 38, 52, 53, 57, 59, 80, 91, 92, 94
Pythagoras 108, 114

Radcliffe Camera, Oxford 78
Ragusa 19
Ramazan Efendi *tekke*, Istanbul 30, 106, *n*.14

Index

Renaissance 13, 31, 35, 37, 47, 110, *n*.7
Rhodes 87
Rome 15, 21, 24
Roxelane *see* Haseki Hürrem
rugs 102
Rum Mehmed Pasha mosque, Istanbul 89
Rüstem Pasha, Grand Vezir 29, 106, 110, *n*.5, *n*.15, *n*.36, *n*.38, *n*.67; *kervansaray*, Edirne 29, 50-1; *medrese*, Istanbul 92; mosque, Istanbul 30, 38, 46, 53, 60, 63, 66, 95, 105, 106; mosque, Tekirdağ 29, 62, 95

Safavids 87, 106
Safiye, Valide Sultan 49, *n*.45
St Clement Danes church, London 20
St Paul's cathedral, London 24, 76, 109, 111
St Peter's, basilica, Rome 24, 109; Piazza San Pietro 90
SS Sergius and Bacchus church (Küçük Aya Sofya mosque), Istanbul 47, 114
San Marco, basilica, Venice 104
Scott, G. 2, 84, 85, *n*.49
Şehzade Mehmed 33, *n*.19; mosque, Istanbul 33, 35, 36, 37, 64, 76, 89, 91, 92, 112, 114, *n*.7
Selim I 16, 17, 20, 33, 58, *n*.28; mosque, Istanbul 17, 33, 72, 89, 92, 100, *n*.51, *n*.69
Selim II 31, 49, 63, 68, 80, 106, 107, *n*.15, *n*.45; mosque, Edirne (Selimiye) 13, 17, 24, 31, 63, 65, 69-70, 72, 76, 80, 81, 85, 88, 89, 92, 94, 107, 110, 111, 114, *n*.26, *n*.36; royal gallery 82, 83; unique 109; mosque, Karapınar 57-8, *n*.42; tomb, Istanbul 45, 107
Seljuks 19, 20, 79
Semiz Ali Pasha mosque, Babaeski 62
Şerefeddin mosque, Konya 89
Shahnama 87, *n*.61
shell 45, 47
Silentiary, Paul the 84
Sinan *passim*; career 13, 14; houses 40; family 17, 63; offices 43, 56, 57; Royal Architect 17, 29, 31ff, 56ff, 89, 104; tomb 19, 43, 56
sites 29, 31, 49, 51-2, 61, 63, 95-6, *n*.44
Sivas 79
slaves 15, 18
Sokollu Mehmed Pasha, Grand Vezir *n*.38; mosque, Bor 57; mosque, Azapkapı 53; mosque, Kadırga 29, 52-3, 63, 95, 96, 111; and decoration 52, 53, 100, 106-7, 111; mosque, Lüleburgaz 54, 62, 95
space 13, 20, 26, 35, 49, 53, 54, 64, 66, 69, 72, 74, 82ff, 90, 91, 95, 98ff, 112
Spain 88
spires 111
squinch 21

stability 68
stalactites 45, 69, 79, 102
subscription lists 29
Süleyman Kanuni, the Magnificent 17, 21, 31, 33, 45, 49, 56, 87, *n*.15, *n*.19; mosque, Istanbul (Süleymaniye) 14, 15, 17, 18, 29, 31, 36-45, 51, 56, 66, 69, 76, 78, 79, 80, 83, 87, 89, 92, 94, 98, 99, 108, 109, 114, *n*.3, *n*.23; decoration 45, 102, 104, 105; domes 47, 98, 99, *n*.52; mosque, Damascus 58; tomb 45, 99, 100, *n*.23
Süleyman Pasha mosque, Cairo 60, 78
Süleymannama 87
Sultan Ahmad mosque *see* Ahmad I, mosque
supplies 15

Tabriz, craftsmen 35
Takkeci Ibrahim Çavuş (Agha) mosque, Istanbul 106, *n*.69; tiles 106
Taksim, Istanbul 87
Tekirdağ 29, 62, 95
Thrace 20, 29, 57, 70
Three Balconies, mosque of the *see* Üç Şerefeli
tiles: *cuerda seca* 45, *n*.27; excess 50-1, 105-6; fake windows 79; floor 102; Iznik 30, 31, 45, 50-1, 53, 58, 61, 70, 82, 99ff, 104-7, 110, *n*.14; roofing 26; Syrian 58
Timur 21, 29
Timurids 87
Todi *see* Consolazione, Tempio della
Topkapısaray, Istanbul 29, 63, 88, 90; Enderun Kolej 16; fire (1574) 55, 63; library *n*.61; studio 58
Tosya 89
triangles 21, 38

Üç Şerefeli mosque, Edirne (mosque of the Three Balconies) 23, 24, 47, 80, 92, 114
ulema 23, *n*.46
Ulu Cami (Great Mosque), Bursa 79
Umayyads 88
units 26, 36

valide sultans and mosques 49
Van 59
Vatican 90
vaults and foundations 33, 36, 40, 46, 51, 52, 53, 55, 56, 79, 99
Venice 15, 21, 104; glass 46, 64
Vicenza 21, *n*.11
Vienna 21
Visegrád, bridge 19
Vitruvius 15, *n*.7, *n*.8
void *see* space

Index

windows 18, 26, 46, 49, 50, 52, 66, 85, 104; large 46, 51, 61, 62, 66, 70; leaning 61, *n.*44
Wittkower, R. *n.*8, *n.*21
Wootton, Sir H. 84
Wren, Sir C. 76, *n.*52

Yakupşah bin Sultanşah *n.*53
Yakut bin Papas *n.*53
Yeni Cami (New Mosque), Tosya 89
Yeni Saray *see* Topkapısaray
Yeni Valide mosque, Istanbul 49, 56, 63, 64, 78, *n.*4
Yeşil Cami (Green Mosque), Bursa 23, 95

Zal Mahmud Pasha *n.*37; mosque, Istanbul 29, 51–2, 86, 107, *n.*14
zaviye-mosques 20, 21, 73, 89

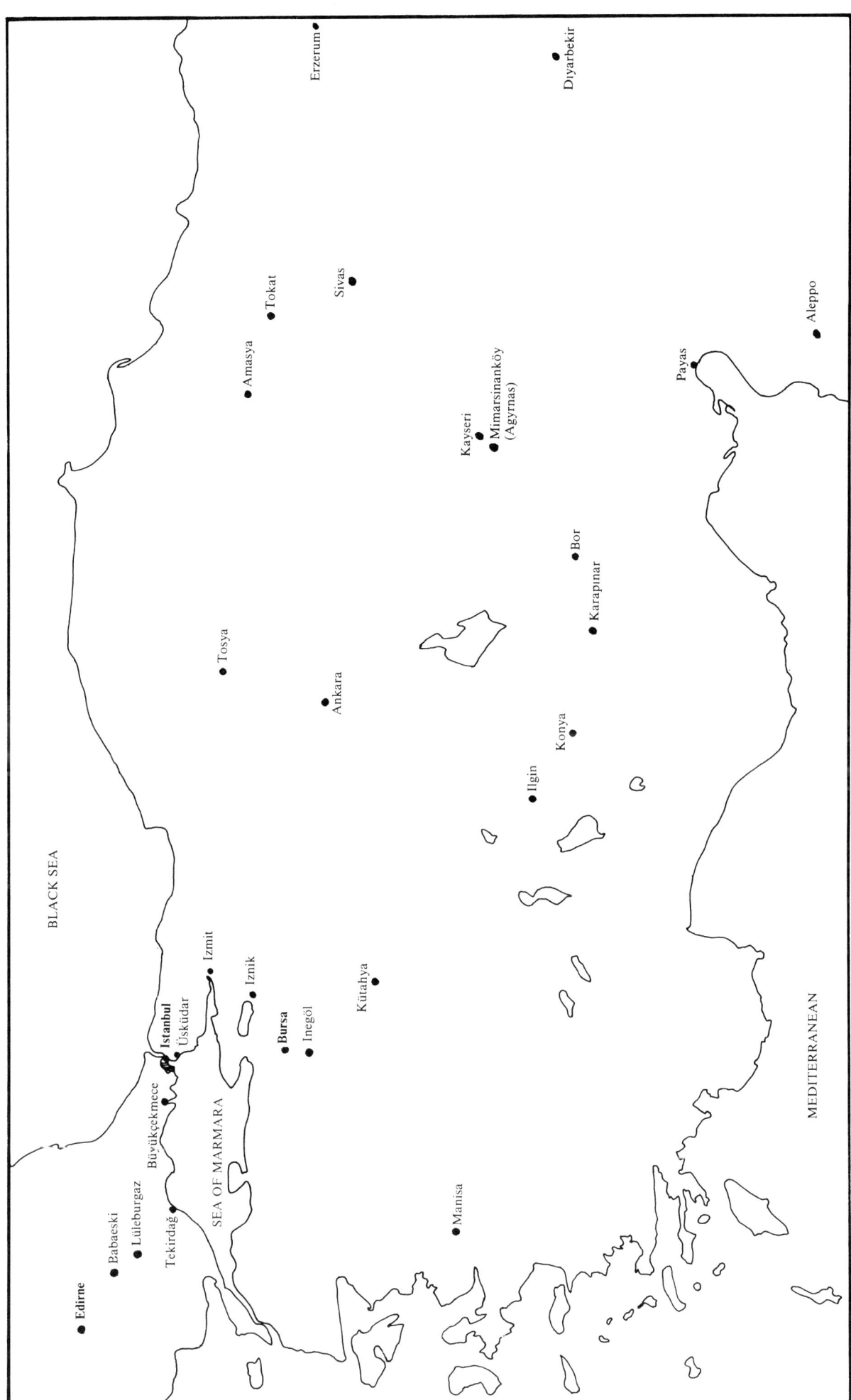

Map 1. Sinan's Turkey

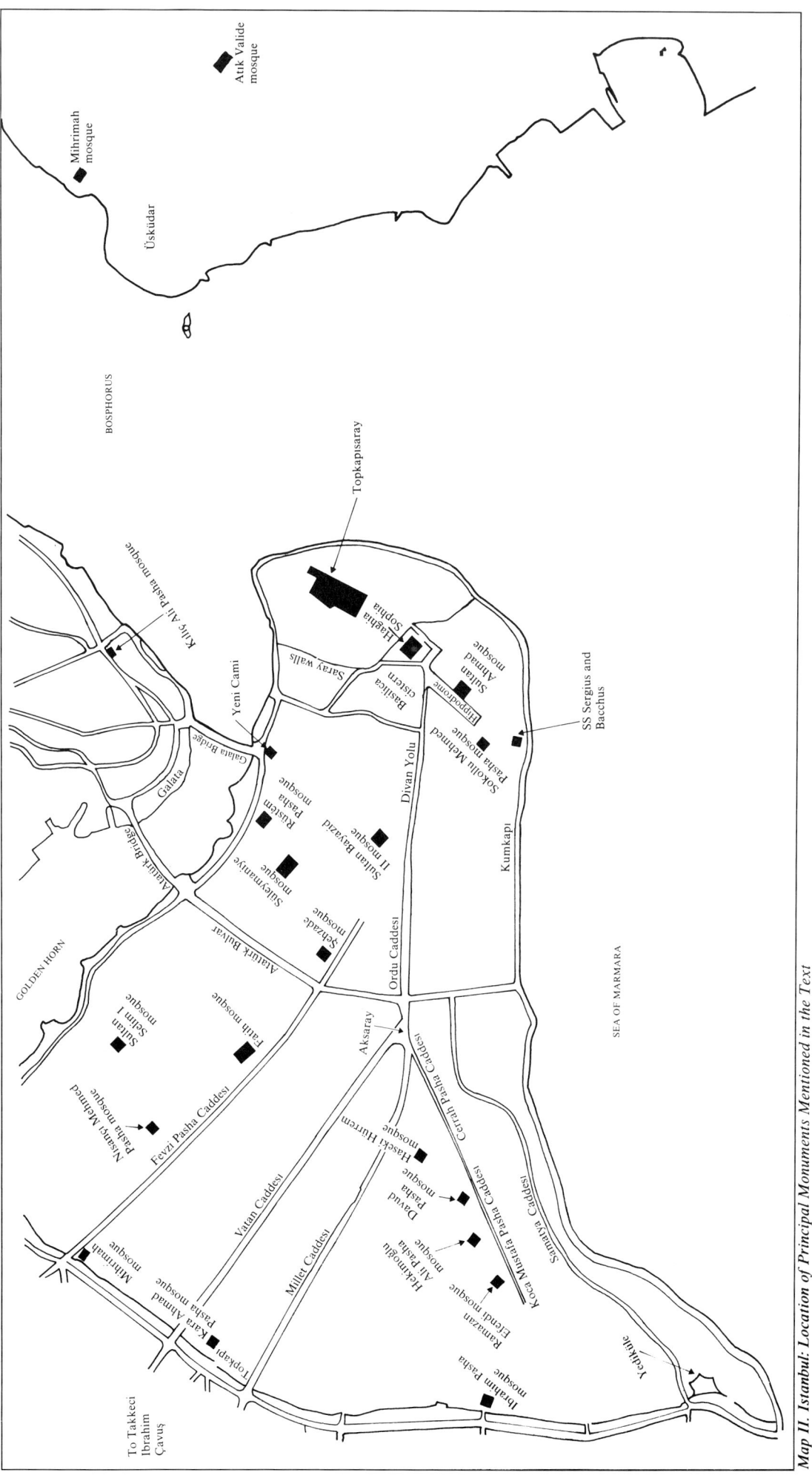

Map II. Istanbul: Location of Principal Monuments Mentioned in the Text

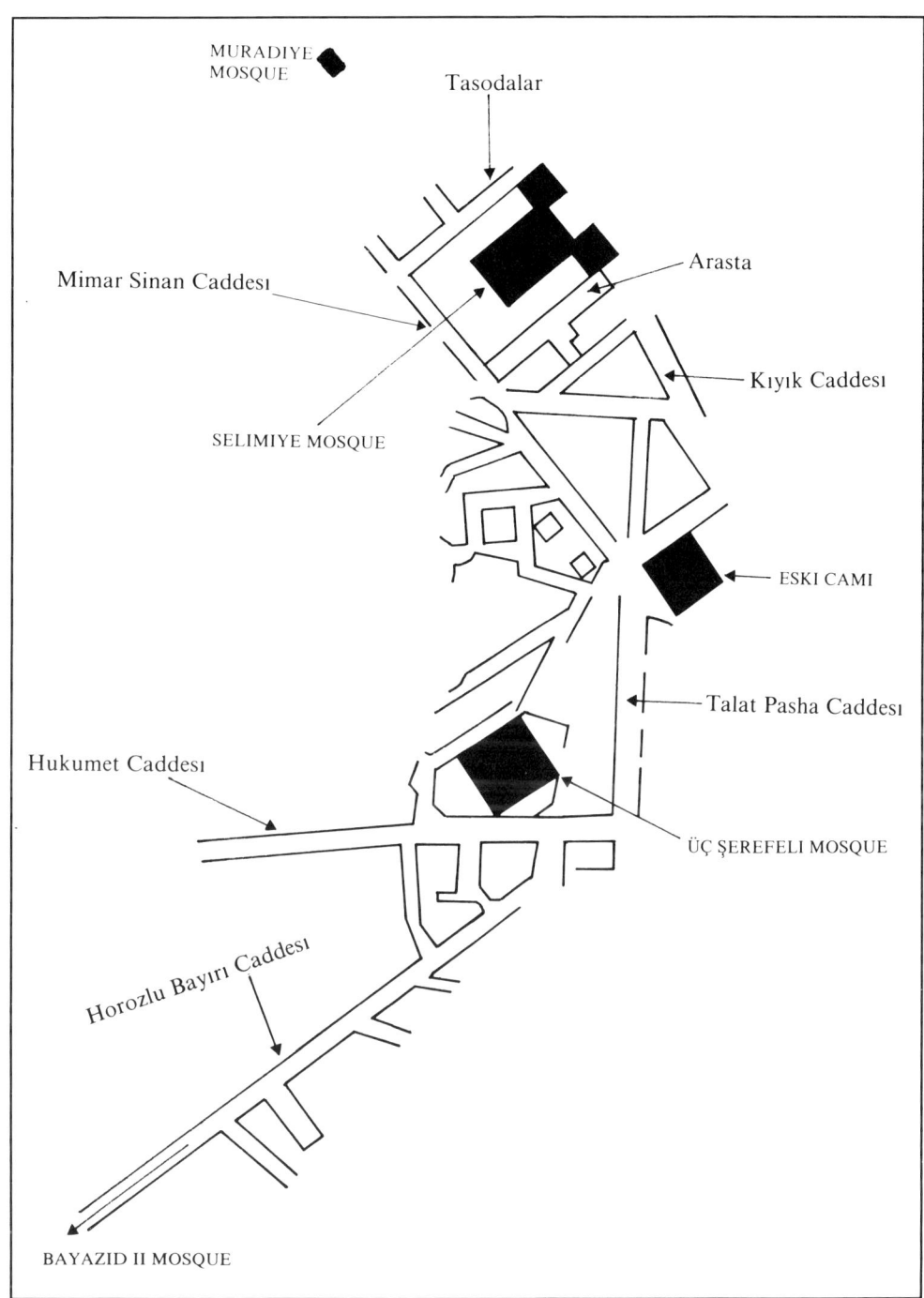

Map III. Edirne: Location of Principal Monuments Mentioned in the Text